# IN THE PUBLIC'S
# INTEREST

# Geographies of Justice and Social Transformation

# IN THE PUBLIC'S INTEREST

## Evictions, Citizenship, and Inequality in Contemporary Delhi

GAUTAM BHAN

THE UNIVERSITY OF GEORGIA PRESS
*Athens*

Published by the University of Georgia Press
Athens, Georgia 30602
www.ugapress.org
© 2016 by Gautam Bhan
All rights reserved

Most University of Georgia Press titles are
available from popular e-book vendors.

Printed digitally

Library of Congress Control Number: 2016946700
ISBN: 9780820350097 (hardcover: alk. paper)
ISBN: 9780820350103 (paperback: alk. paper)
ISBN: 9780820350080 (ebook)

A version of this text for distribution in India and
South Asia was published by Orient BlackSwan.

*For Delhi, For Dilli.*

हमने माना डक्कन मे  हैं ,
बहुत  से क़द्र -ए -सुखन ,
पर कौन जाये, ए ज़ौक ,
ये  दिल्ली  की गलियां  छोड़कर।
- मोहम्मद  इब्राहिम ज़ौक

*In absentia, for Priya Thangarajah.*
*You are yearned for, still.*

# Contents

# Tables, Figures and Maps

## Tables

## Figures

## Maps

# Publisher's Acknowledgements

For permission to reproduce copyright material in this volume, the publisher wishes to make the following acknowledgements.

State Bank of India for permission to use images from its advertisement campaigns, appearing as Figure 3.1 'Banker to Every Indian' and Figure 3.2 'Welcome to a Cashless World' in this book.

Bennett, Coleman & Co. Ltd. for permission to use a creative of a building of The Times of India used in the Times Chalo Dilli campaign, appearing as Figure 3.3 'From Walled City to World City' in this book. © BCCL. All Rights Reserved.

# Abbreviations

| | |
|---|---|
| AAP | Aam Aadmi Party |
| AIR | *All India Reporter* |
| ASUS | Ambedkar Slum Utthan Sangathan |
| BJP | Bharatiya Janata Party |
| CPI | Communist Party of India |
| CWP | Civil Writ Petition |
| DDA | Delhi Development Authority |
| DLT | *Delhi Law Times* |
| DSS | Delhi Shramik Sangathan |
| EWS | Economically Weaker Sections |
| FICCI | Federation of Indian Chambers of Commerce and Industry |
| HIC | Habitat International Coalition |
| HIG | High Income Group |
| HPEC | High Powered Expert Committee (on Urban Infrastructure) |
| HLRN | Housing and Land Rights Network |
| HRLN | Human Rights Law Network |
| ITR | Intent to Reside |
| JNNURM | Jawahar Lal Nehru National Urban Renewal Mission |
| LIG | Low Income Group |
| MISA | Maintenance of Internal Security Act |
| MCD | Municipal Corporation of Delhi |
| MIG | Middle Income Group |

## Abbreviations

| | |
|---|---|
| MPD | Master Plan of Delhi |
| NAPM | National Alliance of People's Movements |
| NASSCOM | National Association of Software and Services Companies |
| NSSO | National Sample Survey Organisation |
| NULM | National Urban Livelihoods Mission |
| NUSP | National Urban Sanitation Policy |
| PUDR | People's Union for Democratic Rights |
| PIL | Public Interest Litigation |
| PUCL-K | People's Union for Civil Liberties, Karnataka |
| RAY | Rajiv Awas Yojana |
| RTI | Right to Information |
| RWA | Resident Welfare Association |
| SCC | *Supreme Court Cases* |
| SFS | Self-Financing Scheme |
| SPARC | Society for the Promotion of Area Resource Centers |
| SBI | State Bank of India |
| UNESCO | United Nations Educational, Scientific and Cultural Organization |
| ZEIS | Zone of Special Social Importance |

# IN THE PUBLIC'S
# INTEREST

# Introduction

*'How did we get here?'*

R afiya Khanum sticks in your mind. Of slight build and boundless energy, she is endlessly on the move—her hands seem unable to stop themselves. As we talk, she cleans, stirs a pot of rice, strings another bead into a necklace she will sell to a supplier, and watches her sleeping son. From the corner of her eye, she keeps anxiously glancing upward to check the distance between my head and the ceiling fan, rightly afraid that if I stretch my hands too far upward I'd meet a rotating blade. 'You're too tall for this house,' she says to me, laughing. 'But then, who isn't?'[1]

She and I are seated on the mud floor of her ten-foot-by-twelve-foot thatch, tin and mud hut in Bawana, a 'resettlement colony' on the northwestern periphery of New Delhi. Bawana was created to house families evicted from the place Rafiya still calls home—a string of *bastis*[2] that housed 30,000 households (nearly 150,000 people) by the river Yamuna in the northeast of the city. The bastis were colloquially just called 'Pushta', or riverbank. Between February and April 2004, in a series of operations involving hundreds of armed policemen, Pushta was demolished (see Figures I.1 and I.2). Only 30 per cent of evicted households received any form of resettlement or rehabilitation. Rafiya was one of the luckier ones.

A notice had appeared in the basti two weeks before the evictions began. The notice was not from any of the institutions of the Executive, i.e. the city's planning agencies, any of its multiple urban authorities, public utilities, or the state or central governments that Rafiya had voted to power and which jointly rule the National Capital Territory of Delhi. Not from, in other words, what Rafiya referred to as the 'sarkar'.[3] The notice, she said, was from the *adalat*—the Court. 'I didn't even know there was a case against us!' she said to me. 'In fact, I still don't know if there was one, or what it was.' The notice and the eviction at Pushta was indeed the implementation of an order of the Delhi high court. There wasn't just a single case, however; the order was issued in hearings on a group of petitions being adjudicated together by the Court. Though they raised multiple issues, each of these cases had one important thing in common: they were all, without exception, Public Interest Litigations (PILs).[4]

A PIL is an innovative judicial mechanism established by the Indian judiciary in the late 1970s explicitly to protect the fundamental rights of the marginalised. Its founding purpose was to enable vulnerable and marginalised citizens to access justice in the highest courts of the land through significantly eased legal procedures and rules of standing. Through PILs, the Supreme Court aimed to become, as one of its own judges argued, 'the last recourse for the oppressed and the bewildered'[5] who could approach the Court to protect the infringement of their constitutionally-guaranteed fundamental rights. In some of the earliest PILs, the Supreme Court treated even a simple letter as a legal petition, taking upon itself the task of fact-finding, gathering evidence, as well as framing legal arguments.[6] Through the 1980s, PILs were indeed the sites of an expansion of rights for the poor in what Upendra Baxi described as no less than a 're-democratizing of the processes of governance and the practices of politics' (1997: 351). PILs were seen as filling a democratic vacuum as the 'Supreme Court *of* India' became a 'Supreme Court *for* Indians' in what Baxi called 'chemotherapy for the carcinogenic body politic' (Baxi 2002: *xvi*, emphasis in the original). The Court was seen as a site where rights—

particularly the rights to life (Article 21), equality (Article 14), anti-discrimination (Article 15) and freedom of expression (Article 19)—were interpreted, expanded and enforced.

In March 2003, however, a two-judge bench of the Delhi high court told a different story. The judges lamented that the river Yamuna 'which is a major source of water has been polluted like never before. [The] Yamuna bed on both the sides of the river has been encroached by unscrupulous persons with the connivance of authorities.'[7] It had, they argued, 'to be cleared of such encroachments immediately.' Arguing that 'the citizens of Delhi are silent spectators to this state of affairs,' they ended their orders with a direction to all the institutions of the sarkar—'the Delhi Development Authority [DDA], the Municipal Corporation of Delhi, the Public Works Department, the Delhi Jal Board,[8] as well as the Central Government'—to 'remove encroachments up to 300m from both sides of River Yamuna in the first instance. No encroachment either in the form of *jhuggi-jhompri* clusters or in any other manner by any person or organization shall be permitted.'

Unlike in previous evictions, this clearance was explicitly delinked from resettlement, i.e. the provision of an alternative dwelling or plot of land to evicted households. 'Under the garb of resettlement,' the judges argued, 'encroachers are paid a premium for further encroachment.'[9] The court's ire against resettlement was part of a broader critique of urban development in Delhi per se. In previous orders in the same case, they had argued that, 'the whole concept of urbanized development of land in Delhi has almost collapsed as a consequence of such haphazard development and irrational policies. Any person can sit wherever he wants. Squatting on the land gives a right to get another allotment which allotment also he sells and after selling comes back on the same land. The policy itself gets defeated.' While agreeing that 'it was the duty of the government to provide shelter for the underprivileged,' the judges argued that '[the government's] lack of planning and initiative' cannot 'be replaced by an arbitrary system of providing alternative sites and land to encroachers on public land.'

Figure I.1: Yamuna Pushta, 2004

Figure I.2: Yamuna Pushta, 2014

Outside the courtroom, the state and central governments remained silent as the Slum and JJ Department of the Municipal Corporation of Delhi began the process of eviction. Activists and Pushta residents scrambled to respond. Some tried to mobilise their elected representatives; the night before demolitions, local *pradhans*[10] claimed, in fact, that a deal had been struck and demolitions would not occur.[11] They were wrong. An emergency appeal filed in the Supreme Court by activists and Pushta residents to get a temporary injunction on the Delhi high court's orders was summarily dismissed. A large public protest at the offices of the DDA by members of Sajha Manch—a coalition of nearly forty organisations, basti associations and unions—was followed by another outside the residence of the then-President A. P. J. Abdul Kalam by nearly 500 children asking that the evictions at least be postponed until after their school year exams. Both failed to elicit even an acknowledgement from the sarkar. In the weeks before and after the evictions, digital renderings of a rumoured riverside promenade to be built in place of the settlements as well as a grand design for the entire Yamuna riverbank began to appear in city newspapers. The evictions themselves and the lack of any resettlement options for those displaced got little coverage. In a matter of months, the land was cleared.

You can, and often have to, tell this story another way. Both Rafiya and Pushta are also data points. Between 2002 and 2010, a series of evictions reduced the total number of bastis in Delhi by the largest margin since sweeping evictions during the Emergency in 1975–77, the 'dark hour' of Indian democracy where fundamental rights stood suspended (see Figure I.3). Estimations of the number of households evicted in the last two decades start at no less than 70,000 and rise to over 150,000. Conservatively, this means 350,000 to 750,000 people spread across at least 216, but possibly up to 283, different sites (for estimations, see Chapter One; Bhan and Shivanand 2013; Dupont 2008; HLRN and HIC 2011).

The quantum is such that it is marked by no less than the decadal census. Recording a 25 per cent fall in population from two central districts, the 2011 census says quite directly:

**Figure I.3: Number of Bastis/'Slums' in Delhi, 1951–2010**

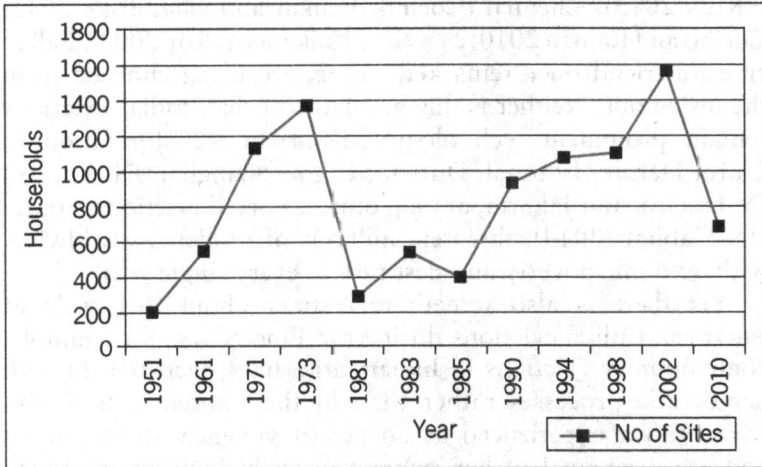

*Source*: Combined, unpublished lists from Food and Civil Supplies Department, Municipal Corporation of Delhi, Delhi Urban Shelter Improvement Board and Government of Delhi (2009). Copies on file.

'It has been established that removal of slum clusters is the primary reason for the fall in population in the New Delhi district vis-à-vis 2001' (Government of India 2012: 44).

Millennial Delhi is a city whose landscape has been scarred by the repeated, frequent and seemingly inevitable evictions of the homes of some of its most income-poor residents. Taken together, these evictions have reversed nearly two decades of the steady, incremental growth of bastis in the city. In the slow rise of the graph's line between 1981 and 2000, many like Rafiya were born, educated and came of age in bastis like Pushta, Nangla Machi, Himmatpuri, Trilokpuri, Banuwal Nagar, Sanjay camp, Sanjay basti and Ambedkar Colony. These bastis grew as the city did—master plans and changing elected governments notwithstanding. None of them stand today.

Delhi lies at perhaps the extreme end of what is arguably a more generalised phenomenon across Indian megacities of urban restructuring through eviction, marking Mumbai (Ramanathan

7

2005), Ahmedabad (N. Mathur 2012), Bangalore (PUCL-K and HRLN 2013), Chennai (Coelho, Venkat and Chandrika 2012; Coelho and Raman 2010) as well as Kolkata (A. Roy 2003). Indian cities, a friend once remarked to me, are being churned from the inside out. Neither is this peculiar to urban India. Evictions remain prominent technologies of urban transformation in Cairo, Harare, Istanbul, Durban, Lagos, Shanghai, Dhaka, Rio De Janeiro, and Jakarta, among others. Forced evictions, argues UN-Habitat (2014), threaten 'millions of residents worldwide' with 'extreme poverty and destitution' every single year.

Yet there is also something distinct about this cycle of evictions. Unlike evictions during the Emergency, for example, contemporary evictions in Indian cities have occurred through democratic processes rather than in their absence. In Delhi, what Rafiya experienced as an act of violence, displacement and the disavowal of her rights, the Delhi high court argued was an act in the public interest—an act of governance, urban development and order. How did the judges determine that the eviction of vast numbers of citizens was within the 'public interest', ruling against their claims to shelter? Bastis are not covert—Pushta stretched nearly a kilometre in the heart of the city and had been in existence for nearly thirty years. Its existence was not a matter of stealth. How then did it suddenly become both necessary and possible to read its presence as a violation that must be erased? How did this occur through a judicial innovation created precisely to be the 'last resort for the bewildered and the oppressed'? 'How,' as Rafiya once asked me, 'did we get here?'

## Bastis, Evictions and Urbanism

*What is a basti?* At its simplest, an archetypical basti is a settlement that houses residents who are often income-poor in a built environment that reflects some measure of their impoverishment. Characterised by relatively poor environmental services and infrastructure, it consists of houses often built of what are considered 'temporary' or *kuccha* (literally, raw) materials like thatch, bamboo and plastic or tarpaulin sheets though a significant number may just as well be made in brick and concrete, particularly in older bastis. Master plans as well as municipal and other laws variously consider bastis as 'informal' or 'illegal' because they are built in violation of planning norms and standards, and usually through the occupation and settlement of public or private land that basti residents do not own in title. In Delhi, in part due to a historic public land acquisition known as the 'Delhi Experiment,'[12] most bastis are on public land.

Rafiya was aware that she did not 'own' the land her house in Pushta was built on. She did, however, feel like she had a claim to it. It was empty swamp land, she argued—'it was poor people like my father who put bricks and sand and made it strong enough to take the weight of a hut. Who else is public land meant for but the public? Where else am I meant to go?' Her arguments are familiar ones. Income-poor urban residents occupy land both out of need and right, implicitly and explicitly pointing out the state's failure to provide (or ensure the provision of) adequate and affordable low-income housing. In claiming the right to the basti, Rafiya is exercising what James Holston has described as a mix of 'text-based, special interest and contributor rights' (2008: 253)—claims, as I shall argue, of citizenship, no matter how fragile.

These claims are inextricably and simultaneously also claims to development. 'The developmental ideology,' Partha Chatterjee reminds us, 'was a constituent part of the self-definition of the post-colonial state.' The state's claim to legitimate rule was based not just on electoral representation but also on the promise of development, on 'directing a program of economic development on behalf of the nation.' It was through this framing of development as the 'universal goal of the nation' that the post-colonial state broke with colonial rule (1997: 277). India's developmental story has always been seen and assessed as a national one—the city has, until recently, played an ambiguous role in the politics of a country that 'lives in its villages' as Gandhi (1967: 302) once famously put it. Yet in the two decades after the Emergency in Delhi, the slow rise of the line of the graph in whose shadow Rafiya was born represents precisely the management of the promise of development in the Indian city.

This management has been complex and contradictory. In Rafiya's lifetime, metered electricity, schools and water connections came to Pushta, all provided by the local government usually after significant struggle by basti residents and often in implicit and explicit exchange for electoral support. Internal streets were paved over, temples and mosques built. Pushta residents had built a paper trail of their lives—they had Voter Identification cards, entitlement cards to the local food distribution centre, utility bills with their names and addresses on them, school leaving documents, certificates that marked lower caste status or declared them to be 'Below the Poverty Line' and bank accounts. They existed (and invested a great deal in existing) on paper. The basti thus is a site where different and often contradictory orders and temporalities of claims, governmental forms and rationalities seemed to co-exist, for years and even decades. A de facto security of tenure grows amidst layers of an emerging and dense urban life making the legibility and enforceability of the de jure 'illegality' of the occupation fade though never entirely disappear.

This relatively stable co-existence of seemingly contradictory logics and orders that defines a significant process of inhabiting the city for many residents is not just a story of Delhi. It is how *favela*s in Rio, *colonias populares* in Mexico City, *musseque*s in Luanda, *amchi wasti*s in Pune, *ashwa'iyyat* in Cairo, shacks or '*mjondolos* in Durban, *sukumbhashi basti*s in Dhaka, *katchi abadi*s in Karachi, *kampung liar*s or *hak milik*s in Kuala Lumpur, and the *sahakhum*s in Phnom Penh, have been built.

Teresa Caldeira writes of this process as a shared history of what she calls auto-construction, the production of the city by residents and communities building and constructing their own homes and neighbourhoods. Auto-construction, she argues, is marked by 'transversal engagements with official logics of legal property, formal labor, colonial dominance, state regulation, and market capitalism' (Caldeira 2014). This does not mean, she reminds us, that such auto-construction is a spatial or temporal 'exception' to a city that is otherwise legible within the orders of land markets, master plans, governance codes, norms and laws. In fact, it is auto-construction rather than planning that is the dominant mode of the production of urban space. Empirics would prove her right in Delhi: in 2000, only 24 per cent of Delhi's population lived in what the master plan called 'planned colonies'. A majority of the city's residents inhabited and settled the city with, to use Caldeira's term, transversal logics.

As Chapter One will argue in detail, these are not just 'slums' or bastis, but a range of elite settlements as well. Seeing the basti as a type of an auto-constructed urban form changes its signification. It no longer refers to just the materiality of its housing, a spatial form or a planning category. It must be read instead as the territorialisation of a political engagement within which subaltern urban residents negotiate—incrementally, over time, and continuously—their presence in as well as right to the city. This engagement is complex. It is based on a mix of political, ethical and moral claims that draw upon on both rights and needs. It is an engagement with (but not limited to) the institutions of the sarkar that often involves their implicit and explicit patronage and, at times, even their active participation. It works through as well as despite the law and regimes and practices of planning. It takes just as often the form of resistance and opposition—through, for example, vigorous social movements resisting eviction or pursuing greater legitimacy and security of tenure—as it does the more institutionalised forms of state–citizen relations such as the ballot. It constructs and attributes meaning and value to urban space through symbolic and discursive practices, telling its own narrative of both the city and the basti within it.

It is, in short, a particular form of urbanism. In defining urbanism, Ananya Roy offers us three inter-twined registers: (a) the production of space in the territorial circuits of late capitalism; (b) a set of social struggles over space, value and meaning; and (c) the object of the public apparatus designated as planning (A. Roy 2011). The basti shapes each of these registers. It moves across them, bringing them together but also pulling them apart. In its eviction, it also marks how they change over time as a new set of configurations undo long held engagements. If a basti marks a pattern of urbanism, an eviction signals its possible transformations.

It is these transformations that this book seeks to read. Evictions signify a moment of closure for the political, legal, social and economic negotiations that allowed the basti to settle and survive for decades. They mark an altered urban politics where a set of familiar referents—development, order, governance, citizens and the public—are redefined to not only enable evictions but also to see them as acts of good governance, order and planning. They signal a shift in management of Chatterjee's 'developmental ideology' as it re-articulates through the 'urban turn'—Gyan Prakash's (2002) evocative description of the political, economic and cultural emergence of the city in contemporary India. They indicate a new set of emergent forms, technologies and rationalities through which another urban generation will inherit the vulnerabilities of their parents rather than the fruits of their sacrifices.

*Inquiry from the South:* I will argue in this book that the basti and its eviction are critical sites to understand dynamics of contemporary urbanism not just in Delhi but across cities of the global South. This is not just because auto-construction represents a significant empirical reality in many, if not all, of these cities. It is also because prioritising the basti as a site and object of inquiry is, I argue, a way to 'see from the south' (Watson 2009), to privilege a set of questions that challenge our understanding of the urbanism of all cities but emerge from place.

In doing so, I follow a set of scholars determined to interrogate the urban post-colony and trace the questions that its 'stubborn realities' (Yiftachel 2006) asks rather pressingly of urban theory. This set of scholars—let me loosely call their distinct but shared work 'southern urban theory'—argue that place matters in shaping geographies of theory as well as those of authoritative knowledge (A. Roy 2008; Watson 2009; Yiftachel 2006). Drawing often from post-colonial theory, they seek to unsettle the meta-narratives of urban theory told from the great cities—New York, Chicago, London, Paris—and locate them in place and time rather that allow them a place-less universalism as 'T'heory, or what Tim Mitchell (2002) once described as 'principles true in every country'.

The goal of southern urban theory is not to study cities of the global South, the 'developing world' or the 'third world' in order to add a greater empirical diversity to our roster of global cities. 'It is not enough,' Roy argues, 'to simply to study the cities of the global South as interesting, anomalous, different, and esoteric empirical cases' (2008: 2). Indeed, this has more often than not been the case. When AbdouMaliq Simone titled his seminal volume on changing life in four African cities *For the City Yet to Come* (2004), he was pushing back against a history of writing that treated African cities always still awaiting economic development, structural transformation, networked infrastructure, cultural modernity and full personhood. Cities, in other words, always judged on the forms, rhythms and times of other places. The goal of what Comaroff and Comaroff (2012) call 'theory from the south,' is then far more ambitious: 'to "dislocate" the Euro American centre of theoretical production' (A. Roy 2008: 2) in order to build theory anew in a manner that reflects the experiences not just of global cities, but also of ordinary ones (Robinson 2006).

This is a contested assertion. Critics argue that while studying cities in the global South is certainly pivotal, it is unclear that such analyses cannot be done within the existing theoretical forms that inform urban theory as we know it today. Example of such critiques from two widely differing ideological positions makes this clear. From Marxism, Andy Merrifield argues that between 'Paris and Palestine, London and Rio, Johannesburg and New York,' there are merely 'differences of degree not substance' (2014: 29) in a new (but still singular) urban question. Within urban economics, Scott and Storper also insist on a 'coherent' conception of the urban, arguing that '*all* cities can be understood in terms of a theoretical framework that combines two main processes namely the dynamics of agglomeration and the unfolding of an associated nexus of locations, land uses and human interactions' (Scott and Storper 2014: 1; emphasis in the original). In her response to Scott and Storper,

Ananya Roy (forthcoming) reflects: 'Households, firms, market mechanisms, agglomeration, land nexus ... this is precisely the "universal" grammar of urbanism that failed me during my dissertation fieldwork in Calcutta.'

Across disciplines that study the urban, these debates are vibrant and diverse sites of knowledge production. Even a brief overview shows immensely enriching contributions: Vanessa Watson and Oren Yiftachel's challenge of 'deep difference' and 'urban ethnocracies' against formulations of communicative action and collaborative urban planning (Watson 2006, 2009, 2012; Yiftachel 2006); Faranak Miraftab's (2009) notions of insurgent planning emerging from the global South; Jennifer Robinson's (2006) call for ordinary cities against the narratives of planetary urbanism and global cities; AbdouMaliq Simone's (2004) notion of 'people as infrastructure' against urban theories of networked infrastructure and systems thinking; Parnell and Pieterse's (2010) challenge to the limits of neoliberalism as an analytical framework to understand shifting urban political economies; Barbara Hariss-White and Prosperi's (2014) insistence on treating informal employment as a end-game rather than a transitional stage of modernisation and economic development; James Holston's (2008) provocation on urban citizenship from the peripheries of large southern megacities; Teresa Caldeira's (1996, 2000) framing of peripheral urbanisation and the changing politics of social relations and collective life it engenders; Partha Chatterjee's (2004b) meditations on citizens, civil society and rights in 'much of the world'; James Ferguson's (2013) investigation of dependence read against the settled liberal valorisation of freedom and development in conceptions of urban welfare; Gidwani and Reddy's (2011) provocation of using 'waste' as a key analytical category to understand production and consumption in cities; and A. Roy and Ong's (2011) conception of 'worlding' practices as against narratives of globalisation, to name just a few.

I list a sample of this scholarship not to take us into a discussion of its arguments or to suggest that there is any one 'southern urbanism' that emerges from them. Such a formulation risks simply reversing the valorisation of a dualism of North and South while keeping its parochialism intact. Instead, I see southern urban theory as a shared ethos of inquiry among this scholarship. One part of such an ethos is an insistence on building theory from places that have so far been considered peripheral. I mean peripheral in multiple senses: peripheries of the world economic and political system both historically and today; peripheries within cities themselves; peripheries of geographies of authoritative knowledge.

The periphery, Caldeira and Holston argue, is a conceptual rather than physical location that not just enables certain inquiries but insists upon them.[13] Seen as a periphery, the 'global South' is then a relational geography. It is not just a collection of previously underdeveloped countries or the boundaries of the post-colonial world but a dynamic and changing set of locations. As Brazil, India, China and South Africa emerge, for example, it is clear that southern urban theory is not simply a study of precarity or difference but equally of ascendance, emergence and a re-configured global geo-politics. I see 'the global south' then as a 'project' (Urban Poverty and Inequality Collective 2015) rather than a place, an 'ex-centric location' that allows a different 'angle of vision in telling the history of the ongoing global present' (Comaroff and Comaroff 2012).

One final note that bears repetition: the inquiries, theories and concepts that emerge from southern urban theory intend to—as they must—travel. They must offer insight into the urbanism of all cities even as they emerge from place. Such work is already well underway as studies of informality influence writing on New York (Devlin 2011) and post-colonial urban theory informs work on London (Jacobs 2002) to take just two examples. Often though by no means always, northern scholars using concepts that emerge from southern urban theory do so to understand their own peripheries—from Detroit to the east side of London, from the *banlieu* of Paris to coping mechanisms amidst scarcity and austerity regimes in Athens. In doing so, they perform the task of bridging our strategic and admittedly essentialist North-South divide: of letting ideas and inquiries travel but doing so in a way that does not erase their origins, contexts and histories.

In this book, within this ethos and community of inquiry, I ask questions *from* Delhi—and within it, from its own peripheries in the basti—rather than just *of* it. Studying the basti and its eviction, I argue, provoke six clear lines of inquiry and conceptual reflection. Not unexpectedly, each is a familiar theme within studies of urbanism in the global South.

The first is the now long-standing debate to understand urban informality/illegality (I shall interrogate the '/' in the chapters that follow) including their impact on conceptions and practices of urban planning, the production of space and the regulation of value. The second is a set of debates on 'good governance,' read through their rationalities, modes and, particularly, their intersections with ideas of 'planned development' within rapidly transforming cities. The third is the political field of urban citizenship and the possibilities of substantive rights and belonging in the city. The fourth is resistance and the ability of subaltern residents to struggle against exclusion from the cities they inhabit and, in many cases, built. Each of these four inquiries forms a substantive chapter in the book.

The two remaining inquiries cut across these four, and, in a sense, bring them together. The first is the role of the Judiciary and a broader set of questions about the relationships between law and urbanism in cities of the global South. The second is to study the relationship between democracy and inequality in the city. I frame the concluding chapter of the book around these two inquiries, drawing in my arguments to see whether they are able to speak together as more than the sum of their individual parts. In the rest of this introduction, I turn to each inquiry in some detail, laying out some of the arguments that are to come.

## One: Planned Illegalities

In urban theory, the narrative of 'informality' has been a particular marker in theorising cities of the global South, particularly 'megacities' that are 'big but not powerful' (Robinson 2006) and beset by 'problems'. In this depiction, the informal is seen as one of the key drivers of the 'dysfunctional landscapes of Southern cities' (Rao 2006). Until recently, the bias in urban theory has been to see informality more as 'a domain of survival by the poor and marginalized' (A. Roy 2008: 2). In this reading, it is often quickly reduced to the 'slum', which itself is the object of multiple readings. In one, it is a 'demographic and territorial form' that is the 'spatial manifestation of the informal proletariat that has emerged from over a decade of structural adjustments' (Davis 2006: 28). In another, it is the 'distorted substance' that changes the 'urban into a dysfunctional stage for violence, conflict and the iniquitous distribution of resources' (Rao 2006: 231). It is that which is out of reach of the state and of modernisation, that which stubbornly refuses to 'bow out' of modernity's way (Nandy 1998).

Recent urban theory has both challenged the reduction of poverty to the 'slum' as well as sought to re-cast informal urban spaces and lives not just as sites of marginalisation but of enterprise, resistance and resilience (for three comprehensive review articles, see Kudva 2009; McFarlane 2012; Varley 2013). Some even argue that the tactics of survival and flourishing 'here' could pre-figure future urbanisms as precarity becomes more widespread in the North (Bhan and Roy 2013; Comaroff and Comaroff 2012; Koolhaas 2007) and ecological horizons find common cause with informal lives (Mehrotra 2010). Yet the entrepreneur and the impoverished slum dweller still form a dualism, argues Varley, and usefully goes on to remind us that, 'reversing the valorization of a dualism does not undermine the binary opposition itself' (2013: 16).

Roy, however, has sought to make a different argument through an influential body of work. She argues that urban informality is not, in fact, a 'bounded' space or sector at all, but a type of governance. She understands it as the state's ability to suspend order, to 'decide what is informal and what is not, to determine which forms of informality will thrive and which will disappear' (2005: 149). This is a 'new spatial vocabulary of control, governance and territorial flexibility' (A. Roy 2003: 157), a mode of the production of space. In her more recent work, she refines her analysis: 'While I wish to maintain the idea of informality as a mode of discipline, power, and regulation, I now seek to reject the designation of extra-legality. That terminology implies that informality is a system that runs parallel to the formal and the legal. Yet, the formal and the legal are perhaps better understood as fictions, as moments of fixture in otherwise volatile, ambiguous, and uncertain systems of planning' (A. Roy 2009b: 81).

Evictions challenge these narratives in many ways. In the first chapter of the book, I argue that it is within illegalities rather than within the false binaries of formal/informal and legal/illegal that the production of space in Delhi—and indeed in cities of the South more broadly—must be understood. I do so through historicising the history of inhabitation in Delhi in order to situate and locate the basti amidst a broader history of housing in the city. Through this history, I argue that the 'formal' and the 'legal' are, in fact, far from 'fictions' in the production of space in contemporary Delhi or indeed in the urbanism of auto-constructed cities more generally.

As a starting point, I use a set of categories—specifically, settlement typologies—shown in Table I.1. In an environment where data is hard to get and even harder to verify, this table appears and re-appears with remarkable consistency across the policy landscape in Delhi. The *Economic Survey of Delhi, 2008–2009* (Government of Delhi 2009) shares it with the *City Development Plan* (Government of Delhi 2006), the *Master Plan for Delhi-2021* (DDA 2007), and the *Delhi Urban Environment and Infrastructure Improvement Report: Delhi 21* (MoEF and Government of Delhi 2001), for example.

Though its data dates back to 2000, the table is still the most (and indeed the only) cited set of statistics on the types and relative quantum of housing in the city. It is then both an empiric and an artefact—used as much as for its representation and categories of enumeration as for its numerics. Its categories are the terms used to speak about housing in the city—by the courts, planners within the DDA, the city and central governments, the municipal authorities, the media and by city residents themselves.

## Table I.1: Settlements in Delhi

| Type of Settlement | Estimated Population in 2000 ('000s) | Percentage of Total Population of City |
|---|---|---|
| JJ Clusters | 20.72 | 14.8 |
| Slum Designated Areas | 26.64 | 19.1 |
| Unauthorised Colonies | 7.40 | 5.3 |
| JJ Resettlement Colon es | 17.76 | 12.7 |
| Rural Villages | 7.40 | 5.3 |
| Regularised-Author sed Colonies | 17.76 | 12.7 |
| Urban Villages | 8.88 | 6.4 |
| Planned Colonies | 33.08 | 23.7 |
| Total | 139.64 | 100 |

*Source:* Drawn based on data from statement 14.4 of Government of Delhi (2009).

Even a bare glance at the table indicates a peculiar fact—only 23.7 per cent of the city lives in what are called 'planned colonies'. What does that tell us about the 'unplanned,' 'illegal' and 'informal'? To answer this question, I historicise and visualise—as far as it is accurately possible to do so using a series of geo-spatial maps—where housing within categories of any legal status was built in Delhi from the issuance of the first master plan in 1962 to the present moment, juxtaposing this history of inhabitation against the city's three master plans. I spatialise, in other words, each of the categories of the table. I then use this data to assess how these categories themselves are constructed—their definitional principles, in-built exclusions and their application in everyday life.

I draw two conclusions from the data. First, I show that the 'unplanned' is not the domain of the poor or the slum. If the 'dysfunctional landscapes of Southern cities' are indeed caused by the 'dominance of informal, unplanned growth,' as Rao argues, then this dysfunction must take into account not just the 'slum' but the production of illegal housing by the middle and upper middle classes as well. In fact, the data reminds us that the illegal construction of housing is, in fact, the dominant mode of production of housing and shelter in the city. The reduction of

urban dysfunction to the 'slum' or the 'informal settlement' in policy and everyday discourse as well as within urban and planning
theory, I argue, has played a key political and intellectual role
that is, in David Harvey's (1973) use of the term, 'counter-
revolutionary'—it not only asks the wrong question, it prevents
the real question from being asked. It has allowed the dualisms
that Varley describes and that Roy challenges to reproduce,
creating the fiction of the 'informal city' as an autonomous,
distinct object.

I suggest then a different field of inquiry—if illegality is
indeed the dominant mode of production of urban housing
as the data suggests, then we must understand and account
for the differentiated implications of various illegalities when
exercised by different urban actors. This reframing insists that
analyses of urban politics be relational, looking at the ways in
which particular kinds of urban practices and actors are framed
as 'illegal' relative to others and what work such a framing
is meant to do. To do so, I argue, the conceptual terrain of
'legitimacy' offers a stronger foundation than the many lives
of 'urban informality'.

Legitimate housing or settlements can be legal/illegal or
formal/informal, and are usually a complex mixture of all of
the above. What defines them is their resilience against arbitrary
eviction through either a de facto or de jure security of tenure
that need not, and indeed often does not, derive from inclusion
within law or the master plan. Legitimacy allows us to explore
how different settlements inhabit the city within illegalities
rather than create false separations between what are deeply
porous categories.

Theorised more generally, legitimacy can be seen as a marker
of the probability of reaching certain desired outcomes—secure
tenure, basic services, but also greater wealth, for example, or
access to capital and resources. Practices that enhance legitimacy
increase the probability of reaching the desired outcome and
sustaining it, though neither is guaranteed. These practices are
diverse, working through law or custom; de jure rights or de
facto gains; negotiation or confrontation. They are irreducible
to (in)formal/(il)legal either spatially, in their form or as a

descriptor of actors wielding them. They are, however, shaped by and intertwined with material, discursive and institutional structures of the 'formal' and 'legal'. There is, in other words, no autonomous 'outside' that they inhabit.

My second conclusion from the data is that it is planning itself that produces and regulates illegality. I show how practices of planning determine which settlements will be legal and which illegal, which will thrive and which will not be allowed to exist. The production and regulation of illegality is thus part of, and not outside, what we understand as planning. Planning then is indeed a technique of rule, what Roy calls a 'a spatial mode of governance' where the state exercises a 'calculated informality,' to 'decide what is informal and what is not, to determine which forms of informality will thrive and which will disappear' (2005: 182).

Yet this ability to be discretionary and 'calculated' has limits. This is particularly true when different institutions within the 'state' choose to exercise competing discretions within the city. Contrary to what Roy argues, within the courtroom, the 'formal and the legal,' are perhaps not better understood as 'fictions'— they take concrete, judicial form that is based on the categories and stipulations of the 'plan in its legal position'. It is this judicial translation of the master plan, planning and the idea of 'planned development' that is the focus of the second chapter.

## Two: Urban Governance and the Crisis of Planned Development

Contemporary writing on urban governance in India has focused largely on the executive when they have spoken of the 'state,' be it in claims and critiques of a neoliberal turn[14] and the emergence of a new developmentalism,[15] critiques of co-option masquerading as participation,[16] the World Bank's elaboration of 'good governance,'[17] or writers tracing the emergence of elite civic government.[18] Even those seeing to disaggregate within the state have done so largely through seeking to move across scale— verticality, as Ferguson and Gupta term it (Ferguson 2002)—to urge a focus on local government, on everyday practices and

21

mundane functioning that produce the state (Gupta 2012) or that shape urban outcomes outside it (Benjamin 2004; A. Roy 2009a).

Yet there has yet been an insufficient analysis of the critical role played by the judiciary in shaping governance. Such an analysis is extremely timely in contemporary Indian politics as an active judiciary intervening in everything from forest rights to urban displacement is accused of a 'judicial activism' that breaches the separation of powers imagined in the Constitution. Courts, argue scholars like Sathe (2002: 238), pass increasingly administrative decisions that obliterate the line between law and policy (Muralidhar and Desai 2000), moving the 'character of the judicial process from adversarial to polycentric, and adjudicative to legislative' (Sathe 2002: 235). Manoj Mate (2013) has termed this as the 'judicialisation of governance'.

Delhi is a particularly rich site within which to study such judicialisation as an urban phenomenon. Evictions are only one marker of an increasing judicial presence in the city shaping everything from industrial closures to energy sources in public transport; from solid waste to the enforcement of land use and zoning regulations; from environmental rulings to illegal construction and peri-urban land acquisition. Contemporary Delhi is a city significantly shaped by judicial decisions taken in the public interest.

In this chapter, I seek to locate the 'judicialisation of governance' in the city. I argue that urban case law within PILs has not been sufficiently seen as a site that produces the city as a scale and object of government. I show how Court-ordered evictions make visible broader judicial efforts to make the city into what Nikolas Rose (1999) calls a 'governable space'. Using a Foucauldian analytics of government, I argue that the courts are a site of the production of new governmental rationalities that emerge within the construction of a particular understanding of the city as a site of crisis marked and caused by the failure of, on the one hand, what the courts repeatedly call 'planned development' and, on the other, of 'Government'.

How do we understand the crisis *of*, *in*, and even *as* the city? Within the case law on evictions, the crisis of the city is repeatedly defined as a failure—pressing, immediate and urgent—of what the courts call 'planned development'. This failure, they argue, is the primary question of public interest. What is this 'failure'? Two intertwined elements form the answer. The first is what is termed in the case-law as 'encroachment': the 'illegal' and 'unauthorised' occupation of land, unauthorised construction in individual building units, and the violation of permitted land use, especially within residential colonies. As the most visible symptom of the failure of planned development, encroachment is what separates the complexities of the real city from the imagination of the planned city—it is the multiple disjunctures between the city and its plan. The courts perform a particular reading of these disjunctures—one that marks them as scars, gaps to be filled, violations that must be undone.

Both the 'slum' and 'encroachment' perform the work of city-making within the Court. When the Court argues that the failure of planned development through encroachment turns the city into a 'slum,' it creates the slum as a shorthand of all that is not planned, not orderly and, therefore, neither legitimate nor desirable. The problem that the slum represents then shifts: it marks neither the vulnerability of its residents nor the history of state failure to build adequate affordable low-income housing. The lives within it are flattened into the land the settlement sits on. From a basti, it becomes a slum—something whose erasure is an act of 'good governance,' of order, and of public interest.

The second part of the crisis of the city is the failure of what the courts call the 'Government,' i.e. the world of policy, institutions of representative and electoral politics, and statutory public bodies including city utilities, municipal authorities, and developmental authorities. It is, in other words, the failure of the sarkar to manage the city and protect it against encroachment. This failure allows the Court to position itself as a powerful urban actor, legitimising its interventions within the city and its attempts to actively subject the Executive to its power. In fact, this subjection becomes framed as inevitable and necessary precisely because of the Court's portrayal of an inefficient, corrupt and unreliable 'Government'. This shift marks a clear break from PILs in the 1980s where, as scholars have noted, the courts may have held the 'Government' responsible for failing to do its duty but they saw their own role as being limited to the determination of this failure. Redressal and further response remained the responsibility of executive authorities—the work of policies and programmes, the work of 'Government'.

The crisis of the city—visibilised by encroachment and understood as the failure of planned development and 'Government'—legitimises judicial urban interventions. The need to address these intertwined failures, to restore order, and to intervene in the idiom and temporality of crisis becomes not only the primary meaning of public interest but also an ethico-moral imperative, what Rose might term the moral form of the rationality of judicial government. This imperative reads judicial action and the rule of law itself as an act of restoring order and governance to a city in crisis. It is not coincidental that, as they order evictions, the courts argue that, 'no city, no democracy can survive without law and order. Public interest requires the promotion of law and order, not its degeneration and decay.'[19]

Yet even if the courts see themselves as legitimate urban actors and create a governmental rationality that allows them to intervene into the city, what is the basis by which the Court decides what to do? If encroachment is the anti-thesis of something called 'planned development,' what is the latter meant to be? To govern, argues Nikolas Rose, it is necessary to 'render visible the space over which government is to be exercised' (1999: 36). Acts of mapping, drawing, scaling and rendering visual, therefore, are particular acts that spatialise government. Within case law on evictions, the Court privileges a particular representation of the city: the three Delhi master plans—1962, 2001 and 2021—that are transformed into what the courts call 'the Plan in its legal position'. How does the Court use a document produced by one of the authorities of the very 'Government' that it accused of failure? What does it mean for the plan—an instrument of policy—to act as 'law'? What is, in other words, the 'legal position' of the plan?

In its legal position, the Plan's boundaries both create and bind the city as a governable space. The Plan in its legal position spatialises governmental thought. Its categories of land use and ownership—in their visual, two-dimensional allocations—reduce the complexity of the city to a neat binary of all that *does* or *does not* ally with the Plan at any given point of time. It becomes the framework, in other words, of the legal and the illegal rather than the legitimate. The 'legal position' of the Plan is what James Scott describes as a 'simplification'—the reduction of complex relations and processes to 'a single element of instrumental value' (1998: 77).

The Plan as seen by the Court is reduced to the spatial order it represents—a two-dimensional system of classification of land use. Perhaps more importantly, it is simplified to what this spatial order represents within the crisis of planned development in the city: a legible, enforceable sense of order. The Plan stands both as law and as ideal, the singular basis of the Court's intervention into the city. It becomes the benchmark of how the city must be ruled in order to escape the crises of infrastructural decay, the breakdown of order, the lack of housing, increasing migration and the proliferation of 'slums'. Within the Court, an ordinary land-use plan becomes a mark of a spatial, aesthetic, social and political urban order that must be attained. The implementation of the Plan becomes not just the mechanism of government but its rationality, a defining component of public interest. As it does so, it impacts not just governance, but conceptions and practices of citizenship and rights—the subjects of the third chapter.

## Three: Citizenship and Spatial Illegality

Recent writing suggests that cities of the global South could be sites of a more egalitarian politics, be it through Arjun Appadurai's (2001) notion of a 'deep democracy' that represents efforts to 'reconstitute citizenship in cities,' or James Holston's (2009) writing on the possibility of insurgence that he describes as 'a counter-politics that destabilizes the dominant regime of citizenship and renders it vulnerable.' Urban citizens, Holston argues, see the city rather than the nation as the 'primary community of reference' (2008: 23) for claims to rights and belonging. This claim is particularly important, argue Holston and Appadurai, in post-colonial societies where a 'new generation has arisen to create urban cultures severed from both colonial memories and nationalist fictions' (Holston and Appadurai 1999: 3). Holston gives us a compelling definition of an *urban* citizenship:

> where urban residence is the basis for mobilization, rights claims addressing the urban experience compose their agenda, the city is the primary community of reference for these developments, and residents legitimate this agenda of rights and participatory practices on the basis of their contributions to the city itself. (2008: 23)

Has Lefebvre's oft-quoted 'right to the city' indeed 'moved south, so to speak' (Holston 2009: 245)? Holston reminds us that 'insurgent citizenship' is not necessarily 'progressive' or 'egalitarian' space. Citizenship as 'a means of organizing society,' he argues, has always been 'both subversive and reactionary, inclusionary and exclusionary, a project of equalization and one of maintaining inequality' (2008: 21).

Indian cities seem to heed his caution. On the one hand, there is no doubt that the urban has emerged both as a site and context in contemporary India. Yet the 'urban turn' that Gyan Prakash heralded nearly a decade ago remains immensely debated. Many scholars have argued that the dominant discourses of citizenship in urban India reflect, in fact, the rise of a new growth coalition that sees cities as the 'engines of national development' (HPEC 2011: *xii*). Within this new urban political economy, Jayal (2013) argues, lies an 'unsocial compact'. Gidwani and Reddy term this a 'post-development social formation' within which even the 'nominal ethical relationship' between the state, elite and the poor of a previous developmentalism stands fractured (2011: 1640). As a self-fashioned 'middle class citizen' becomes the object of what Deshpande (1993) once eloquently called the 'imagined economy' at the heart of any developmental imagination, Drèze and Sen (2013) argue that this citizen becomes the new *aam aadmi* or 'common man' in our cities—not necessarily elite but certainly not poor given the demographic realities of both poverty and destitution in Indian cities. Indian cities, to twist an older argument from Partha Chatterjee (2004a), seem indeed to have become bourgeoisie at last.

In this chapter, I argue that while the power of the claims of the 'middle class' and the emergence of a new urban political economy are well documented, the specificity of how subaltern urban residents have been displaced from a developmental imagination remains relatively understudied. Put simply: how have the claims, presence and resistance of a significant proportion of urban residents been managed and even evaded within urban politics? Negotiating the claims of differentiated citizens takes particular forms in different citizenship regimes, places and times. To explain and challenge what Satish Deshpande has described as the 'elusiveness of counter-hegemonic politics in urban spaces' (2013: 39) in India today, understanding this particularity matters.

To do so, I utilise a second analytical category: impoverishment. Upendra Baxi has argued that, 'people are not naturally poor, but are made poor.' He argues that 'poverty' and the 'poor' are passive words that invisibilise the processes by which poverty is produced and reproduced. He argues instead for a perspective based on 'impoverishment'—'a dynamic process of public decision-making in which it is considered just, right and fair that some people may become or stay poor' (1988: *viii*). In this chapter, I trace processes of impoverishment through looking at evictions. I show that the principle mechanism of impoverishment that evictions make visible is how more familiar loci for accessing citizenship in India—for example, caste and poverty—can be rendered ineffective within the urban through the rising salience of a third: spatial illegality.

Following from earlier chapters where I show the relational nature of this illegality and argue that its correction was a cornerstone of planned development and good governance, I shift my focus to take spatial illegality seriously as a logic that mediates contemporary urban citizenship. In doing so, I argue that such illegality impacts not just the legal status of settlement forms such as the basti but the conditions of possibility for politics for the residents within them. I locate this argument

27

as a significant shift within the particular context of historical configurations of citizenship within Indian constitutionalism where group-differentiated citizenship has long been enshrined as a political principle and practice. In the move from nation to city, and from national to urban development, evictions make visible how status categories based on the production of space and spatial location foreclose claims to citizenship based on more familiar loci of economic and social marginalisation such as caste or poverty with crucial implications for inclusive urban politics.

In the first part of this chapter, I outline specific process of such impoverishment within case law on evictions. First, I trace the emergence of an elite insurgent urban citizenship that produces and claims the city as its primary community of belonging. I show how petitioners representing elite associations describe themselves as 'citizens of Delhi,' and use this location to articulate the right to a certain quality of life, or as some authors have termed it, a 'lifestyle' (L. Fernandes 2004), as opposed to basic needs in the determination of the meanings and bounds of the constitutionally-guaranteed Right to Life.

Second, I argue that the courts' description of basti residents as 'encroachers' enables an *act* of occupation to translate into the *identity* of the basti resident. To use the term 'encroacher' is to characterise personhood. Building on the work of Usha Ramanathan (2004), I argue that an 'encroacher' is the antithesis of the 'citizen'. Each is produced in contradistinction to the other as the judges differentiate between 'unscrupulous elements in society' and 'honest citizens who have to pay for a land or a flat;'[20] or argue, when basti residents demand justice, that they 'cannot forget' that they are, after all, 'encroachers on public land'.[21] As an identity, 'encroacher' performs exactly the same function as 'citizen'—it supersedes other claims and sites of belonging. Within the Court, it becomes the primary and often the only identity of a certain set of urban residents. The use of the 'encroacher' reduces the basti resident to the slum dweller. It is not just the slum as encroachment then that represents Rao's 'distorted urban substance,' it is the encroacher himself that is no longer legitimate nor desirable. Personifying illegality, the encroacher becomes unworthy of rights. He cannot possess what Chatterjee calls, 'the moral connotation of sharing in the sovereignty of the state' that is implied within citizenship (2004a: 136).

Third, I trace an altered representation of the poor through an erasure of an older basis of making claims—need and vulnerability. I show how the courts misrecognise the basti as a space of 'commercial activity' rather than shelter; as *pucca*—formed, built, improved—rather than kuccha, i.e. temporary, vulnerable, still unmade. Within the Court, the basti no longer marks vulnerability and deprivation. The move from kuccha to pucca that, in any other context, would translate into a desirable indication of a marginal but important rise in the economic security of income-poor residents is interpreted instead as a sign of their diminished vulnerability. The basti is thus emptied. It is reduced to an image—flattened of the people who live within it, erased from its historical origins and its structural location within the political economy of the production of space in the city.

The processes of impoverishment I have been describing above are made visible through the case law on eviction but they originate and extend beyond them. In the second part of this chapter, therefore, I juxtapose the arguments of the judges against two sites beyond the courtroom. I do so in order to trace how discourses and imaginations of poverty, vulnerability and inequality move between the courtroom and the city. I am particularly interested in showing how these discourses shape who can be an urban citizen, what kind of claims different citizens can make, and what they are entitled to. These sites are: (a) emergence of new urban aesthetic regimes of poverty and the city itself; and (b) emergent discourses and institutionalised policy directives on 'citizen participation'.

In conclusion, I argue that urban citizenship in contemporary Delhi appears to be a site not of equity and insurgence, but of inequality, impoverishment and differentiation. To imagine new futures, I argue, a new and more inclusive politics for the city must take seriously the role that spatial illegality plays as a mode of impoverishment. In moving from the nation to the city, it must look beyond familiar categories of identity and status such as labour, caste and poverty to new locations for insurgent urban politics that take seriously the urban not just as a location but a context for the determination of citizenship. In doing so, it must begin, following Richard Pitthouse (2014), to see the basti as a 'site for and of politics' in order to re-configure how it is viewed, valued and imagined. It must follow Vinay Gidwani in asking: what is an urban politics that 'pivots around the waste-picker, the shack-dweller and the informal vendor'[22] so that a new political personhood can be framed that is spatial as well as economic, cultural and political, and emerges from the realities of fighting for substantive citizenship within auto-constructed cities.

## Four: The Judicialisation of Resistance

The fourth chapter of the book then shifts our focus from the Court's rulings to the residents and activists of the bastis themselves. It asks: how did social movements react to and resist evictions? What were the sites and forms of their struggle? What strategies did they employ and what claims to rights, relief or resources were embedded within these strategies? Particularly, it asks: how, if at all, did the fact that these evictions were ordered by the Delhi high court and the Supreme Court of India rather than the sarkar, impact resistance?

Conceptualising resistance lies within the fault lines between a Lefebvrian conception of the right to the city and what Zerah, Lama-Rewal et al. (2012: 2) describe as rights in the city—a retake on the right to the city that argues that a bundle of rights can be obtained 'only by engaging with the institutions of the developmental state.' The right to the city, Lefebvre argued, was 'the right to *oeuvre* (the city as a work of art), to participation and to appropriation (clearly distinct from the right to property)' as a claim to the city (2002/1968). In recent and influential work, James Holston (2008, 2009, among others) suggests that it has not been, as Lefebvre expected, the working classes of the cities of the North Atlantic that brought about the right to the city. For Holston, it is within the contemporary moment of extraordinary urbanism in cities of the South that the right to the city finds some realisation. It is precisely in the 'peripheries of these cities,' he argues, 'that residents organize movements of insurgent citizenship to confront the entrenched regimes of citizen inequality that the urban centers use to segregate them' (Holston 2009: 245).

'Not all peripheries, of course,' concedes Holston, 'are insurgent' (ibid.). Susan Parnell and Edgar Pieterse, in fact, argue that the 'notions of urban citizenship have been little applied to the fundamental development questions of how cities of the South might be imagined or governed'—a lacuna made apparent by 'the absence of an articulated rights-based agenda for cities of the South' though they mark Brazil as a strong exception (2010: 148). For them, the challenge of using rights-based approaches amidst an urbanisation of poverty underscores the need for a different political practice: an engagement with the 'state' and the 'downscaling' of 'the developmental state to the city scale' especially in the 'large cities of the South' (ibid.: 146).

Parnell and Pieterse argue that socio-economic rights require 'bringing the state back into development debates' (ibid.: 153). They are writing against what they see as the marginalisation of the state as a development actor through the undifferentiated charge of 'neoliberalism'. Their understanding of the nature of engagement with the state deserves close attention. They argue that

> citizen action that relies exclusively on an oppositional logic or a political stance of perpetual resistance is unlikely to achieve reforms in the mundane functioning of the state, which we have shown from the Cape Town experience to be a precondition for cumulative changes that can transform the political economy of opportunity and provide institutional access to resources. (ibid.: 158)

This tension, or perhaps more accurately this calculus, between negotiation and confrontation as modes of engagement, as well as the relationship of this calculus to rights to and in the city, are at the heart of this chapter. This calculus became evident in Indian cities in 2005 in Mumbai when the city witnessed a series of brutal evictions of informal settlements and pavement dwellers that displaced nearly 300,000 people. The Alliance—the network of Society for the Promotion of Area Resource Centers (SPARC), the National Slum Dwellers Federation and Mahila Milan written about extensively as a new form of 'deep democracy' and resistance to dispossession and urban evictions (see Appadurai 2002; Burra, Patel and Kerr 2003; Patel, D'Cruz and Burra 2002)—famously and to much public criticism did not mount a campaign of public resistance. It said instead that, 'our experiences in the past and the outlook of the poor communities that we work with have propelled us to eschew the path of righteous indignation and protest' (Mitlin and Patel 2005: 3–4) in what they described as an 'on-going war of attrition between the poor and the state' (ibid.: 2–3).

Ananya Roy has argued that this 'politics of patience' (Appadurai 2002) can also be read as a 'politics of compensation' that creates a 'distinctive political subjectivity' (A. Roy 2009a). This politics, she argues, is steeped in the 'morality of collaboration, participation and mediation. To protest, to confront, is to stand outside the parameters of citizenship' (ibid.: 173). When seen from the perspective of urban social movements within settlements facing eviction, how do we understand this calculus between negotiation and confrontation?

Drawing upon a series of interviews conducted with activists who are members of urban social movements resisting evictions in Delhi from the late 1990s, I argue that existing fault lines within urban social movements on choosing between (or simultaneously using) multiple strategies of resistance are further complicated when the object of resistance is the Judiciary rather than the Executive. Already complex divisions on axes of gender, class and vulnerability continue to play out in the decision of how to resist a Court-ordered eviction even as activists additionally struggle with the belief that a Court order cannot be contested at all, on the one hand, or arguing that it is not a site where the poor can and should voice their demands, on the other.

Strategies of resistance are further compromised as the right and obligation to contest the Executive or sarkar is contrasted with the sense among activists that they don't have a right to fight the Court. This sense is strongly rooted in a sense of distance from the Court—both in the literal barriers to access as well as the symbolic distance in the imagination of the social and political position of the Court in the lives of residents of the basti. This sense of distance is constituted in part by the role played by lawyers as both interlocutors but also symbols of the barriers to entry within the legal process. It also manifests itself in the very composition of right-claims that are made by and on behalf of those facing eviction. Rights in their 'legal sense' are bound by the limits of arguments that lawyers believe the Court will recognise as legitimate. Arguments made by residents in movements spaces—particularly those challenging the cut-off dates and questioning the public purpose for which basti land is required—therefore cannot be 'legally sensible' though they form a core of right-claims outside the courtroom.

I argue that Court-ordered evictions alter the forms, claims, sites and strategies of urban social movements in advocating for the rights and citizenship of those facing the threat of eviction. Specifically, the emergence of the Court shapes the choice of strategies used by urban social movements, introduces new actors and decision-making processes into movement spaces, alters the content of rights claims and forecloses certain kinds of claimants just as it shapes the political identity, narratives and history of bastis and basti residents themselves. It is this that I term the *judicialisation of resistance*.

## Five: On Law and Urbanism

Comaroff and Comaroff (2008) argue that, across the post-colonial world, politics is increasingly constituted in and as law. Using a range of examples from the drug trade to real estate, generic drugs to evictions, they describe this as a 'judicialisation of politics'. Politics itself, they argue, is 'migrating to the Courts. Conflicts once joined in parliament, by means of street protests, mass demonstrations, and media campaigns, through labour boycotts, and other instruments of assertion, to name a few—now tend more and more to head to the Courts' (ibid.: 27).

To engage with the law, they argue, is no longer a choice but an inevitability.

Studying Delhi indeed does make the study of law seem inevitable. The last two decades, as chapters across this book will argue, have seen the Judiciary emerge as a critical site in shaping almost every facet of the city's urbanism. These are a set of diverse interventions: intervening in the state's discretion within informality as it insists rather on illegalities; reading policies such as the master plan 'in their legal position'; shaping notions of 'good governance'; intervening in the production of the built form of the city; mediating state-citizen relations; reflecting as well shaping public discourse on urban development; and altering practices of resistance and activism, among others.

The fifth inquiry from Delhi then is to study the relationship between law and urbanism. It is to ask: What does it mean for a series of urban questions, interventions, and process to come to be articulated, institutionalised and addressed within the logics of law? How do the judicialisation of governance described earlier and the judicialisation of politics locate themselves in the city? Taken together, do they suggest what we may call a *judicial urbanism*? In the conclusion of the book, I will return to this question.

## Six: The Persistence of Poverty

The final inquiry is perhaps the book's most central ethical pre-occupation and what, quite frankly, provoked its writing. When theorising not just from Delhi but also from the basti within it, questions of poverty, vulnerability and inequality are inescapable. The basti represents the slow, incremental and fragile process of producing the city for subaltern urban residents. Its courage and resilience are real as are its vulnerability, marginalisation and structural exclusion. It is equally a marker of slow progress towards as well as the continual denial of claims to equalities of outcome and opportunity—to basic services, core human development capabilities, rights, economic security, as well as belonging and citizenship. Evictions mark a moment when both this set of incremental gains as well as claims to at least progressive realisation of equality are erased. As a generation thus inherits the poverty of their parents rather than the fruits of their sacrifices, poverty and inequality are undeniably reproduced. They become, to use Tilly's (1998) frame, 'durable'.

Throughout this book, I will show the processes by which such reproduction was made possible. My interest in doing so is, following Tilly, and Mosse, is to begin to attempt to 'explain rather than just describe durable poverty' within a 'relational approach to poverty' (Mosse 2010: 1157). Such an approach, argues Mosse, 'views persistent poverty as the consequence of historically developed economic and political relations' and emphasises 'the effect of social categorization and identity in reproducing inequality' (ibid.).

In the concluding chapter, I return to this attempt, thinking through about what evictions in particular can tell us about the persistence of poverty and the reproduction of inequality within contemporary urbanism.

## On Methods and Archives: The View from the Basti

*The cities of which we are citizens are cities in which we want to intervene, build, reform, criticize and transform. We cannot leave them untouched, implicit, unspoken about.*

—Teresa Caldeira (2000: 8)

*It is precisely because we are dealing with 'social worlds of massive and extreme inequality that it is not just necessary but imperative to ask how inequalities are socially institutionalised'.*

—James Ferguson (2013: 233)

My fieldwork started several years before I began my research for this book. I am both a native and citizen of Delhi—it is my place of origin as well as where I legally, morally, emotionally and culturally belong. I discovered the bastis of my own city through their eviction. For many years, I was a part of anti-eviction social movements, present both in the street and the courtroom, trying to resist. When Pushta was evicted, I followed families like Rafiya's to Bawana. For two years, I led a local research team in a study to quantify the impact of resettlement on these families. The research became a book and an annexure in multiple court challenges to evictions as evidence of what we had described as the 'permanent poverty' of the resettlement colony (Bhan and Menon-Sen 2008). Evictions had angered, hurt and horrified me. I went to Bawana seeking something: an outlet, some absolution, some answers. Those years changed the basti for me. An object of inquiry became an ordinary, everyday place. Its vulnerability was obvious. As time passed, so was its resilience. As more time passed, neither became the defining trope of the basti for me—the 'slum' had left my imagination both as space of hope and a space of despair. I was now, I felt, finally ready to understand it on its own terms. The first thing I learnt to do was to stop looking at the basti, but rather look from it. In a sense, this book represents that moment.

The study of the periphery in contemporary urban theory is too often just that: an attempt to explain what occurs at the periphery, looked at, inevitably, from the gaze of those who live outside it. My intention here is not to debate the politics of either representation or location. It is instead to suggest a new kind of native informant: the elite, organic intellectual who uses the periphery as a site to study his own locations: the academy and planning theory, the authority and institutions of planning practice as well as himself. Let me put it simply: to look at the basti from within planning theory or practice, for example, is to tell a tale of exception. To look at planning from the basti is to tell a tale of the fiction of the rule. As I argued earlier, peripheries both allow and compel us to ask different questions—the task for our inquiries is to take these questions and construct bodies of theory from and with them.

This book is, in its essence, one part of a broader project to create an ethnography of inequality. It is so because, for me, questions of the (re)production of inequality are arguably the most pressing questions that the basti asks of the city—that it asked of me in the years I spent within it. The longue durée task of my research—far beyond the capacities of this book—is then an explicitly political exercise: to build a theory of the inequality and the city from the periphery, reflecting its priorities and concerns. It is then to take these concerns to the academy, the government, the public and the city to hold them/us answerable. The ethnographer is then native informant and Trojan horse, seeking to unravel the 'foundationalist fictions' of the presumed centres of power from within.

My research thus began with trying, quite literally, to find the evicted basti. How does one search for the site of a settlement that no longer exists? Over a period of two months in October and November 2010, a team of research assistants and I went out everyday into the city searching for absences. Armed with a list of eviction sites with very approximate geographical locations, we reached neighbourhoods and then began to ask residents if they remembered a basti that once stood somewhere in the area. Rickshaw pullers, street vendors, labourers and taxi drivers, we quickly realised, were the best informants. Their memories were amazingly clear: they knew sites, names, the number of households and where the evicted bastis had been resettled, allowing us to verify official lists and find the locations of bastis to geo-code onto maps. Searching for evictions, I realised that there were two cities everywhere we went—one that still stood, and one whose memory still marked local narratives of space.

As I created the map of evictions, I began to see the patterns that I present in Chapter One. The evictions clustered in the centre of the city—leaving large white spaces that seemed implausible. I plotted existing bastis next that made another pattern emerge. Unauthorised colonies, resettlement colonies, regularised colonies—one by one I mapped all the housing typologies that defined Delhi's built environment, provoked by the pattern that evictions had thrown up. The basti did indeed provoke its own questions, allowing me to rebuild the city from within it, and reconstruct planning in the city in doing so.

The evictions then led me to the courts. I knew of Pushta and Nangla Machi as two Court-ordered evictions. Curiosity took me to the Delhi high court to find the original petitions that resulted in the order for evictions. I realised then that the orders that led to the evictions at Pushta were given in a clustered litigation that brought no less than 63 different PILs together. That first petition led me to another, and then another. The primary archive that this book draws upon is now a set of 24 PILs filed in the Delhi high court and the Supreme Court of India that led directly to evictions. I accessed copies of the lead original petitions, interim orders, court transcripts and committee reports filed in the process of hearing. I focused on the *dicta*, the text of the judges' verdicts where they outlined their reason and the logics of their determination of rights and the public interest. As the judgments were reported in the media, I followed them, seeing how the judges' words travelled through the city.

The last part of the fieldwork was, in many ways, the most difficult. In seeking to understand resistance to evictions, I turned back to open-ended interviews with activists in urban social movements, and particularly, to key figures in a coalition of individuals, basti associations, organisations and unions called Sajha Manch. They were all, without exception, friends and colleagues. They were used to researchers but not to one of their own. Interviewing them felt, at times, like questioning myself, voicing out loud many of my own doubts about our strategies and campaigns together. At times, I struggled to keep myself out of the conversation as I believed I should. Halfway through my first set of interviews, I decided to stop trying. I traded interviews for conversations, offering my own reflections but marking the conversations that I led and those that came unaided. In writing transcripts of the interviews, I sorted and contextualised each statement and attempted to indicate this contextualisation. I still do not fully know how far I succeeded.

### Speaking of the 'Court'

How does one speak of the 'Court'? Throughout this Introduction and through this book, I speak of the Delhi high court and the Supreme Court of India as the 'Court' well aware that within them judgments are given by individual judges with varied locations, opinions and styles. I continue to speak of these diverse individual judgments as emergent from the 'Court' for two reasons. The first is that within the Indian legal system, a single case often rotates among benches of judges. In other words, in the course of its hearing, several judges will have presided over a case until it is reserved for judgment by a particular bench of anywhere between one and three judges, or, in rarer cases, a full bench of five or more judges. Orders may be passed by multiple judges, especially within a PIL that continues for several years. The case law, therefore, does not permit attributing a single judgment to a single bench.

This structural phenomena of the Indian courts lies behind the second and more important reason for speaking of the 'Court' as an entity. A high court advocate, Jawahar Raja, once described to me something he called the *hava* of the Court. 'Hava' in Hindi literally means 'air' or 'wind', but colloquially is often used to describe a prevailing atmosphere. The hava of the Court, he said, is the sense you get of what the political climate of the Court is, what arguments they are open to hearing and what they won't take. You have a clear sense of it at most times, he said, and it shapes the tactics you take. These tactics, he argued, are not tailored to particular judges—'the bench will just change', he argued, so you 'frame your arguments for the Court itself, prepared for whomever you will get.'[23] A recently retired judge of the Delhi high court, Justice A. P. Shah, echoed Raja's thoughts. 'Judges are very aware of what the other is saying,' he said, 'you notice trends in judicial judgments and you have a sense of where the Court is in periods of time.'[24] It is in writing of this hava that I speak of the Court, though I am careful therefore to not attribute motive or agency to it as if it were an actor whose motivations could be thus plainly read.

## How Did We Get Here?

Contemporary evictions capture a moment in which rights are lost, where citizenship is inegalitarian and differentiated, the promise of development is refused, and poverty and inequality are reproduced and deepened. For any effective conceptualisation and realisation of a just city, we must understand this moment in all its particularities, continuities and discontinuities from both previous claims to inhabitation as well as experiences of eviction. The task at hand then is not just to explain evictions but also to listen to what they are telling us—about the city that is as well as the city that can be.

Sitting that day on the floor of her house, as I was trying to escape being maimed by the ceiling fan, Rafiya asked me: 'How did we get here?' It was a question I had been unable to escape—as a resident of Delhi, as a member of social movements resisting evictions, or as an ethnographer. 'Here' as in Bawana where, to me, life seemed nearly impossible either to recreate or start anew though I knew both would happen. 'Here' as in a moment where the evictions of nearly a hundred thousand people in a basti nearly three decades old occurred seemingly without a ripple in the everyday life of the city—without governments falling, without newspaper headlines, without outrage. 'Here' where these same evictions were seen as acts of good governance, planning and public interest. 'Here' where social movements seemed to lose both slogans and surety as they struggled to resist. 'Here' where a judicial innovation seeking to further access to justice for the poor had become precisely the site of their exclusion. 'Here' where neither a claim of poverty nor one to rights seemed sufficient to guarantee a right to the city for the majority of its residents.

Rafiya's question animates, inspires and haunts this book. It also, however, points to its *raison d'etre*. If we do not understand how we got 'here', we cannot understand how to move 'there'— towards a city of inclusion, justice and shelter, even if the latter is made of a small square sheet of thatch, slightly fraying on its sides with a ceiling fan that's uncomfortably close to your head.

# Notes

1. Personal interview, dated 11 February 2010.
2. The Hindi/Urdu word *basti* (related to *basna*, to settle; plural: bastis) means settlement. It is the word most commonly used by residents of urban poor settlements to describe their homes and hence it is the word used throughout this book. Colloquially, bastis are

understood to represent settlements typically marked by some measure of physical, economic and social vulnerability. It is these settlements that are often called 'slums'. Within planning paradigms in Delhi, however, a 'slum' refers specifically to a settlement designated as such under the 1956 Slum Areas Act. I use the word 'slum' only to either refer to this specific planning category or to report its use in English when necessary. In relation to planning, bastis cover three types of settlements: Slum Designated Areas, Resettlement Colonies and jhuggi-jhompri (JJ) clusters. See Chapter One, this volume, for a detailed discussion of these categories.

3. *Sarkar* is often translated as 'government' or even the 'state' but, in this book, I will argue and use it explicitly as the institutions of the Executive.

4. In referring to legal documents in this book, I use short form citations of the name of the petitioner in italics for ease of reading. I refer, for example, to *Wazirpur Bartan Nirmata Sangh vs Union of India (2002)* as *Wazirpur*. Where a reported judgment exists, I cite its record. For example, in this case, the citation 108 (2002) DLT 517 is the record of the reported judgment. If a reported judgment does not exist or when I am directly referring to the original petition filed in the case, I use the citation for a petition. Such petitions are then cited often as 'CWP' or Civil Writ Petition and are marked to indicate the year in which they were filed. For example, *Hemraj* is the 3419th civil writ petition filed in the year 1999. Hence, it is cited as CWP 3419 of 1999. When I cite interim orders in a petition that precede a final, recorded judgment, I give the date of the order. For example, 'Orders of 29 February 2010'.

5. Justice Goswami in *State of Rajasthan & Ors vs Union of India* 1978 SCR (1) 1 (hereafter, *State of Rajasthan*).

6. Letters to the Supreme Court were indeed treated as PILs in *Sunil Batra vs Delhi Administration* (1980) 3 SCC 480 (hereafter, *Sunil Batra*); *Dr Upendra Baxi vs State of UP* (1983) 2 SCC 308 (hereafter, *Dr Upendra Baxi*); *Veena Sethi vs State of Bihar* (1982) 2 SCC 583 (hereafter, *Veena Sethi*); *People's Union for Democratic Rights (PUDR) vs Union of India* (1982) AIR SC 1473 (hereafter, *PUDR*); *Bandhua Mukti Morcha vs Union of India* (1984) 3 SCC 161 (hereafter, *Bandhua Mukti Morcha*); and *Nav Kiran Singh vs State of Punjab* (1995) 4 SCC 591 (hereafter, *Nav Kiran Singh*); among many others.

7. All citations in this paragraph are from the orders of 3 March 2003 in *Okhla Factory Owner's Association vs Government of National*

*Capital Territory of Delhi* CWP 4441 of 1994 (hereafter, *Okhla*) and *Wazirpur Bartan Nirmata Sangh vs Union of India* CWP 2112 of 2002 (hereafter, *Wazirpur*).

8. The Delhi Water Board, the public water utility in the city of Delhi.

9. All citations in this paragraph are from the orders of 29 November 2002, *Okhla*.

10. *Pradhan* refers to the (usually) elected leader of a basti *panchayat*, or council. Though unofficial from the perspective of government, the pradhan is usually recognised as a local political leader. Pradhans are, at times though not always, affiliated, loosely or through direct membership/affiliation, with national political parties like the Congress, Bharatiya Janata Party (BJP) or Communist Party of India (CPI).

11. Personal interview, Kalyani Menon-Sen, member, Stop Evictions campaign, 12 February 2011. See also Chapter Four, this volume.

12. In 1959, the Government of Delhi acquired nearly 39,000 acres of land in the heart of the city, including already built-up areas as well as enough land as planners believed would be needed to account for the city's expansion till 1980. The aim of this acquisition was, in line with the Delhi's first master plan issued in 1962, to enable state control over land to ensure equitable development. See Chapter One, this volume, for a detailed discussion.

13. I draw this argument from personal conversations in Berkeley between 2012 and 2014 on emerging work by these two scholars.

14. For both proponents and particularly its critics writing from the South, see Harvey (2005), Ong (2006), Parnell and Pieterse (2010), Parnell and Robinson (2012), Peck, Theodore and Brenner (2009) and Tickell and Peck (1992).

15. See Bhan (2009), L. Fernandes (2004), Chatterjee (2004a), Deshpande (2013), Gidwani and Reddy (2011), Goldman (2011), Harriss (2007) and Peck, Theodore and Benner (2009).

16. See Coelho, Kamath and Vijayabaskar (2013), Cooke and Kothari (2001) and Harriss (2007).

17. See Santiso (2001) and World Bank (1992).

18. See Anjaria (2009), Ellis (2012) and D. A. Ghertner (2011a).

19. *Pitampura Sudhar Samiti vs Government of the National Capital Territory of Delhi*, CWP 4215 of 1995 (hereafter, *Pitampura*).

20. *Maloy Krishna Dhar vs Government of National Capital Territory of Delhi*, CWP 6160 of 2003 (hereafter, *Maloy*).

21. *Satbeer Singh Rathi vs Municipal Corporation of Delhi* (2004) 114 DLT 760 (hereafter, *Satbeer*).

22. Remarks made at the inaugural meeting of the Urban Poverty and Inequality Collective at the University of California, Berkeley, August 2014.
23. Personal interview, dated 4 May 2011.
24. Personal interview, dated 6 May 2011.

# 1

# Planned Illegalities

## The Production of Housing in Delhi, 1947–2010*

> The City was not planned as it is, but the City is an outcome of planning.
>
> —Lisa Peattie (1987: 15)

In a room full of luminaries on a spring day in Delhi, the city searches, yet again, for illumination. The workshop is another of what seems like an endless number in the unfolding of the urban agenda in India across the academy, policy and government, private enterprise, as well as in the media. The 'Urban Turn' seems complete (Prakash 2002). On the masthead this day is the '21st Century Indian City'.[1] The lead author of the latest urban manifesto—the High Powered Expert Committee Report on Urban Infrastructure (HPEC 2011)—is the lead panelist of the

---

* An earlier version of this chapter appeared as 'Planned Illegalities: Housing and the Failure of Planning in Delhi, 1947–2010' in *Economic and Political Weekly* 48, no. 24 (2013): 58–70. The article has since been revised.

opening session of the workshop. She speaks eloquently about the need for growth in urban infrastructure and the mechanisms by which these are to be attained. At the end, almost as an afterthought, she sums up one of the reasons why her work was, in a way, 'simple'. The committee's approach to infrastructure provision, she says, was 'obvious' because, 'planning, as we all know, has failed in Indian cities'.

The 'failure of planning' has become a ubiquitous and commonsensical refrain uniting voices from across sectors, disciplines and ideological positions. In 2006, the then Prime Minister Manmohan Singh inaugurated the Jawahar Lal Nehru National Urban Renewal Mission (JNNURM)—India's largest urban programme and policy intervention in her history— saying the cities needed to 're-think planning'.[2] Global analysts McKinsey & Co. root India's 'poor state of urban planning' in urban and regional plans that are 'esoteric rather than practical, rarely followed and riddled with exemptions' (McKinsey Global Institute 2010). Members of social movements representing the urban poor go further, describing and protesting what some have called the 'total bankruptcy and arrogance of the planning process' that has led to a 'systemic failure of modern planning' and deep exclusions in Indian cities (D. Roy 2004). Decades apart, Ashis Nandy (1998) and Jai Sen (1976) both famously described Indian cities as 'unintended'.

The planners' desire to 'effect a controlled and orderly manipulation of change' has been, argues Amita Baviskar, 'continuously thwarted' by the 'inherent unruliness of people and places' (2003: 92). Urban planning is considered, at best, 'hopelessly inadequate' in terms of being able to tackle this chaos (Patel 1997) though inadequacy is the gentlest of the charges levelled against planning. Citing the twin jaundice and cholera epidemics in Delhi in 1955 and 1988, Dunu Roy argues that the worst aspect of the failure of planning was that, in fact, 'planners did not even understand the implications of what they themselves had done' (D. Roy 2004).

Crisis-ridden as well as crisis-inducing, chaotic, irrelevant, incompetent, exclusionary: planning in India indeed does indeed seem to have failed. In Indian cities, this 'failure' has acted as a reason, impetus and justification for a range of diverse urban practices—increasing judicial intervention into urban governance by the higher courts; political action by civil society organisations and resident associations; the emergence of new forms of public-private governance mechanisms within urban reform; and policy paradigms as well as trenchant critiques by social movements seeking rights to and in the city. Narratives of 'failure' also critically inform the main subject of this book: the evictions of bastis[3] through judicial orders in the name of public interest. In ordering evictions, the Delhi high court and the Supreme Court of India frequently used the terms 'planning' and 'planned development' with an air of familiarity, resting on the assumption that their meaning and representations were both obvious and commonly shared. As they did, in the same breath, they repeated their diagnosis that 'planning' and 'planned development' had indeed 'failed'.[4] It is here then that we must begin.

How do we assess the 'failure of planning'? Narratives of 'failure' are simultaneously narratives of planning. Accusations of chaos, irrelevance, incompetence and exclusion, in other words, each rely upon an imagination of what functional, relevant, competent and inclusionary planning could and should look like within an Indian city. 'Failure is,' in Ravi Sundaram's (2009) words, 'a diagnostic of planning'. In this book, I take Sundaram seriously. I ask not if planning has indeed failed but instead frame a different inquiry: What is the work done by the idea and discourse of 'failure'? What, in other words, does the idea of 'failure' itself make possible within and as planning?

In this chapter, I am interested particularly in the ways in which failure intertwines with some more familiar objects of urban theory when studying cities of the global South: informality and illegality, both of which are closely seen as the most visible manifestations of the failure of planning. I thus interrogate failure within a specific aspect of urban development: the production of housing in the city. My questions become narrower and more specific: what is the relationship between planning, the nature of its single or multiple 'failures', and the production of housing in the city? In particular, how does planning relate to conceptions of illegal and informal housing closely associated both with urban marginality as well as with narratives of failure? What, in other words, does planning and its 'failures' tell us about the 'slum'?

I seek answers to these questions through constructing a necessarily partial but illuminating history of inhabitation in the city. Using a series of geo-spatial maps, I visualise where housing across the city's planning categories was built from the issuance of the first master plan in 1962. On these maps, I then transpose Delhi's three master plans, using the result along with additional housing data to assess the relationship between these master plans and the building of actually existing housing stock. I seek to map, in a sense, the magnitude and textures of the gaps between imagination, intention and actual practice—arguably one of the most commonly understood 'failures' of planning. Finally, I map evictions in the city from 1990 to 2007 in order to juxtapose sites of eviction, existing housing stock and the master plans to further interrogate the idea of 'planned development'.

In doing so, I argue that, in Delhi, the 'chaos that is urban development' (Verma 2003) is not planned but it is, to twist Peattie's phrase, an outcome of planning. Plans do not control but they influence, determine and limit. Problematising planning's failures allows us to find what I am calling the *traces* of planning—its legacies both historical and contemporary and its presence in the contemporary city either in absence or presence, in failure or success. These traces challenge the ideas of a 'politics of stealth' (Benjamin 2008) as a narrative of subaltern urbanism in cities of the global South. They also reject simplistic diagnoses of 'failure' built upon the misrecognition of assumed distinctions between formal/informal and legal/illegal, and the association of informality and illegality as exclusive domains of the politics of the marginalised. Looking at the actual practices of settling the city, I argue, suggests instead that it is between illegalities practiced by a diverse range of urban residents where we must look to understand the urbanism that lies beneath a 'failed' plan. These illegalities are not 'outside' planning or a mark of its 'failure', but are produced and regulated within

47

planning itself. I conclude by arguing that urban practitioners in a city like Delhi must, therefore, engage with planning precisely because of the continuing relevance of what are considered its 'failures'. The terms of such engagement require new conceptual categories. I propose the idea of *legitimacy*, rather than legality or formality, as a more useful conceptualisation for a more relational urban politics that also more accurately reflects the history of the production of space in southern cities.

*Histories and categories of inhabitation*: To assess housing, I return to a table I used in the introduction. It is based on data from the chapter 'Urban Development' in the *Economic Survey of Delhi, 2008–2009*, presenting 'description' of 'types of settlements' in Delhi in order to 'explain the situation' in the city (Government of Delhi 2009).

As I argued earlier, this table is still the most (and indeed the only) cited set of statistics on the types and relative quantum of housing in the city, used equally by the Judiciary, planners within the DDA, the city and central governments, the municipal authorities, the media and by city residents themselves. In our assessment of planning's failures and the particular history

**Table 1.1: Settlements in Delhi**

| Type of Settlement | Estimated Population in 2000 (100,000s) | Percentage of Total Population of City |
|---|---|---|
| JJ Clusters | 20.72 | 14.8 |
| Slum Designated Areas | 26.64 | 19.1 |
| Unauthorised Colonies | 7.40 | 5.3 |
| JJ Resettlement Colonies | 17.76 | 12.7 |
| Rural Villages | 7.40 | 5.3 |
| Regularised-Unauthorised Colonies | 17.76 | 12.7 |
| Urban Villages | 8.88 | 6.4 |
| Planned Colonies | 33.08 | 23.7 |
| Total | 139.64 | 100 |

*Source*: Drawn based on data from statement 14.4 of Government of Delhi (2009).

of those failures in Delhi within housing, the table therefore represents an ideal starting point.

At first sight, the table seems to confirm a failure of planning: What could be a greater indictment than nearly 75 per cent of the city living in housing that is apparently 'unplanned'? Yet as we problematise this failure, we must ask a different set of questions. From the extensive and interdisciplinary literature on how to think about classification, three key elements are relevant for our purposes. I trace these below.

## Thinking in Categories

The first element is that categories entail choices of what to include and what to leave out. Boundaries must be created, defined and policed for the category to have meaning and be useful. Modern statecraft, argues James Scott, works in part through such simplification—the reduction of 'an infinite array of detail to a set of categories that will facilitate summary descriptions, comparisons and aggregation.' These 'forms of knowledge and manipulation' are particularly characteristic, he says, 'of powerful institutions with sharply defined interests' of which state bureaucracies and institutions are emblematic (1998: 77). These categories, Scott warns, must 'collapse or ignore distinctions that might otherwise be relevant' (ibid.: 81).

It is not just that 'other distinctions' between categories are ignored, argues Amartya Sen, but that they are deemed less important and hence marginalised. Writing about social theories on inequality, Sen argues that different frameworks prioritise a different 'primary variable' that they use to then compare and construct categories. The need 'for ensuring basal equality' in the primary variable, argues Sen, then 'necessitates the tolerance of inequality in what are seen as "outlying perspectives"' (1992: 131).

From Sen and Scott, we get a set of questions about the construction of categories in our table: What is the 'infinite array of detail' that these categories reduce? What do they reduce them to? What are the 'other distinctions' (or similarities) that are erased? Or, in Sen's terms, what is the primary basis of classification of settlement typologies, of separating the 'planned' from the 'unplanned'? What are then the 'outlying perspectives' that this primary basis allows us to consider marginal or less important?

The second element is that categories are often parts of systems and processes of order and ordering. In her seminal study of ideas of pollution and dirt, Mary Douglas argues that dirt is essentially 'disorder'—it is 'matter out of place' (1966: 35). What are order and disorder? Order implies 'restriction', says Douglas, because 'from all possible relations a limited set has been used.' Disorder, in contrast, 'is unlimited, no pattern has been realized in it, but its potential for patterning is indefinite ... disorder symbolizes both danger and power' (ibid.: 94). Categories and the order they are meant to represent must then guard against what Douglas calls anomalies and ambiguities. In culture and through ritual then, 'ideas about separating, purifying, demarcating, and punishing transgressions' play this role, a continuous and fragile attempt 'to impose system on an inherently untidy experience' (ibid.: 4).

From Douglas, we get a second set of questions: What is the dirt—the 'unplanned'—that this system of settlement typologies is trying to keep at bay? What, in other words, is the disorder? What patterns is this 'disorder' capable of and what 'danger' does it represent? How does this system of order guard against ambiguity and anomaly—what are its 'rituals of separation, purification and punishing transgression?'

The third element we must consider is that categories are generative, not just descriptive. In other words, they create and reproduce, albeit imperfectly and incompletely, what they describe or narrate. For Scott, descriptive categories become 'categories that organize people's daily experience precisely because they are embedded in state-created institutions that structure that experience.' They are the 'authoritative tune to which most of the population must dance' because they can be given 'the force of law' (1998: 83). Douglas argues that cultural categories frame experiences just as powerfully. She says that, 'public, standardized values of a community, mediate the experience of individuals [by providing] in advance some basic categories, a positive pattern in which ideas and values are tidily ordered' (1966: 39). It is the 'public character' of these categories that gives them 'authority', which may or may not be enshrined in law.

A third set of questions then arises: How have our housing categories been generative—how have they shaped the built form of the city as well as urban politics? In doing so, how have they impacted and managed the trajectories, subjectivities and claims of resistance to them, or deviance from them?

## Built Categories and Built Environments: A History of and through Settlement Typologies in Delhi

Armed with the set of questions above, I now turn to the analysis of the categories of housing presented in Table 1.1, taking each in turn. Before that, I briefly mark two final necessary contextualisations—a clarification on terms, and a history of Delhi's three master plans.

### Legal, Formal, Planned, Legitimate: A Clarification on Terms

In the analysis that follows, I use a recognisable but often confusing vocabulary to describe settlements: legal/illegal, formal/informal and planned/unplanned. My use of these terms is strategic. I use them despite knowing their limitations and the lack of clarity in their competing definitions. I do so precisely to make these limitations visible, to highlight internalised foreclosures, and to show the political work these perform as terms used widely within legal, planning, academic as well as everyday discourse.

Specifically, I use the term 'planned' only when it is used by the table itself, i.e. in describing the 'Planned Colony'. I limit my use of 'legal' to only refer to housing that is recognised by the Plan to the extent that the owners of the house possess some kind of recognised title or ownership that can be registered with local authorities and is recognised by the state. To describe documented transactions of sale and purchase of property or built housing whether or not the resultant titles are legally recognised, I use the term 'formal'. To describe violations of building norms, developmental controls, and layout plans, regardless of the legality or planning status of the settlement, I again use the twin terms 'formal/informal'. As I will argue later, this separation in terming the violations of certain norms as 'illegal' and others as 'informal' is one that emerges from the settlement typologies themselves and has significant implications for settlements and their residents alike.

I introduce one additional term to the above vocabulary: *legitimate*. I use legitimate to describe settlements that enjoy a de facto or de jure security of tenure. I mean by this that they are protected—either explicitly within the Plan or implicitly in actual urban development practice—from arbitrary eviction. Settlements that are legitimate need not, therefore, derive their legitimacy only from law (although some can and do). They can be formal or informal, legal or illegal, in the sense of the terms described above.

## Brief History of Planning Time: Delhi's Master Plans and the Delhi Experiment

Delhi has had three master plans. Each was made by the DDA— a para-statal, technocratic institution, appointed (as opposed to being elected) by and reporting to the central ministry of urban development. The first was the master plan of Delhi of 1962 (hereafter MPD '62; Map 1.1), followed by plans in MPD '01 (Map 1.2) and MPD '21 (Map 1.3) Each is a twenty-year plan, intended to capture growth in the city, therefore, during 1962–81, 1981–2001 and 2001–21. The MPD '01 was only issued in 1990, however, and was thus nine years late. The MPD '21 was issued in 2007, six years late.

Each plan marks detailed land use categories but for our purposes it is sufficient to note that the Plan divides the National Capital Territory of Delhi into an 'urban development area' (which is then zoned by use) and 'rural' zones. From the MPD '21, a third category of 'urbanisable area' was added, presumably to mark areas for future expansion.

## Map 1.1: Master Plan of Delhi 1962

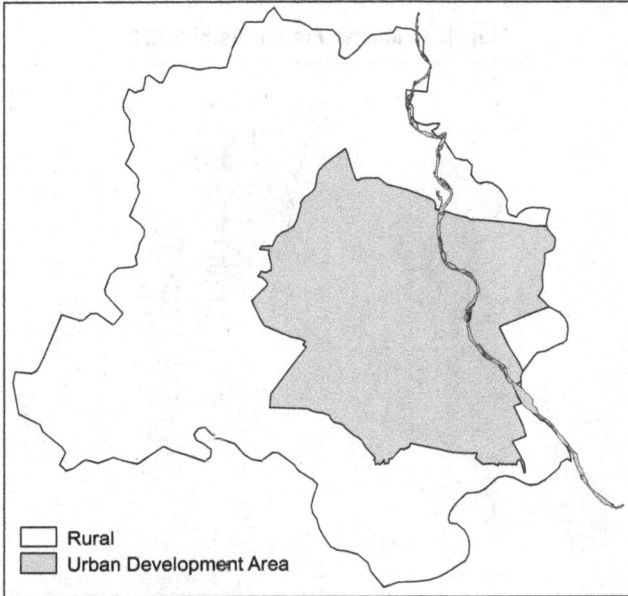

Rural
Urban Development Area

*Source*: Drawn by the author.

## Map 1.2: Master Plan of Delhi 2001

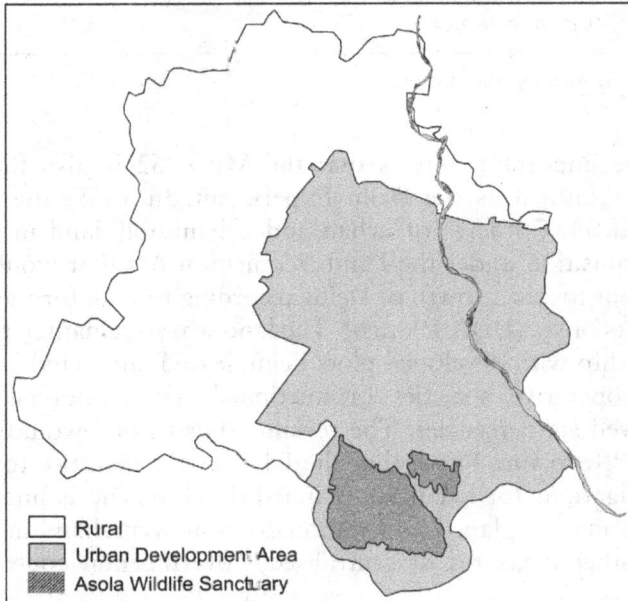

Rural
Urban Development Area
Asola Wildlife Sanctuary

*Source*: Drawn by the author.

## Map 1.3: Master Plan of Delhi 2021

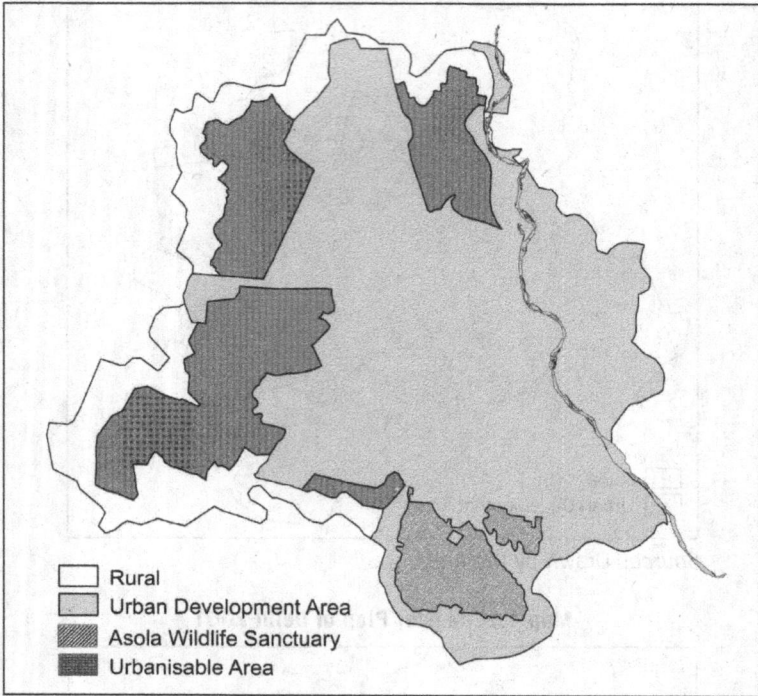

Rural
Urban Development Area
Asola Wildlife Sanctuary
Urbanisable Area

*Source*: Drawn by the author.

One important note is that the MPD '62 is also the site what is known as the Delhi Experiment. In 1959, the DDA notified 34,070 acres of urban and urbanisable land in Delhi for acquisition under the Land Acquisition Act that would 'be sufficient for the growth of Delhi according to plan for the next 10 years or so' (DDA 1962: 6). The land was to remain in public ownership with developed plots being leased out to individuals or co-operative societies or auctioned for development by approved state agencies. The revenue thus earned would enter into a 'Revolving Fund' that the DDA could then use to fulfil its obligations for balanced, planned development as imagined by the master plan. Land nationalisation went hand-in-hand with other measures of centralised, governmental control on

54

urban transformation. In the 1960s, the DDA was imagined as a single actor that would regulate or itself build all categories of housing for what came to be called low, middle and high-income groups/categories. Rent Control and Urban Land Ceiling Acts were passed. The city was to be rationally and centrally controlled towards determined ends. For this to succeed, land had to be under state control. Direct ownership of land, argued the MPD '62

> makes planning and implementation of plans easier and is imperative if slum clearance, redevelopment and subsidized housing and provision of community facilities according to accepted standards have to be undertaken, as indeed they must be in Delhi, in a determined way. (DDA 1962: 7)

The entire grey-shaded urban development area in the MPD '62, therefore, also represents the site of an ambitious modernist project to bring together planning and a centralised welfare state. As the next sections will detail, however, things did not go as planned.

## Planned Colonies

The penultimate row of our table is striking: a category called 'planned colonies' that is only one of eight categories of housing in the city. Even more intriguing is that these planned colonies housed only 23.7 per cent of the population in 2000. Before addressing what seems like a clear failure of planning, it is important to understand what this category of 'planned colony' represents and what it tells us about the 'unplanned', particularly in its relationship to the formal, the legal and the legitimate.

Planned colonies are those that are built on plots marked in the development area of the master plan, in concordance with the use allocated to that plot in the master plan or the zonal plan (if it exists)[5] and that are presumably laid out according to norms and standards defined in the master plan for design, infrastructure and amenities. There is, however, one more critical element—the temporality of *when* all these conditions were met. A 'planned colony' fulfils all of these conditions *at the time that it was built.* It is and has always been planned, legal and legitimate.

The importance of the category of 'planned colony' is in its role as a benchmark. It is the ideal type—the colony that planning imagines as typifying both the norms of the Plan as well as the process for producing housing. The planned colony is at the heart of 'planned development', a marker of the imagined chronology and synergy between the temporalities of building, inhabiting and planning that is taught in planning schools: Plan, Service, Build, then Occupy (Baross 1987). It is housing under the plan's control; built where, when and how it was imagined within it.

Over time, two types of changes have come about in planned colonies: the extension of individual housing units beyond allowed limits of covered and built area (including extensions into public paths, areas and roads) as well as widespread violations of permitted use, particularly the commercial use of residential premises. It is worth remembering here that the Delhi master plans have retained the single use model of zoning imagined in the MPD '62—implying that almost all mixed use in colonies zoned as 'residential' violates Plan guidelines. Successive plans have created layers of exemptions to handle these non-conforming uses. First, they allowed certain kinds of commercial use. Then, individual streets were exempted in otherwise residentially zoned colonies. In the MPD '21, nearly 2183 streets across the city were suddenly declared 'mixed use' though these were not all by any means within planned colonies alone.

In other words, even within the 'Planned Colony', there are layers of unplanned activities and informal uses. The priority—Sen's basal variable—given in the settlement typologies has been to the fact that the colony is built on a plot that is marked on and exists in conformity with the layout and design rules of the master plan at the time it was built. Within individual units, violations of developmental controls and norms of use as per zoning codes are then akin to the 'other distinctions' that Scott argued must be overlooked or Sen's 'outlying perspectives'. The planned colony, therefore, is legal, planned and legitimate, but has both formal and informal uses as well as built structures within it.

*Planned colonies and nousing stock: Looking at the data*: Yet looking more closely at how, when and where planned colonies were built, and more importantly, those that were intended but not built, this ideal type of planned development begins to unravel. Looking at housing data makes two kinds of failures clear: (a) shortfalls in housing built by the DDA or DDA-approved actors that emerge almost immediately after the MPD '62 was issued and proceed to widen till the present day; and (b) the absence of sufficient notified, zoned and development land where planned housing could be built to make up this widening housing shortfall.

There is no disagreement in the data that there is a systemic and widening gap between housing needed and that built by the DDA or DDA-approved actors. Estimates of housing shortfalls vary only in the severity of their estimation. Three aspects of the housing shortfall are relevant to our analysis: (a) mistaken population projections and a gross underestimation of housing need in and of itself; (b) the inability to meet even the inadequate housing targets that were set, and (c) the fact that the gap between need and demand, and then between demand and supply, was highest for those that were income poor. Tables 1.2a and 1.2b show projected population growth for Delhi in the first and second plans and actual population levels. They then further translate these into housing shortfalls.

Yet the DDA failed to create the housing stock to meet even these underestimated needs. This 'failure' was particular: it over-built middle and higher income housing while substantially underbuilding housing for what are termed as the Economically Weaker Sections (EWS). Table 1.3 plots the targeted distribution of housing stock by income category in successive master plans and the actual distribution that resulted.

Others have argued that the data itself severely undercounts the extent of bias towards building HIG and MIG flats. The Self-Financing Scheme (or SFS), started by the DDA in the 1970s, was intended to allow families to expedite the construction of their

**Table 1.2a: Population Projections and Actuals in the Master Plans**

|  | Projected (in million) | Actual (in million) |
|---|---|---|
| MPD '62 for 1981 | 4.59 | 6.22 |
| MPD '01 for 2001 | 12.00 | 13.78 |

*Source*: DDA (1962, 1990, 2007); Government of Delhi (2009); Census of India (1981, 1991, 2001)

**Table 1.2b: Housing Shortfalls by Plan**

| MPD '62 | 100,000 dwelling units |
|---|---|
| MPD '01 | 300,000 dwelling units |
| MPD '21 | 400,000 dwelling units |

*Source*: DDA (1962, 1990, 2007).

**Table 1.3: Housing Stock Allocated vs Built**

|  | Intended % of Total Built Housing | Actual % of Total Built Housing |
|---|---|---|
| EWS | 40 | 30.32 |
| Low Income Group (LIG) | 30 | 27.99 |
| Middle Income/High Income Group (MIG/HIG) | 25 | 22.94 |
| Self-Financed Schemes/Other | 5 | 18.76 |

*Note*: Indicates housing built on by DDA or DDA-authorised actors including government agencies, co-operative societies. Does not include privately built housing.
*Source*: Hazards Centre (2003); DDA and Tiwari (2000).

own DDA flat by paying the entire cost in fewer instalments. Needless to say, only middle and higher income families, and largely the latter, were able to afford unsubsidised housing and raise the required down payments. Given this, we can add SFS housing to the HIG housing stock. This implies that 41 per cent of all housing stock built by the DDA was either middle or high income.

*Shortfalls in planned areas:* The second type of 'failure' that becomes evident when looking at why planned colonies house only a quarter of the city's population is a shortfall in notifying additional land within the development areas of master plan. A planned colony can only be built on land notified within the development area of the master plan and zoned residential. Yet no new land was notified as an urban development area by the DDA between 1962 (when MPD '62 was issued) and 1990 (when MPD '01 was issued). Though it is true that MPD '62 sought to notify enough land to account for urban expansion up till 1981, this still leaves nearly a decade of urban growth for which no additional land was notified within the master plan—a decade in which the city's population increased by 3.2 million people. MPD '01 further added only 4000 hectares to the development area of the MPD '62—a mere 4.5 per cent of the existing development area in the MPD '62. This extension was the only addition until 2007 when the MPD '21 added 20,000 hectares. In the interim, the city's population had grown by another six million people.

This rising population, clearly, could not wait for the Plan to catch-up with the realities of the urban growth and expansion. In 1990, when the MPD '01 was issued, and in 2007, when the MPD '21 was issued, areas far beyond the notified area in the master plan were already built up. Both the MPD '01 and the MPD '21 chose not to notify already built-up areas as development areas within the Plan. For these colonies built in between plans, it was impossible to be a planned colony as they had no way to meet (rather than violate) the basic classificatory principle of the table: the building of the colony on land marked and zoned residential within the development area.

How then do we understand the 'violation' of the plan? The shortfalls in housing for all categories of residents—and the particularly significant shortfall in housing for the income-poor—implies that planned housing stock was, by any estimation, inadequate. The shortfall of notified developed areas within the plans and the long durations between successive plans meant that even building planned colonies was impossible.

Residents therefore were forced to build shelter in what became, by implication, a range of 'unplanned colonies'. There was, in a curious sense, then not the violation of the Plan through 'illegal' acts, but instead, the impossibility of legal and planned inhabitation for the poor and the rich alike. This impossibility is partly a result of the DDA's inadequate housing production but is, in equal part, the result of its refusal to include already built-up areas within the development area of the master plan. It is the Plan therefore that produces and regulates what it itself defines as 'illegal' settlements. Illegality is not outside planning—it is part of its logics, conceptions and practices. What is important to note here is that this 'illegal inhabitation', as I shall argue in the next sections, has defined the processes of inhabitation for the poor and rich alike even as the consequences of these illegalities are markedly different for each.

## Unauthorised Colonies and Regularised-Unauthorised Colonies

The primary classification principle for our housing categories is inclusion within the development area of the Plan in a zone marked for residential use. An 'Unauthorised Colony', then, is precisely one that is built on land not included in the development area in the Plan or one built on land within the developmental area but not zoned for residential use. Before 1975, most of Delhi's unauthorised colonies fell in the latter category as land acquired under the MPD '62 was not fully developed, i.e. infrastructural services were not provided and the land parcels not notified to be ready for planned housing to be built. Since 1975, however, most unauthorised colonies belong to the former category and fall outside the development area of the plan—precisely in the built-up areas that the MPD '01 and MPD '21 selectively included or continued to leave out of the development area.

These colonies are on land considered 'rural' by the master plan at the time they were built—land that, crucially, lay outside developed or even 'urbanisable' land as notified by the then relevant master plan. Rural land belonged either to individual farmers or was common land in the village and belonged to the *gram sabha* (village council). An unauthorised colony gets created when land is bought by an individual—let us call him an 'aggregator'—from either individual farmers or the gram sabha and aggregated into the size of a colony that could be large enough to hold as many as 200 units or as few as 10. This aggregated land is then divided into plots (without any specific or standardised norms of layouts, public areas or infrastructure, but often in some relationship to prevalent developmental norms for planned colonies in the master plan) and sold with written contractual agreements that detail monthly instalments and payment schedules undertaken and completed by individual house owners.[6] Densities, size of dwelling units and layouts vary considerably—unauthorised colonies range from working poor neighbourhoods to elite single-family homes.

What exactly is unauthorised about the unauthorised colony? First, the farmers and the gram sabha cannot sell rural land for non-agricultural use—they can only sell to others who will keep the land under agricultural use; ostensibly, to 'farmers'. Many unauthorised colonies—and in Delhi, the most famous of them all[7]—were thus never called as such by their residents through the 1980s. Their homes were 'farmhouses' and many of them claimed to use them for 'agriculture', going so far as to conforming to layouts where built structures covered no more than 10 per cent of the total layout on the 'farm'. Yet many other unauthorised colonies do not even make such pretence and look, for all purposes, like residential layouts with no claims to agriculture.

The violation here is not one of squatting; that the residents of these colonies paid for their land is undisputed. Such payment and the written documents produced therein are proof of a documented and, indeed, formal process of purchase by the buyer. Yet though the purchase is formal, it is not legal. The violation occurs because the farmer and the aggregator did not have the right to sell the land to the house owners in the first place. Housing units within these colonies are thus both with and without 'titles'; though all house owners have formal documents that show detailed payments for their flats, none of these can be registered with the local authorities as recognised, legal property titles because the colony does not exist on the Plan. Titles cannot be legally transferred. Municipal services cannot be provided to these colonies since they do not exist on the Plan.[8]

Many unauthorised colonies therefore were built without regards to design, infrastructure and service standards, and, in fact, often were built without any municipal or public services at all. In the latest official definition of the unauthorised colony, it is this aspect of Plan violation that the development authorities choose to focus on: 'Unauthorized Colony', according to the DDA, means a 'colony/development comprising of contiguous area, where no permission of concerned agency has been obtained for approval of Layout Plan, and/or building plan.'[9] The illegal sale and conversion of rural land for urban use is deemphasised from the history of the colony, focusing only on the need for norms and standards for layouts and service provisions.

Unauthorised colonies are illegal, both formal (in transaction) and informal (in building codes and developmental norms), and unplanned. Yet they are legitimate. There is no recorded case of an eviction of an unauthorised colony. Unauthorised colonies do, therefore, enjoy a de facto security of tenure if not a de jure one.

Periodically, an unauthorised colony is 'regularised'. Regularisation is a process by which the colony is made *legal*— the property titles are recognised by law and can be registered with the state. The process involves an attempt to align the unauthorised colony as closely with planned norms of the settlement layout (including building codes) as well as the payment of a one-time 'conversion charge'. However, the colony, once regularised can still not be a planned colony for it was not one at the time of its inception. Its journey to legality, via its time as an unauthorised colony, is thus eternally enshrined in its new categorical name: regularised-unauthorised colony, or regularised colony, as it is colloquially known. Regularised colonies are legal and legitimate and must attempt to shift from informal to formal in terms of building and developmental codes as part of the layout process, but are not planned.

## Mapping Regularisation

Why do unauthorised colonies emerge? The previous section detailed the housing shortfalls in planned colonies in Delhi. The sheer inadequacy in housing stock, of land zoned in the developmental area for housing and the inability of many households to wait for allocations of housing stock built directly by the DDA itself are key drivers for the emergence of the 'unauthorised colony'. This market was clearly artificially constrained by regulation that allocated insufficient land for housing and then further prevented private builders to build housing on the land it did notify. In short, some part of the story of the unauthorised colony is simply a matter of supply and demand, of what I have called the impossibility of planned and legal housing.

What then is the relationship of the master plan with the unauthorised colony? It is here that spatial analysis of where unauthorised colonies were built becomes particularly illuminating. Data on where unauthorised colonies exist are hard to come by for both definitional reasons and because of the near absence of systematic surveys. Like in bastis, the survey by the authorities of the government represents a tricky political moment for unauthorised colonies. On the one hand, surveys are necessary for any possibility of 'regularisation'. Yet any surveying sheds light precisely on the extent of illegal building and makes the colony visible to the authority technically responsible for enforcing the Plan and, thereby, taking punitive action against the colony. Periodically, schemes for regularisation will be announced and invite applications from unauthorised colonies. It is at these moments that it becomes possible to map these colonies.

There were three major waves of 'regularisation' in Delhi's history. In the first wave in 1962, as part of the first master plan, 102 colonies were regularised. The second wave was in 1975. Map 1.4 shows 567 unauthorised colonies that were regularised in 1975, plotting them against the boundaries of MPD '62 that was in force at the time. It is important to note that we have no way, using existing data, to know if more unauthorised

63

**Map 1.4: The Second Wave of Regularisation: 567 Unauthorised Colonies, 1975**

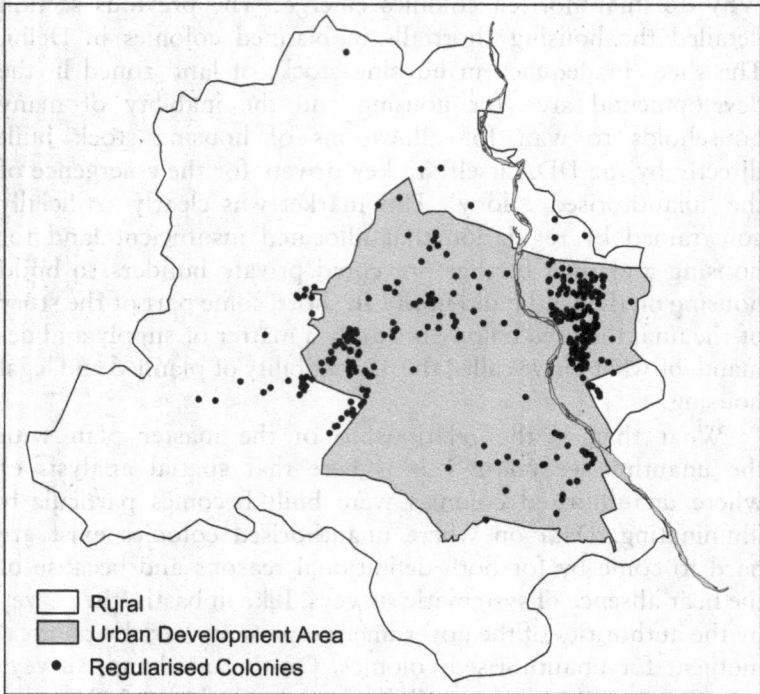

Legend:
☐ Rural
▨ Urban Development Area
• Regularised Colonies

*Source*: Drawn by the author.

colonies existed at this point. It is possible that there were many other colonies that were not regularised but existed at this point of time though it is believed that this first wave of 'regularisation' of these colonies covered most of the existing unauthorised colonies.[10]

What is immediately visible is the colonies lie within urban extensions imagined by the MPD '62 but within areas not zoned or notified for residential use. Yet there is a small cluster to the west, clearly outside the development area of the Plan that has caused a ribbon-effect from the furthest colony to the boundaries of the Plan. These colonies were regularised even as they clearly violated the MPD '62 by being located beyond the urban developmental area. They are then, in our first set of what Douglas would call 'anomalies', housing that was made legitimate and legal though it violated the primary basis of classification of the categories.

This contradiction—where the creator of the system of categories itself violates the primary principle of classification of the categories—repeats itself decades later. In 1993, applications were again invited from unauthorised colonies as part of a regularisation scheme. A total of 1639 colonies applied. In their applications, each colony submitted a layout plan, mapping precisely the boundaries of the colony, the number of units and location. Using this data, Map 1.5a maps these colonies against MPD '01 which had been issued just a few years before the regularisation scheme was announced while Map 1.5b shows where these colonies exist and maps them against MPD '62. Map 1.6a then maps these same colonies against the MPD '21.

A clear spatial pattern is immediately visible. The largest clusters of unauthorised colonies clearly populate areas just beyond the developmental areas of the plan, i.e. areas still considered 'rural' or 'urbanisable'. In this sense, the unauthorised colony marks the immediate 'outside' of the master plan. Yet what is striking is that, even in 1993, these colonies are largely outside the Plan boundaries of the MPD '62! When plotted against MPD '01, a relatively small number in the southern extension enter the development area. The MPD '62 remains, therefore, even in 1993, a boundary to the planned city. The master plans here clearly act as a *bounding condition*. The spatial pattern of where unauthorised colonies are built is not planned but is determined by planning—the clustering of unauthorised colonies at the edge of the development area is not incidental. There is then, in Douglas' words, a very particular 'pattern within the disorder'. I shall return to this argument in more detail later in the chapter.

In 2009, nearly a decade and a half after the colonies had applied for regularisation, 733 of these colonies were regularised in what is considered the third major wave of regularisation. Map 1.6b shows the regularised colonies within the universe of all the unauthorised colonies that applied, mapped against the MPD '21 that had been issued just a few years earlier in 2007.

**Map 1.5a: The Third Wave: 1639 Unauthorised Colonies in 1993 Mapped against MPD '01**

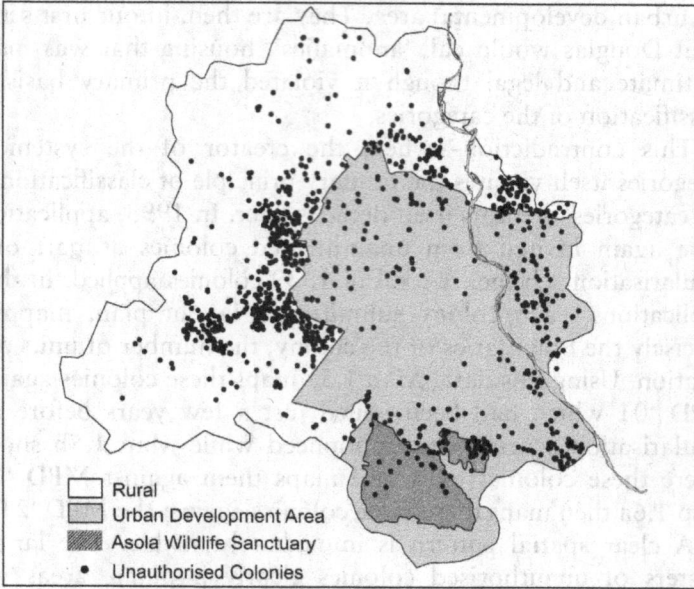

- Rural
- Urban Development Area
- Asola Wildlife Sanctuary
- • Unauthorised Colonies

*Source*: Drawn by the author.

**Map 1.5b: The Third Wave: 1639 Unauthorised Colonies in 1993 Mapped against MPD '62**

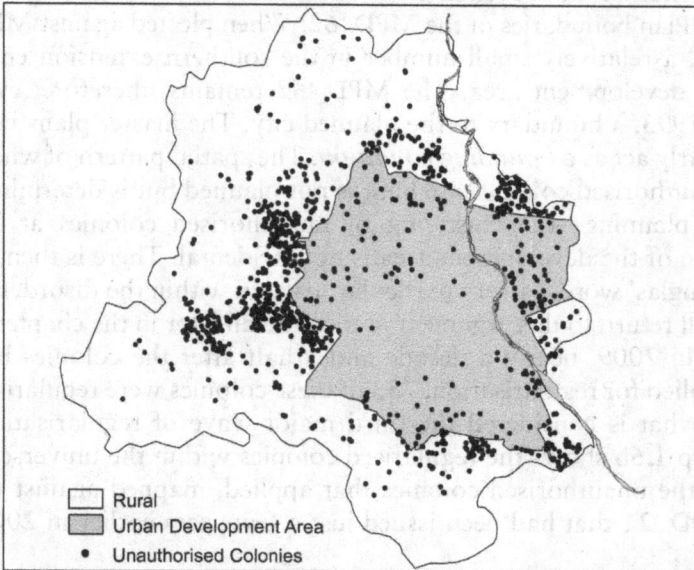

- Rural
- Urban Development Area
- • Unauthorised Colonies

*Source*: Drawn by the author.

**Map 1.6a: The Third Wave: 1639 Unauthorised Colonies Applying for Regularisation, Mapped against MPD '21**

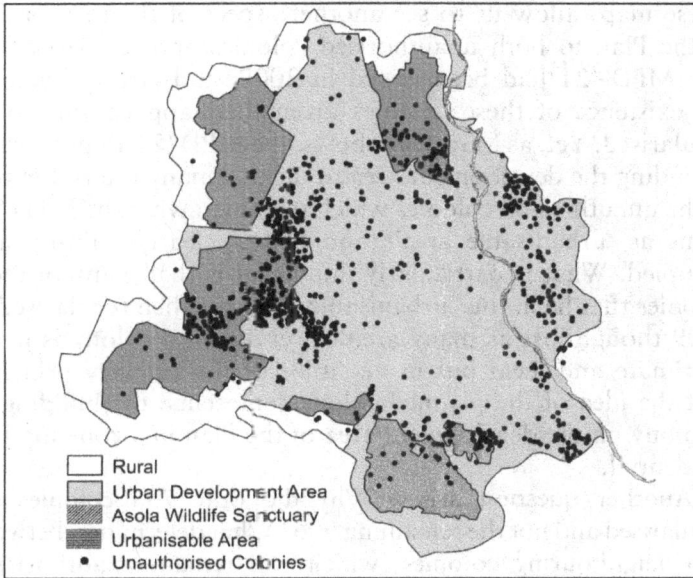

*Source*: Drawn by the author.

**Map 1.6b: The Third Wave: Regularised Colonies in 2009, Mapped against MPD '21**

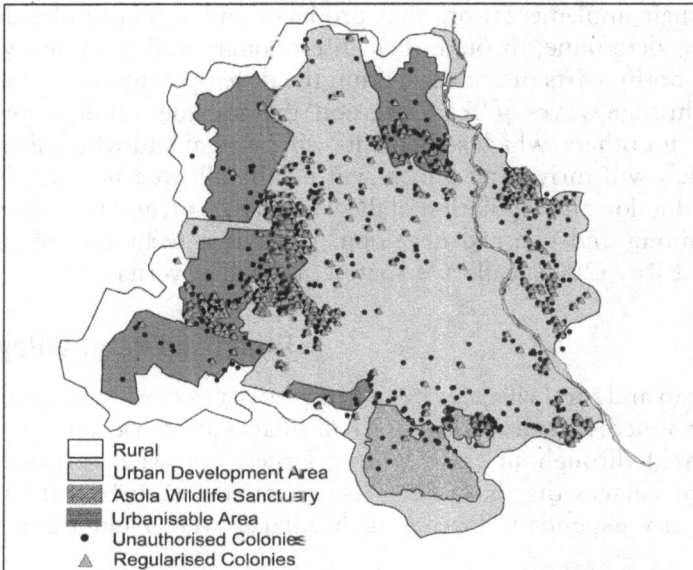

*Source*: Drawn by the author.

These maps allow us to see another aspect of the relationship of the Plan to both unauthorised colonies and regularisation. The MPD '21 had been issued in 2007, and clearly knew of the existence of these colonies given their applications to be regularised. Yet, as Map 1.6b shows, the MPD '21 stops short of extending the development area to include many (indeed, most) of the unauthorised colonies which remain in what the MPD '21 terms as 'urbanisable area' though it is clearly built-up and occupied. What is particularly important is that many of these colonies that lie in this 'urbanisable area' are then regularised in 2009 though just as many aren't. Yet again, a colony is made legitimate and legal but in violation of the primary principle that the idea of the planned colony represents: the building of a colony on the development area of the Plan in a zone marked residential.

Another question arises: Why did only 733 colonies get regularised and not the remaining 906? What determines, between two neighbouring colonies, which will remain unauthorised? In the absence of objective metrics by which the regularisation process functions, it is indeed the discretion of the DDA to decide who will become legal and who will remain illegal, at what time and for how long. Once again, it is the plans, and not the failure of their implementation, that produces and regulates illegality. They determine, through their discretionary ability to notify or not notify parts of the city within the development area, as well as through waves of 'regularisation' that include certain colonies but not others, which settlements will be legal and which illegal, which will thrive and which will not be allowed to exist. The production and regulation of illegality is part of, and not outside, planning and planned development. It is a technique of rule, what Roy (2003) calls a 'a spatial mode of governance'.

## Urban and Rural Villages

Urban and rural villages offer a further twist to our understanding of planned, formal and legal. Urban villages are dense settlements, located throughout the city, and largely consist of previously rural villages that have been incorporated into urban areas as the city expanded. Twenty such villages were included in the

MPD '62, 106 in MPD '01 and 152 in MPD '21. Rural villages are similar settlements but located in the peripheries of the city and still in areas of the master plan marked as 'rural'.

In one sense, urban and rural villages are planned since they are included explicitly within the master plan. This incorporation, however, is on the basis of exceptions: a suspension of the norms and rules of planning. In order to be able to 'retain their character', urban villages are exempt from any building norms, mixed use or single use zoning classifications, or restrictions from any kind of use. In other words, urban villages may build to any height, mix commercial and residential activities, and violate developmental controls for setbacks, parking and street widths. All of these were considered 'inapplicable' to urban villages because they were meant to be the locus of 'village-trades' that the MPD '62 sought to remove from the planned city.

Urban villages today range from income-poor neighbourhoods still practicing 'village trades' including pottery, leather kilns and rearing of cattle, to neighbourhoods providing affordable student housing to some of the cities' most chic fashion and arts districts. They take advantage precisely of their status of exemption from planning and developmental controls to create vibrant mixed-use neighbourhoods. What is ironic about urban villages is that activities that would be considered informal in any other city neighbourhood are permissible in urban villages. The villages are legitimate: residents enjoy security of tenure and cannot be evicted. However, residents of urban villages are meant to be owner-occupiers in perpetuity—no sale or transfer of land or housing is permitted. They are thus legal, in the sense that their property titles are recognised by the state, but within their exceptional status are limitations to their legal property rights. Urban and rural villages are, therefore, formal in name though not in practice, legitimate, planned by decree of exception and legal though with limitations.

## JJ Clusters, Slum Designated Areas and Resettlement Colonies

Images of the 'slum' need little introduction. Temporary, fragile and vulnerable housing materials, the absence of sanitation, waste and sewage services, the income poverty of the residents, the overwhelming density of the 'slum' can be conjured up by even those that have never actually been to one. As argued earlier, I used the term basti to refer to the settlements of the poor for which the 'slum' has become shorthand. Yet what is colloquially called the basti by those who live within it is, in terms of our categories, seen as three distinct categories of settlement: slum designated areas, jhuggi-jhompri clusters (JJ clusters)[11] and resettlement colonies.

*Slum designated areas*: Slums are settlements identified, or 'notified', under the Slum Areas Act, 1956. Slums were considered 'any area unfit for human habitation' by reason of 'dilapidation, overcrowding, faulty arrangement and design of buildings, narrowness or faulty arrangements of streets, lack of ventilation, light or sanitation facilities, or any combination of above factors' (Government of India 1956). Yet no measurable parameters were included in the definition leading to a discretionary rather than objective assessment of which areas would be declared as slums.

This is evident in looking at areas notified as slums under the Act. The last notification under the Act in Delhi was in 1994—no new slum has been acknowledged under the Act in over two decades! In fact, most of the slum designated areas in Delhi exist in the Old City—the walled city of Shahjahanabad that was notified as a slum in the MPD '62. Since then, it has been reclassified first as a heritage zone and in the MPD '01 as a 'Special Area' though many parts of it remain notified as a slum in addition to being both a heritage zone and a 'special area'. What is critical to note is that 97 per cent of notified *katra*s, or small neighbourhoods, in the Old City areas notified as slums are privately owned and have been so since before Independence and the MPD '62. There are almost no notified slums, therefore, on public land.

Slum designated areas are often referred to as notified slums, as opposed to JJ clusters. Notification entitles settlements to an element of protection against arbitrary eviction or eviction without resettlement, and priorities in upgrading. Indeed, several schemes in the 1970s, including the Environmental Improvement in Urban Slums policy, were restricted to notified slums though incremental upgradation policies from the mid-1980s disbanded this practice. Slum designated areas are then legal but with restrictions, legitimate, unplanned, and both formal and informal.

*JJ clusters*: JJ clusters are bastis that have not been declared slums by notification under the Slum Areas Act and that are imagined to retain the physical fragility and deprivation of the slum. Again, there is little clarity on what makes a community a 'JJ cluster'—there are no strict metrics of infrastructural services, income or spatial layouts, for example, to determine whether a settlement is or is not a JJ cluster. The National Sample Survey Organization (NSSO) describes a 'non-notified slum' as 'a compact settlement with a collection of poorly built tenements, mostly of temporary nature, crowded together usually with inadequate sanitary and drinking water facilities in unhygienic conditions' (NSSO 1997). Yet what is important to note is that unlike a notification under the Slum Areas Act for which a denotification exists, there is no mechanism for a settlement to cease to be a JJ cluster. There is no metric of density, services or income that they can clear, for example, that will make the surveyors of the NSSO stop including the settlement in the category of slum. This is one reason why actual JJ clusters vary widely in infrastructural standards, quality of housing and even layouts of settlements.

The categorisation process—and the fact that no new slums are being declared—implies that a settlement can remain a JJ cluster indefinitely. One of the reasons behind this curious practice is that the primary classification principle of our categories is not, in fact, the quality of housing but instead, as I have argued repeatedly, the status of the land the settlement is built on vis-à-vis the master plan. These are planning categories. Whether the quality of the housing stock in a JJ cluster is better or worse than that of an unauthorised colony, a planned colony or a regularised colony, let alone a slum designated area, is then seen as irrelevant. The definitional manipulations and naming practices of the categories of settlements, as I shall argue in detail in the concluding section of this chapter, are techniques of rule, exercised in the name of and as part of planning practice. They are critical in determining the distance between the legitimate and the legal. In other words, they are part of the calculus—beyond the state and its attempts at governance—that determine whether a legal or illegal colony is legitimate or not, i.e. if it can enjoy a de facto security of tenure.

What separates a JJ cluster and an unauthorised colony? The focus of the categorical definition, therefore, to bring back Sen's understanding of the primary principle of classification of the category, remains that residents of bastis are seen to be 'squatting' on land they neither own nor paid for. In Delhi, 95 per cent of JJ clusters[12] are on public land, and the large majority (83 per cent) of them on land owned by the DDA (Government of Delhi 2009). It is this that is seen to make their illegality clear—the land they occupy has a clear owner. Unlike in the case of unauthorised colonies where residents did not have the right to buy rural or private land for urban use but the sale itself is seen as a formal, valid transaction, payments made by some residents of bastis to 'buy' their plots or at least the right to remain on them, are seen as clearly and unambiguously informal. The 'aggregator' who creates the unauthorised colony in this case becomes the 'Slum Lord' for precisely the same set of actions: occupying land, parcelling it, and allowing families to settle in defined and marked parcels for a fee. The JJ cluster, therefore, is unplanned, illegal, informal and not legitimate.

*Resettlement colonies*: The only way for residents of JJ clusters to become legitimate is, ironically, to be evicted from the JJ cluster and resettled into an alternative site, called a resettlement colony.

Terms of resettlement have shifted through the three plans from plot sizes of 80 sq m in the MPD '62 to 18–25 sq m in MPD '01, and back to 25 sq m in MPD '21. Eligibility criteria have also changed dramatically. Displacement without resettlement was 'not an option' in the 1960s, argues Sundaram (2009) when the first wave of resettlement took place. Within and after the

Emergency, however, resettlement shifted from being universal to being conditional. Renters were excluded and only plot 'owners' were allowed even though the ownership of the latter had no legal recognition. Down payments were demanded before families would be allocated plots and, most importantly, only families that could prove that they had been living in a particular site for a certain number of years were eligible. The year chosen was determined as the cut-off date. In evictions from 1990 to 2007, estimates of the number of families resettled averaged only about 25–40 per cent of total families at any given site (Bhan and Shivanand 2013). This offers a further insight into JJ clusters—the only claim to legitimacy that residents of JJ clusters have is the number of years that they have lived in a particular settlement.

Resettlement colonies are the closest category to planned housing. They are planned in the sense that they are explicitly included within the development area of the master plan in a zone marked for residential use, laid out according to standards and norms for resettlement colonies in the master plan and, critically, they fulfil all these conditions at the time they were built. In other words, they are the only other housing category that fulfils all the benchmark conditions of planned colonies. The only difference lies in the nature of the title. Families allocated plots in resettlement colonies are imagined as eternal owner-occupiers. They are given licenses rather than titles that are non-transferable, cannot be sold, and indeed, are often not in perpetuity—some licenses have to be renewed every ten years or so. Though there has been no recorded case thus far of licenses not being renewed, the possibility remains. Resettlement colonies are then planned, formal, legitimate as well as legal, though with restrictions on the last count.

What separates slum designated areas, JJ clusters and resettlement colonies? The only tenable criterion of difference is their tenurial status and their relationship to the master plan. Slum designated areas are protected from arbitrary eviction without resettlement and thereby enjoy a certain de facto security of tenure though not a de jure one. JJ clusters have no security of tenure at all; resettlement colonies are authorised by the master plan but offer security of tenure only to the original allottees of the plot—titles are non-transferable and rentals are illegal though they occur widely in practice. Studies estimate that between 15 and 40 per cent of all resettlement colonies are inhabited by renters or those that have illegally and informally 'purchased' a plot in the colony from the original allottee. Cancellations of allotments and 'recovery' of plots from within resettlement colonies is, therefore, not uncommon.

What is important to emphasise is that distinctions between these three categories are impossible to make in terms of either their built environment, housing stock or of the poverty levels of their residents. Many resettlement colonies are inhabited by residents who may be legal but are more impoverished than those that live in tenurially more precarious JJ clusters. Resettlement colonies have often, in fact, been called 'planned slums' by activists who argue that it is impossible to create anything other than a 'slum' in recent resettlement colonies because of the diminishing size of the plots, the distance from employment and work centres and the abysmal state of infrastructural services.

There are, of course, widespread differences between resettlement colonies depending on when they were built. Many older resettlement colonies are arguably better off than many JJ clusters. Yet, for many of the latter that have existed for many years, even decades, incremental upgradation even without tenure has resulted in a much improved quality of life than in many more formal, legal settlements. A significant part of this distinction is because of the relative locations of these two categories of settlements. As Map 1.7 shows, resettlement colonies are increasingly located more and more towards urban peripheries while JJ clusters remain closer to the heart of the cities. Locational advantages, therefore, can significantly outweigh the benefits of legality in determining the economic development of a settlement (Dupont 2008; Bhan and Menon-Sen 2008). There can be, in other words, no simple correlation between the tenurial security of a settlement, its legal or planned status vis-à-vis the master plan and its poverty and vulnerability. Put quite simply: not all bastis are poor, not all of the poor live in bastis.

## Map 1.7: Resettlement Colonies Before and After 1990

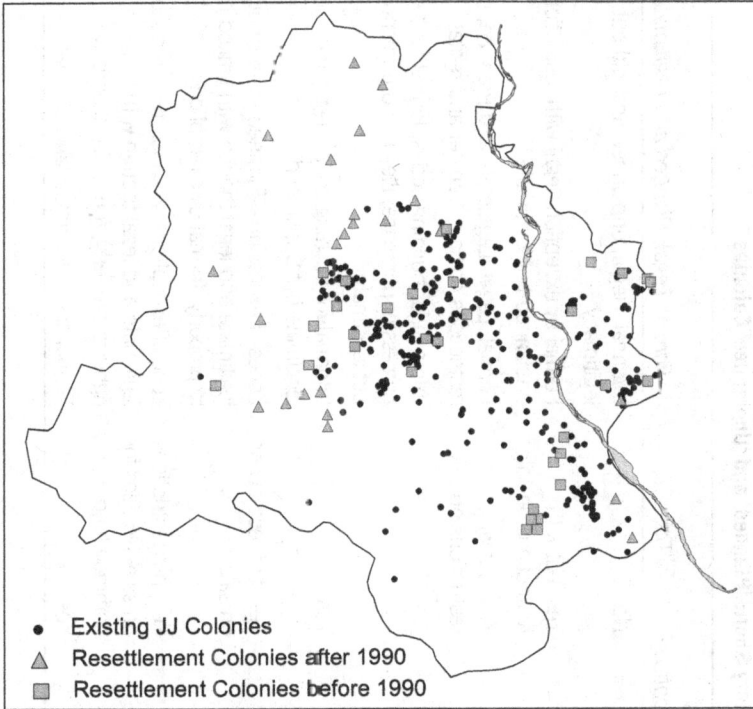

- ● Existing JJ Colonies
- △ Resettlement Colonies after 1990
- ▢ Resettlement Colonies before 1990

*Source*: Drawn by the author.

## Evictions 1990–2007

In Introduction, I described the dramatic rise in the extent, frequency, scale and intensity of evictions between 1990 and 2007. Map 1.8 shows the 217 sites where evictions occurred between 1990 and 2007 *and* some resettlement took place. I have explained the data used to construct these maps in detail elsewhere (Bhan and Shivanand 2013).

What is apparent even at first glance is the white space on the map. The eviction sites cluster to an area in the centre, east and south/southeast of the city. The north, northwest and western parts of the cities are conspicuously blank. What explains this geographical clustering? It is when we put the Plan back into

**Table 1.4: The Long Story Short: 'Planned' and 'Unplanned' Colonies**

| | In the Master Plan? | Conform to Developmental Controls? | Titles? | Formal, Legal, Planned and Legitimate? |
|---|---|---|---|---|
| JJ Clusters | No | No | No | Informal, illegal, unplanned and without legitimacy |
| Slum Designated Areas | Yes | Exempted | Yes, but with restrictions on sale | Formal by exception, legal with restriction, unplanned but legitimate |
| Resettlement Colonies | Yes | Yes | Yes, but with restrictions on sale | Formal, Legal, Legitimate and Planned, but restrictions on sale, transfer and rental |
| Unauthorised Colonies | No | No; Modifications required | No | Informal for building codes, formal for the process of purchase, illegal and unplanned but legitimate |
| Regularised Colonies | Yes | No; Modifications required | Yes | Informal for building codes, legal and legitimate but unplanned |
| Urban Villages | Yes | Exempted | Yes, but restrictions on sale | Zones of exception—Planned by exemption, legitimate and legal though with limited right to property, formal by exemption |
| Rural Villages | Yes | Exempted | Yes, but restrictions on sale; No titles for common land | Zone of exception—Planned by exemption, legitimate and legal though with limited rights to property, formal by exemption |
| Planned Colonies | Yes | Yes | Yes | Formal, legal, legitimate and planned |

*Source:* Prepared by the author.

## Map 1.8: Evictions 1990–2007

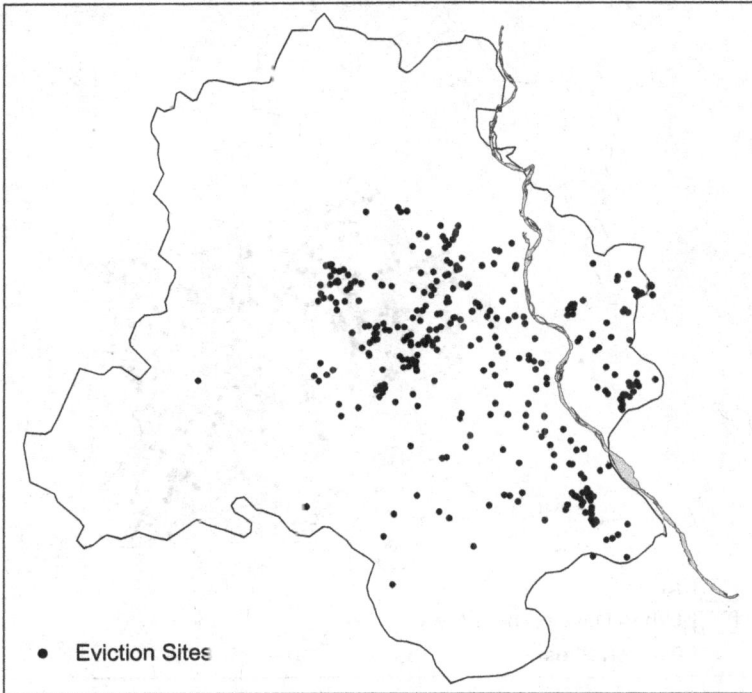

● Eviction Sites

*Source*: Drawn by the author.

the map that a possible answer emerges. Map 1.9 shows the eviction sites as mapped against the development area of the MPD '62. Remarkably, nearly all the eviction sites, even four decades later, fall within the bounds of MPD '62.

Yet that is not the complete story. If we add a third layer to our maps—that of existing JJ clusters that have not been evicted—we see another rather unexpected observation (see Map 1.10). Nearly all the existing JJ clusters also fall within or just on the border of the MPD '62. Put together, this implies that the settlements of the poor—those that exist and those evicted—display a particular spatial pattern of settlement that is determined by the MPD '62. The Plan acts, as it did for unauthorised colonies, as a *bounding condition*. This time,

**Map 1.9: Evictions 1990–2007 Mapped against MPD '62**

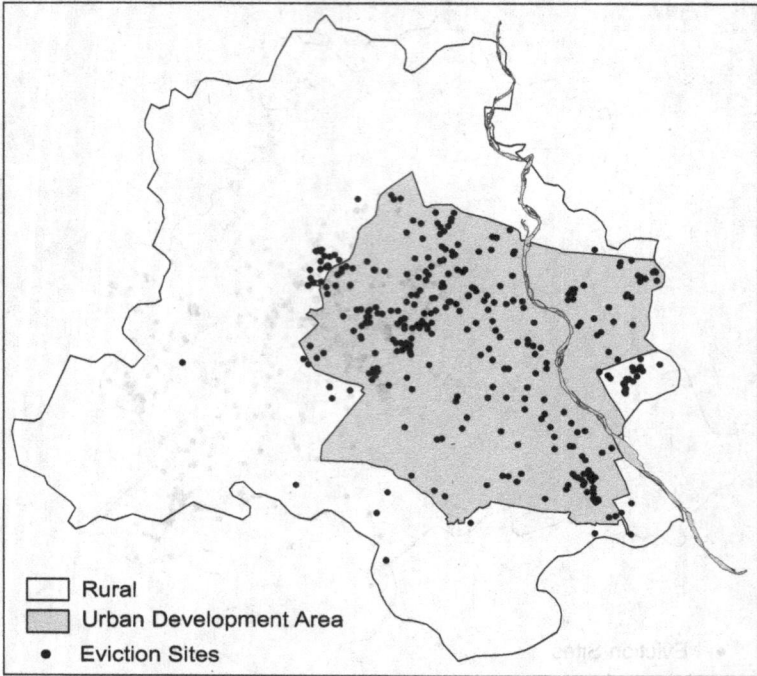

☐ Rural
▨ Urban Development Area
● Eviction Sites

*Source*: Drawn by the author.

it acts as another kind of boundary: one that seems to hold the settlements of the poor within the centre of the city. It is worth remembering here that this centre represents a particular urban footprint—the public lands acquired as part of the Delhi Experiment.

Bastis have been seen to be the single most visible and uncontested sign of the failure of planning. Yet what is clear is that, like unauthorised colonies, bastis may not be planned but their spatial patterns and locations are determined by planning. How do we understand this clear presence of the master plan in the very constitution and production of settlements that are assessed as unplanned, illegal, informal and illegitimate? Those that are, in other words, presumed to exist beyond, outside, despite or in violation of the Plan? What does this

**Map 1.10: Evictions 1990–2007 and existing JJ Clusters (in 2010) Mapped against MPD '62**

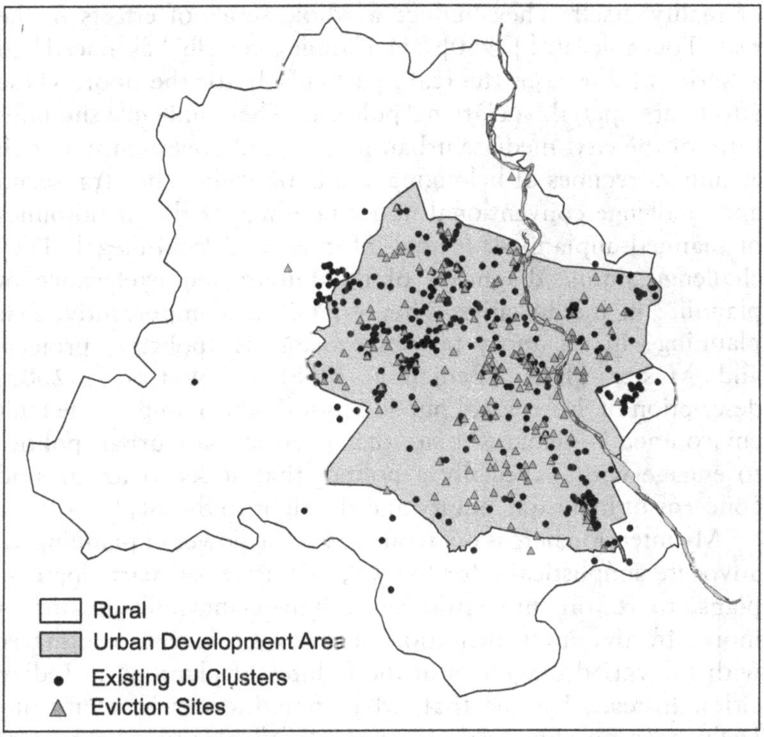

*Source*: Drawn by the author.

tell us about the 'failure' of planning, or narratives of its absence in shaping and settling the city? Importantly, why do bastis cluster not just around the development area of the MPD '62 in particular—the exact footprints of the Delhi Experiment? It is to these questions that I now turn in the concluding section of this chapter.

## Diagnosing Failure

Michel Foucault readily admitted that nothing happens as laid down in programmer's schemes. Yet he insisted that these schemes are not simply utopias 'in the heads of a few projectors'. They are not 'abortive schemas for the creation of a reality' but 'fragments of reality' itself. They 'induce a whole series of effects in the real' (Foucault 1991 [1980]: 81). Planning in Delhi has indeed had a 'series of effects in the real', particularly for the poor. These effects are spatial, social and political. They influence the built form of the city, mediate urban politics and governance as well as impact regimes of belonging and citizenship. They transcend and challenge conventional understandings of the dichotomies of planned-unplanned, formal-informal and legal-illegal. They challenge simple diagnoses of the failure and irrelevance of planning in Indian cities. They argue, most importantly, that planning—in its most tangible forms as 'policies, projects and Master Plans' (Benjamin 2008) or Watson's (2002) description of 'intentional public actions' which 'impact the built environment'—remains a site that is critical for urban politics to engage with, especially a politics that seeks to foreground concerns of inclusion, equity and the right to the city.

My intention here is not to argue for the power of planning, to advocate simplistically for 'better', 'inclusive' or 'participatory' plans, to restore modernist or techno-phantasmic dreams of more effective implementation or control, or even to disagree with the varied diagnoses of the failures of planning in Indian cities. Instead, I argue that urban practitioners in a city like Delhi have no choice but to engage with planning because of the continuing relevance of its failures. The 'chaos that is urban development' that Verma (2003) describes is not planned but it is, to twist Peattie's phrase, an outcome of planning. The task for theory is to conceptualise the terms of this engagement in order to suggest both a useful conceptual terrain as well as a political practice.

This concluding section attempts precisely this by tracing the contours of planning as a site of politics. I do so along four main threads: (a) re-thinking an 'irrelevant' plan; (b) challenging the politics of stealth (Benjamin 2008); (c) re-thinking informality and illegality as theoretical categories; and (d) suggesting 'legitimacy' as a conceptual foundation for a more relational urban politics.

## The Territorial Footprint of an Irrelevant Plan

The Delhi Experiment—the large-scale acquisition of urban land in the MPD '62—has been largely seen as a 'failure'. It is argued that the experiment failed in its primary objectives: to prevent the spatial segregation of the poor and to prevent speculation and vast inequalities in land and housing markets. The land acquisition, particularly because it was not accompanied by corresponding large-scale housing development, is seen to have distorted the land market. These are certainly valid critiques. Yet the data presents another side to thinking about how to evaluate the Delhi Experiment and, indeed, the impact of public land ownership on housing for the poor.

The data shows that while most housing is built illegally and termed 'unplanned', the spatial patterns of the location of where different kinds of housing have been built is indeed significantly determined by the MPD '62. The Plan acts as a bounding condition—it determines, even if it doesn't control, where housing has been built. Two clear examples of this have been shown. As Maps 1.5a and 1.5b show, the largest clusters of unauthorised colonies populate areas just beyond the development areas of the first two master plans. In this sense, the unauthorised colony marks the immediate 'outside' of the master plan. The MPD '62 remains, therefore, even in 1993, a boundary to the planned city. The spatial pattern of where unauthorised colonies are built is not planned but is determined by planning—the clustering of unauthorised colonies at the edge of the development area is not incidental.

Map 1.10 similarly showed us that almost all evictions where some resettlement occurred and all existing JJ clusters are located within the development area of the MPD '62. Plans see bastis as the result of an absence or incompleteness of planning—the result of 'unplanned and unregulated urban growth' (Swamy, Rao and Hegde 2008). They are settlements assumed to exist despite or outside plans. Yet what is clear from the data is that planning determines where bastis have been built. The locational preferences of the urban poor are not independent of an irrelevant or absent plan—bastis are not 'outside' planning

81

even within the context of a 'failed' plan. In the context of Delhi, specifically, bastis are tied to planning in a particular way—their locational patterns are determined by public land ownership.

There is then, in Douglas' words, a very particular 'pattern within the disorder'. The pattern suggests a relationship not just between master plans and housing but, in particular, between the MPD '62 and spatial patterns of 'illegal housing'. Since the MPD '62 is also the site of the Delhi Experiment, this pattern is a relationship between public land ownership and the settling patterns of the poor. It is a pattern that, for the poor, is arguably a beneficial one: a large number of bastis still remain in the centre of the city as imagined by the MPD '62. One could argue, in fact, that as the city has grown around and beyond the MPD '62, the poor have—as Map 1.8 suggests—remained in the core imagined by the first plan. They have done so, importantly, not just during the 1962–81 period when the MPD '62 applied but also well beyond it, through the 1980s and the 2000s. Bastis, in other words, chose to settle on public land in the MPD '62 area rather than in the vast areas in the west and northwest of the city. These areas, as Maps 1.3 and 1.4 showed us, were where large middle and upper middle class colonies were being built through the 1990s. These were by no means peripheral or underdeveloped areas without markets, employment or housing.

The implications of this spatial clustering for interventions in housing are immense. For Delhi, debates on ideas of 'public purpose' determining the use of publicly owned land; the metrics, mechanisms and evaluation of its value; and the determinations of 'public interest' that govern its use thus have a specific and disproportionate importance for the poor. What is important to note is that this importance does not derive simply from having publicly owned land being used as directed by the plans but even despite the 'failure' of planning to control its intended use. Even amidst 'failure', in other words, bastis find themselves in locations in the central city near employment where what I have elsewhere described as an upgrading dividend (Bhan and Shivanand 2013) is still possible. For planners, this implies that the struggle for land banks and greater public land ownership and/or control may indeed be beneficial for an inclusive politics despite implementation gaps. Arguments that place little faith in land reservation tools within contemporary Indian planning, for example, must reconsider the diagnosis of the implementation—another emblematic kind of failure—that is part of everyday discourse on planning and governance in Indian cities.

There are both opportunities and challenges here. The former lies in the far reaching effects state action can still have on building affordable housing even within a time of what Goldman (2011) calls 'speculative urbanism'. The mechanisms to do so exist. If, for example, as current housing policies and particularly the new central housing initiative for the poor under JNNURM suggest, in-situ upgradation is implemented for existing JJ clusters, the locations bastis find themselves in would be tremendously advantageous. However, it is precisely these locations that may make this political imperative difficult. The darker counter-argument suggests that the current trend of increased evictions and peripheral resettlement occurs precisely because of the prime locations of many JJ clusters within the city centre. Further, as Sivaramakrishnan has argued, the ability of planning authorities to exercise such an option is systematically being eroded as deregulation and reform weaken instruments and techniques of public control over land and land use in Indian cities (2011: 175). Yet how far this trend can be countered depends, in large part, on attempts to invest in and strengthen planning from within and recognising it as a site of political practice.

## Challenges to the Politics of Stealth

The territorial legitimacy of the Plan challenges certain contemporary theories of how the poor inhabit cities of the South. Solomon Benjamin (2008) argues, for example, for an occupancy urbanism. Taking 'land rather than the Economy [*sic*]' as his starting point, he argues for a perspective that, 'contests narratives that view cities as passive stage sets, acted upon by a macro-narrative' (ibid.: 720)—a critique made often of modernist planning embodied by the MPD '62. Occupancy urbanism, Benjamin argues, focuses on other materialities, the incremental nature by which land is actually settled. In more recent work, he has added the tagline 'an anti-planning manifesto' to the argument (Benjamin 2014).

Benjamin's argument is both correct and insightful. I seek to add to it only a sense of its limits as well as possible new engagements in response to these limits that take us further in thinking about, as Benjamin is interested and committed to doing, subaltern and micro-politics in the southern cities. Large-scale evictions in Delhi significantly challenge the narrative and possibility of 'occupancy', 'the politics of stealth' or even 'the quiet encroachment' suggested by Bayat (2000), whether these work through vote-bank politics, complex negotiations with local and municipal politics, or knowing how to 'work' the system. 'Macro-narratives' are indeed unable to control the city, as Benjamin suggests, but this does not mean that they do not determine many aspects of inhabitation in the city, by rich and poor alike, or that the political techniques of negotiation, stealth, subversion and resistance are not applicable to these macro-frames just as powerfully. In other words, different plans fail to control the city at different times in different ways. Understanding these differences is necessary whether one seeks to support or resist planning, and certainly if one believes that planning is 'irrelevant' for those who 'live outside it'. What the data suggests is that none of these housing categories, and particularly not those considered 'unplanned', are or can be 'outside' planning.

Benjamin shows how elite civil society organisations in Indian cities pit 'planned development' against 'slums' but planning and the master plans do not seem to be important sites of engagement or resistance for him. Planners, he argues, 'are duty bound and cajoled into declaring [particular] land settings as illegal' (2008: 724). What makes planners 'duty-bound' other than the terms of the Plan and planning process? How could challenges to and problematisations of these terms and the categories they work through act as a form of resistance? Can planners not practice occupancy urbanism, focusing on politics, materialities and open-ended complexities? Benjamin's concern with respect to planning is to show its inability to control the city. Yet the counter-narrative of this 'failure', as I have argued, is as incomplete as the modernist planning's claims of success.

This is dangerous ground to cede. Benjamin argues that planning and policies have become the domain of elite engagement—it is business associations like NASSCOM or FICCI[13] and elite city associations like the Bangalore Action Task Force and Mumbai First that are calling for 'comprehensive planning'. Yet this is precisely a reason to reclaim planning as a site of subaltern urban politics. This chapter, in deconstructing the 'failure' of planning to show how traces of the Plan continue to impact the city and the lives of the vulnerable and income-poor urban residents within it, has attempted to make a case that planning is a site that subaltern politics must engage with. It certainly must not cede it to, or dismiss it as, a terrain of state rule, as an irrelevant set of archaic and forgotten modernist ambitions or a site of elite capture set in opposition to 'complex negotiations at the local level' that are seen as the primary domain of subaltern political engagement.

I am arguing, instead, for urban political practices that grapple with places for which, as Sheppard, Leitner and Maringanti argue, 'it is difficult to plan and yet where planning cannot be abandoned' (2013: 895). Imagining the contours of such a practice, however, first requires us to re-think some foundational relationships in both urban theory and the study of urban poverty and marginality. I turn to this next.

## Informality, Illegality and Poverty: Re-thinking Planning Theory

From its roots in economics and the theory of dual labour markets, informality has been traditionally represented as 'a sphere of unregulated, even illegal, activity, outside the scope of the state' (A. Roy 2008). In urban theory, the narrative of 'informality' has been a particular marker in theorising cities of the global South, particularly 'megacities' that are 'big but not powerful' (Robinson 2006) and beset by 'problems'. In this depiction, the informal is seen as one of the key drivers of the 'dysfunctional landscapes of Southern cities' (Rao 2006).

Until recently, the bias in urban theory has been to see informality more as 'a domain of survival by the poor and marginalized' (A. Roy 2008: 2). In this reading, it is often quickly reduced to the 'slum'. The slum then is read as a 'demographic and territorial form' that is the 'spatial manifestation of the informal proletariat that has emerged from over a decade of structural adjustments' (Davis 2006: 28). It is the 'distorted substance' that changes the 'urban into a dysfunctional stage for violence, conflict and the iniquitous distribution of resources' (Rao 2006: 231).

Recent urban theory, however, has both challenged the reduction of poverty to the 'slum', as well as sought to re-cast informal urban spaces and lives not just as sites of marginalisation but of enterprise, resistance and resilience.[14] Yet, as Varley reminds us, the entrepreneur and the impoverished slum dweller still form a dualism (2013: 16).

Roy has argued instead that urban informality is not, in fact, a 'bounded' space or sector at all, but a type of governance. She understands it as the state's ability to suspend order, to 'decide what is informal and what is not, to determine which forms of informality will thrive and which will disappear' (2005: 149). This is a 'new spatial vocabulary of control, governance and territorial flexibility' (A. Roy 2003: 157), a mode of the production of space. It is, in fact, she argues, 'the formal and the legal that are perhaps better understood as fictions, as moments of fixture in otherwise volatile, ambiguous, and uncertain systems of planning' (A. Roy 2009b: 81). How does our data respond to this set of debates?

First, the data certainly show that 'unplanned' growth is not the domain of the poor or the slum. If the 'dysfunctional landscapes of Southern cities' are indeed caused by the 'dominance of informal, unplanned growth,' as Rao argues, then this dysfunction must take into account not just the 'slum' but the production of illegal housing by the middle and upper middle classes as well. In fact, the data reminds us that illegal construction of housing is, in fact, the dominant mode of production of housing and shelter in the city. The reduction of urban dysfunction to the 'slum' in policy, everyday discourse as well as within urban and planning theory, I argue, has played a key political and intellectual role that is, in David Harvey's use of the term, 'counter-revolutionary'—it not only asks the wrong question, it prevents the real question from being asked (Harvey 1973). It has allowed the dualisms that Varley describes and that Roy challenges to reproduce, creating the fiction of the 'informal city' as an autonomous, distinct object.

I suggest a different field of inquiry. If illegality is indeed the dominant mode of production of urban housing as the data suggests, then how do we understand the processes within, as well as implications and management of, different kinds of illegalities when exercised by different urban actors? Such a reframing insists that analyses of urban politics be relational, looking at the ways in which particular kinds of urban practices and actors are framed as 'illegal' relative to others and what work such a framing is meant to do. In other words, it argues that how the dirt is kept at bay—'ideas about separating, purifying, demarcating and punishing transgressions' (Douglas 1966)—matters in the differential impact these have on urban politics and particularly a politics of resistance.

How do these differentiated illegalities emerge, and how are they related to planning? Let us take two examples. First, the MPD '01 and MPD '21 deliberately chose not to include already built-up areas within notified development areas of the Plan. Since we know that the only way to be legal and planned within our settlement typologies is to be within the development area, built up housing in this area is thus rendered illegal by plans choosing not to include them. Second, the waves of 'regularisation' of unauthorised colonies to make them legal regularised colonies equally embody acts of discretion as authorities decide 733 colonies of the total 1639 will be regularised and which will remain unauthorised. In the absence of objective metrics by which the regularisation process functions, it is indeed the discretion of the DDA to decide who will become legal and who will remain illegal, at what time and for how long. The construction of the categories of housing complements this discretion. Since the typologies are not based on objective metrics of what makes one colony a JJ cluster, a slum designated area or an unauthorised colony; or even what differentiates a planned colony from a resettlement colony, categorisation becomes flexible, a mode of control that cannot be contested against a set of objective criteria.

Put simply: it is plans, and not the failure of their implementation, that produces and regulates illegality. They determine, through their discretionary ability to notify or not notify parts of the city within the development area, as well as through waves of 'regularisation' that include certain colonies but not others, or even in patterns of eviction that evict certain bastis but not others, which settlements will be legal and which illegal, which will thrive and which will not be allowed to exist. The production and regulation of illegality is part of, and not outside, planning and planned development. It is a technique of rule, what Roy calls 'a spatial mode of governance'.

Yet there are limits to this mode of governance—limits that are embedded within and exercised through the Plan and, therefore, must be engaged with through planning itself. What are these limits? The first is the unintended consequences of planning as outlined above. Once plans are notified, even if they 'fail', their traces still determine the spatial patterns of housing. This implies that there are constraints to the state's own ability to wield a flexible governance model. In the gaps between intention and outcome lie the possibilities of different political imaginations as well as the practices that are celebrated as part of informal urbanism.

The second limit is that discretionary governance—what Roy calls a 'calculated informality'—exercised by the state still uses and is thus bound by the categories of planning. I showed in multiple instances in this chapter that the DDA often violated its own principles of categorisation. As Chapter Two will argue in detail, this violation has consequences. The ability to be discretionary and 'calculated' has limits. This is particularly true when different institutions within the 'state' choose to exercise competing discretions within the city. In the chapters to come, the advent of the Judiciary and their understanding of the Plan as statutory law, for example, will greatly compromise the ability of the Executive to exercise discretion as a part of rule. Contrary to what Roy argues, within the courtroom, the 'formal and the legal', are perhaps not better understood as 'fictions'—they take concrete, judicial form that is based on the categories and stipulations of planning. To be both understood as well as resisted, this judicial form will have to, at least partly, be deconstructed from within planning itself. To do so, I argue, the conceptual terrain of 'legitimacy' offers a stronger foundation than the many lives of urban informality.

## Thinking through Legitimacy

Responding to Partha Chatterjee's celebrated formulation of political society and civil society, Nivedita Menon (2010) argued that Chatterjee errs in seeing them as 'empirical spaces'. A neat distinction, she says, between 'civil society consisting of citizens with rights; the zone of corporate capital' and 'populations which are the object of development policies, people with no legal rights; the zone of non-corporate capital,' flounders on empirical examination. Citizens of civil society groups can just as well be treated as populations and the objects of welfare and development, and people in political society often make rights-claims using the institutions of the state that Chatterjee describes as the domain of civil society. Menon argues that the two terms should be understood as 'conceptual distinctions' rather than as empirical groupings. There is, therefore, not 'political society' or 'civil society' to be found, but 'two styles of political engagement' that are available to all people (ibid.).

Seeking the 'informal city' or the 'illegal city' runs the same danger of seeking empirical spaces rather than modes of politics, and ignoring the ways in which loosely coded 'formal' and 'informal' practices actually intertwine and are related to one another (McFarlane 2012). AbdouMaliq Simone has argued that even as 'everyday practices of adaptation' and survival celebrated as informal urbanism should be recognised, they must be set against, 'a backdrop punctuated by fragmented infrastructures, social divisions and partial forms of urban governance' (2008: 197).

I take Simone's argument one step further: we must ask how this 'backdrop' shapes these forms of practice and, therefore, how its different configurations make (im)possible different forms of everyday urban life. We must understand, in other words, what Heller and Evans call, the 'weapons of the powerful' that are 'a vast repertoire of techniques (material and discursive) that reproduce inequality' (2010: 436) just as they also shape the 'weapons of the weak' (Scott 2008).

Yet how do we assess these intertwined sets of formal and informal practices and the impact they have on the lives of different urban residents? It is here that legitimacy offers a useful conceptual location. Legitimacy can be seen as a marker of the probability of reaching certain desired outcomes: secure tenure, basic services, but also greater wealth, for example, or access to capital and resources. Practices that enhance legitimacy increase the probability of reaching the desired outcome and sustaining it, though neither is guaranteed. These practices are diverse, working through law or custom; de jure rights or de facto gains; political society-type jockeying or civil society-type lobbying; negotiation or confrontation. They are irreducible to (in)formal/(il)legal either spatially, in their form or as a descriptor of actors wielding them. They are, however, shaped by and intertwined with material, discursive and institutional structures of the 'formal' and 'legal'. There is, in other words, no autonomous 'outside' that they inhabit.

Let us take an example. Viewed from the lens of legitimacy, the 'slum question' cannot be framed as merely a question of regularisation or formalisation, i.e. the conversion, De Soto style, of the informal/illegal into the formal/legal. Instead, it asks a different set of questions: What allows one settlement a longer tenure even as its neighbour is evicted? Through what set of practices does one settlement gain enough legitimacy to survive twenty years without eviction while another merely lasts five? What explains the different levels of access to basic services and infrastructure amidst two illegal settlements? What makes one group of basti residents choose to negotiate and another to confront when faced with the threat of eviction? How will regularisation impact these existing ways of ordering everyday life—does becoming legal increase access to infrastructure or make no discernible impact?

Seeking to increase legitimacy rather than simply seeking to make legal/formal opens up a range of practices—securing tenure through non-title based claims and/or rights; using different kinds of networks and political connections; lobbying to separate provision of basic services and infrastructure from questions of spatial illegality (Bhan, Goswami and Revi 2014), among many others—that impact the socio-material realities of everyday life beyond just formal/legal status. These practices may even choose to avoid such status if it hinders existing practices that have secured legitimacy though they may just as well seek to use such status selectively.

Legitimacy thus rejects the idea of an 'outside' to instead embrace change from within constrained degrees of freedom that seek to move to more desired ends incrementally. Practices seeking to further legitimacy can be fleeting or can slowly embed themselves iteratively to form new norms, laws and structures over time. Importantly, such movement can be generated not just through subaltern resistance but from within the structures and institutions that wield power and by elite actors themselves.

This implies a certain 'moral ambivalence' (Jeffrey and McFarlane 2008) to legitimacy. Certainly, elite actors seek to enhance their own legitimacy—in unauthorised colonies, for example, jostling for regularisation, or in the actions of real estate brokers transforming peri-urban areas in a grey zone with respect to the law—just as much as subaltern residents. They often do so with an equally creative, adaptive and dynamic relationship to the 'formal' and 'legal'. Legitimacy is therefore not unproblematically available as a foundation for an emancipatory politics. Yet it compels those seeking such a politics to locate their struggles in the 'thicket of contestations', to use Chatterjee's description, where urban outcomes are shaped and the sociomaterial fields of possibility are determined. If both subaltern and elite actors are jockeying for legitimacy using both civil and political society styles of engagement, then the site and forms of struggle must navigate this contested field to be effective.

For those of us interested in a more egalitarian city, we may choose to be more specific about the kind of legitimacy that interests us. In such a formulation, one could argue, in Rawlsian fashion, that an inclusive politics must judge itself by whether its practices increase the possibility of legitimacy *for subaltern urban residents*. Yet even then, such a politics is possible only if it can take root in the relationships between and beyond 'formal' and 'informal' practices, engaging with both as well as with competing claims and practices by other, often more powerful, urban actors. Legitimacy forces us to see and address these other practices and not assume that they lie undifferentiated and bound within 'civil society'. Without such engagement, an inclusive politics will run aground. Subaltern resistance that does not seek to impact even porously formal/legal structures and rules—the 'political stance of perpetual resistance' (Parnell and Pieterse 2010)—or that believes it can act outside them, will be unable to better the material conditions of everyday life where it matters the most. On the other hand, change from 'within' the system that is not in engagement with the existing practices of everyday life will be doomed again to 'fail' or be undone, at best, and be a violent exercise of dominant power, at worst.

Searching for the 'concreteness of subaltern political action' (Guha 1988: 5) implies looking beyond familiar locations for a politics of resistance and change. If political society is not an empirical space and the 'slum' is not the territorialisation of marginality, then a new set of actors, sites and scales for inclusive urban politics need to be imagined. I have argued in this chapter that the idea of increasing the capacity to seek and enhance legitimacy imagines political practices that can occupy both institutional structures as well as everyday life. Such practices would emphasise the intertwining of these two realms, refusing the power of plans to control everyday life but equally refusing the ability of an autonomous everyday life 'outside' even failed, imperfect and porous institutions.

## Notes

1. The conference was held in March 2011, at the India International Centre and titled 'Developing an Agenda for Urbanisation in India'. See http://indiancities.berkeley.edu/ (accessed 14 April 2012).

2. See the full text of the speech on the JNNURM website here: jnnurm.nic.in (accessed 1 September 2011).
3. For my use of the term 'basti', see note 2 in Introduction, this volume.
4. See Chapter Two, this volume, in particular.
5. Delhi is divided into fifteen zones—eight urban, six rural and Zone 'O' for the riverbed. Zonal plans were introduced under the MPD '21. There are currently sixteen zonal plans prepared for Delhi. These are available at http://dda.org.in/planning/zonal_plans.htm (accessed 19 April 2012). Most of these plans have been made in the last five years. In 2009, when I began fieldwork, only six zonal plans had been notified. The number rose to 11 by 2011, and up to 15 by April 2012.
6. Personal interview with Sunil Mehra, Senior Town Planner, Municipal Corporation of Delhi, 11 October 2010.
7. A colony called Sainik Farms has, for nearly two decades, arguably been the best-known example of a rich, illegal colony. The government is widely seen as powerless to act against the powerful residents of the colony. See, for example, http://articles.timesofindia.indiatimes.com/2009-12-04/delhi/28059937_1_affluent-colony-illegal-colonies-unauthorized-colony (accessed 13 April 2011).
8. Recent urban policies like JNNURM and the National Urban Sanitation Policy have moved towards providing environmental services regardless of legality of tenure. This has allowed public utilities to legally provide services even in 'illegal' settlements.
9. See dda.nic.in (accessed 23 June 2011).
10. Personal interviews with A. K. Jain, former director of planning, DDA, 2 January 2011, Sunil Mehra, Senior Town Planner, Municipal Corporation of Delhi, 11 October 2010, and Viresh Bugga, Chief Town Planner, Municipal Corporation of Delhi, 15 February 2011.
11. In Hindi, *jhuggi-jhompri* refers to temporary, fragile housing shacks typically made of temporary materials like tarp or thatch, though its use can be more general and just refer to poor settlements. Along with basti, it is the closest translation of the everyday use of the English word 'slum'.
12. Estimates range from 95 to 98 per cent.
13. The National Association of Software and Services Companies (NASSCOM) is a 'premier organisation that represents and sets the tone for public policy for the Indian software industry.' See www.nasscom.org (accessed October 2015). FICCI stands for the

Federation of Indian Chambers of Commerce and Industry, an industry lobby that describes itself as 'the voice of India's business and industry'. See www.ficci.com (accessed October 2015).

14. For three comprehensive review articles, see Kudva (2009), McFarlane (2012) and Varley (2013).

# 2

# Planned Development and/as Crisis

*Evictions and the Politics of Governance in Contemporary Delhi*

> *What is to be done in this never-ending drama of illegal encroachment in the capital city of our republic?*
>
> —Supreme Court, *Wazirpur*[1]

> *It quenches the thirst of the thirsty, such is Nangla, it shelters those who come to Delhi, such is Nangla.*
>
> —Nangla's Delhi[2]

'There is an encroachment,' said the Delhi high court, 'on the Ring Road, on the left side of the T-Junction on the Ring Road-Bhairon Road crossing.' To the people who lived there, the 'encroachment' was a basti[3] called Nangla Maachi, or as in the couplet cited above, just 'Nangla'. Over nearly twenty years, Nangla had been transformed from a swamp area near the River Yamuna in the south-eastern part of Delhi into a settlement housing over 2800 families (nearly 15,000 people). Like other bastis in Delhi, its residents were mostly service providers to the city: domestic workers, recyclers and ragpickers, small business and trade owners, construction workers, tailors, rickshaw pullers, and craftsmen and women.

In the Delhi high court, Nangla was both hypervisible and invisible. In a case called *Hemraj vs the Commissioner of Police and Ors*[4] (henceforth, *Hemraj*), the court noted its presence and ordered its demolition in no less than eleven different orders between 2001 and 2006. Yet in not a single one of these eleven orders was Nangla ever mentioned by name. It remained simply, each time it was mentioned, a full sentence geographically accurate and devoid of life: 'an encroachment on the left side of Bhairon Marg on the way to Noida' or 'the remaining encroachment on the left side of the T-Junction going from Pragati Maidan to Noida.'

'Unauthorized occupants,' the judges said, 'have encroached upon the valuable land and opened commercial shops.'[5] It is 'shocking', they argued further, that on 'the main arterial road of Delhi, i.e. the Ring Road, unauthorized encroachment is allowed.' These unauthorised occupants had 'buffaloes and other animals' that not only created a 'problem of hygiene' but also created a 'hindrance for the smooth flow of commuters' that the judges specifically pointed out 'are in lakhs'. These unauthorised occupants used the land 'not for shelter' but 'for commercial activities'. The court was irate that 'tax payers money' was being spent on 'widening on the road' on one hand and on the other, 'illegal encroachment was allowed for commercial benefits.' The reason for the encroachment was clear. As a result, the Court argued, 'of passing the buck from one government agency to another, [no one] came forward to own responsibility to get the encroachment cleared.' This gave 'ample time' to the 'encroachers' who 'further proliferated on the land' as if it 'was no man's land'.

Yet in the original petition filed by Mr Hemraj on behalf of the residents of Deragaon, an urban village in entirely another part of the city, Nangla—in fact, any basti or any type of encroachment at all—isn't even mentioned. The petition is not about 'slums' or 'urban poverty', let alone about Nangla in particular. It is, in fact, about traffic. Not even 'traffic' per se, but the movement of large vehicles/trucks across a particular stretch of road outside the petitioner's house during a particular set of hours in the day. Its main prayer is simple: 'to impose restrictions on the movement of heavy and medium goods traffic on the entire main road from Chattarpur Mandir leading towards Bhatti Mines during peak hours in the morning as well as in the evening.'

In August 2006, under the orders of the Delhi high court, Nangla was demolished. Less than half of the residents were eligible for any form of resettlement. Some were excluded because they did not meet the 'cut-off date'—only those that had documents that proved that they had been residents of the basti before 1998 were eligible for resettlement.[5] Complex tenurial agreements between 'owners' and 'renters' meant that many renters were instantly excluded from even the possibility of being eligible. Many of those eligible were unable to afford even the minimal down payment required to get an alternate plot. Those that were resettled were sent to Savda Ghewra, no less than fifty kilometre away on the northwestern periphery of the city, and housed in 18 sq m plots for families with an average size of five. Amenities were scarce if not absent, especially compared to Nangla, where the community had built up its own environmental services over two decades.

★ ★ ★

Evictions are not new to cities in general or Delhi in particular. Yet Nangla is one of a series of evictions that have scarred contemporary Delhi which, as I have argued in this book, are different not just in degree but in kind from previous evictions. These evictions were not ordered by planning agencies, the municipality, development authorities or either of the state- and central-level governments that govern the national capital. They were ordered by verdicts in the Delhi high court and the Supreme Court of India, each in a unique legal innovation ironically intended to democratise access to justice in a country marked by entrenched inequalities—the PIL.

Authors that have previously looked at the case law on evictions have looked closely at the Court's portrayal of the poor as 'encroachers' (Dupont 2008; Ramanathan 2004; Chapter Three, this volume); the use of 'nuisance' laws (A. Ghertner 2008); changing environmental mores that portray the poor as 'dirty' in what one scholar has termed 'bourgeoisie environmentalism' (Baviskar 2003); a shifting political climate in Indian cities that seek global transformations into 'World-Class Cities' where there is little, if any, place for the poor (Chatterjee 2004a; Menon and Nigam 2007), or simply the 'anti-poor' nature of the judiciary[7] (Bhushan 2004; Rajagopal 2007). In this chapter, I build upon these explanations but suggest both a different focus and purpose of inquiry. I argue that Court-ordered evictions are a privileged site through which to assess urban governance. Specifically, I argue that urban case law within PILs has not been sufficiently seen as a site where a set of 'active processes' (L. Fernandes 2004) produce the city as a scale and object of government as well as fashion a set of altered governmental rationalities. Case law on evictions, in particular, as I will show, makes visible how one set of these emergent rationalities are based on conceptions of planning and planned development as both ethico-moral imperatives of judicial intervention into the city as well as the modes and technologies of its implementation.

Such an analysis is extremely timely in contemporary Indian politics as the Judiciary engages and acts in ways scarcely imagined in the constitutional separation of powers: from fiscal federalism to forest rights; urban management to environmental determination; freedom of speech to the Right to Education. The Court's active and dynamic engagement has been described as judicial activism (or 'judicial adventurism' by its critics) that breaches the separation of powers as the courts pass orders that are increasingly 'administrative' (Sathe 2002: 238) in character. The PIL processes often, some argue, 'obliterate the line between law and policy' (Muralidhar and Desai 2000) moving, argues Sathe, the 'character of the judicial process from adversarial to polycentric, and adjudicative to legislative' (2002: 235). Manoj Mate (2013) has termed this as the 'judicialisation of governance'. This chapter seeks to unpack one part of this judicialisation by tracing its rationalities, idioms, modes and technologies as it locates itself in the city.

Studying Delhi insists on such an analysis. Evictions are only one marker of an increasing judicial presence in the city. PIL decisions emerging from the courts have been responsible for many of the major changes to the city's urban systems since the mid-1990s: the closure and relocation of 'hazardous' industries to outside the city limits;[8] the conversion of all public transport and private commercial transport to the use of compressed natural gas;[9] decisions on municipal solid waste disposal;[10] the 'sealing' of unauthorised commercial units in residential neighbourhoods in violation of the city master plan;[11] and, more recently, the cancellation of a number of residential developments in peri-urban Delhi by nullifying the process of land acquisition of previously agricultural land from farmers.[12] Contemporary Delhi is indeed a city shaped by judicial decisions taken in the public interest.

In what follows, I argue that case law on evictions makes visible broader judicial efforts to make the city into what Nikolas Rose calls a 'governable space'. Using a Foucauldian analytics of government, I show that the courts are a site of the production of new urban governmental rationalities based on altered understandings of a familiar set of concepts—the 'city', 'public', 'inequality', 'slum', 'governance' and 'development'—through the introduction and privileging of others: 'encroachment', 'planned development', 'crisis' and 'order'. These rationalities emerge within the construction of an understanding of the city as a site of crisis both marked and caused by the failure of what the courts repeatedly call 'planned development'. This crisis comes to not only define the threat to public interest but also becomes both the basis as well as the object of the judicial interventions into contemporary Delhi.

To do so, I analyse an archive of twenty-four PILs that have resulted in evictions in Delhi between 1990 and 2007 in either the Delhi high court or the Supreme Court of India. I focus not just on the verdicts in these judgments but the *dicta*, i.e. the detailed texts of the judges' orders in which they locate their decisions within and as the public interest. I look not just at the judgments and orders of eviction issued by the judges but also at the original petitions that initiated the PIL, affidavits filed by petitioners, interveners and other impacted parties, reports by Court-appointed expert committees as well as attempts to appeal or stay the orders of the Court by communities threatened with eviction.

This chapter is structured in four parts. The first lays out the theoretical frame, i.e. an analytics of government. The second then presents a history of the emergence of PIL within Indian jurisprudence, focusing on urban case law within Delhi. The third—the main section of the chapter—analyses the case law on evictions to show how the courts legitimise eviction within new urban governmental rationalities based on particular notions of planning and planned development. The final, concluding section then discusses the implications of these emerging governmental rationalities in thinking about contemporary urbanism and urban governance in Delhi at a time of political and economic transformation.

## An Analytics of Government

The work of Michel Foucault on the art of government is much studied. Foucault, in looking at Western European societies in the sixteenth–eighteenth centuries marked what he called the 'governmentalisation of the state': the 'tendency, the line of force, that for a long time, and throughout the West, has constantly led towards the pre-eminence over all other types of power—sovereignty, discipline and so on—of the type of power that we can call "government"' (1991 [1979]: 102). The shift, in other words, from centralised power to 'those thousands of spatially scattered points where the constitutional, fiscal, organizational, and judicial powers of the state connect with endeavours to manage economic life, the health and habits of the population, the civility of the masses and so forth' (Rose 1999: 18). Foucault's work went on to speak of governmentality, what is now widely known as the 'conduct of conduct'.

Dean (2010) argues that governmentality, in Foucault's work, marks the emergence of a 'distinctly new form of thinking about and exercising power' though one that is still in a certain relationship with older forms such as sovereignty and discipline. In this historically specific manifestation, Foucault described the rise of the art of government as a 'distinct activity' based on certain forms of knowledge concerned with a new object, the 'population', in a particular register, the 'economy'. The welfare of the population as well as the forms of knowledge and technical means appropriate to optimise it became, he argued, the concern of government.

My interest here is not to translate historically specific observations about power and rule from early modern Europe to the post-colonial global South nor to take from Foucault's work a general theory of power to argue for a similar shift in the balance of sovereignty-discipline-governmentality to understand evictions in an Indian city. I am interested, following Nikolas Rose, in a 'looser relation' to Foucault's conceptualisations; to being committed instead to a 'certain ethos of enquiry' embodied in his work that Rose (1999) calls an 'analytics of government'.

An analytics of government, argues Dean, views 'practices of government in their complex and variable relations to different ways in which "truth" is produced in social, cultural and political practices' (2010: 27). It asks, quite simply, 'how we govern and are governed within different regimes, and the conditions under which such regimes emerge, continue to operate and are transformed' (ibid.: 33). An analytics of government is based then on what Dean calls the 'general meaning' of governmentality in contrast to its historically specific manifestation.

In a useful formulation, Jonathan Inda argues that such an analytics has been usually approached through three broad themes: reason, technics and subjects. *Reason* explores the rationalities of government. Studies of the rationalities of government are concerned, argue Rose and Miller, with 'the changing discursive fields within which the exercise of power is conceptualized [and] the moral justifications of particular ways of exercising power by diverse authorities' (1992: 178). Governmental rationalities, argues Rose, are thus the means by which 'governance is legitimised in relation to truth.' These rationalities, he says, have: (a) a distinctive *moral form*, i.e. 'ideals or principles that should guide the exercise of authority, such as justice, equality, or citizenship, among others'; (b) an *epistemological character* in that they are 'articulated in relation to some understanding of the spaces, persons, problems, and objects to be governed'; and (c) a distinctive *idiom* or language (1999: 25–27). *Technics* refer to the mechanisms, techniques and technologies by which authority is constituted and rule established. It is the 'complex of techniques, instruments, measures and programs' that endeavour to translate 'thought into practice' and 'actualize political reason' (Inda 2005: 9). Finally, *subjects* refer to the forms of individual and collective identity—the types of selves, persons, actors, agents or identities—that arise from and inform government.

This chapter undertakes an analytics of government by looking at case law on eviction. It asks a distinct set of questions: What rationalities, reasons, 'changing discursive fields' and 'moral justifications' underlay the framing of evictions as acts of public interest? What 'distinctive moral form' or 'principles' shaped the Court's interpretation of public interest? What techniques or instruments emerged to put these rationalities into practice? In particular, what technologies and forms made the problems and objects of government visible within the Court? How were the objects of government—the 'poor', the 'slum', the 'city'—understood? What was their 'epistemological character' within the courtroom? And, finally, what regimes of government become intelligible through this analytics?

Before we proceed, it is important to understand the context of our analysis itself—a unique judicial innovation practiced within the regional high courts and the Supreme Court of India called the PIL.

## Public Interest Litigation

*The rule of law does not mean that the protection of the law must be available only to a fortunate few or that the law should be allowed to be prostituted by vested interests for protecting and upholding the status quo under the guise of enforcement of civil and political rights. The poor too have civil and political rights and the rule of law is meant for them also, though today it exists only on paper and not in reality.*

—Supreme Court, *PUDR*

In the late 1970s, the Judiciary in India, led by the Supreme Court, fashioned itself as a front line in the defence of rights and social justice, particularly for the poor. It would not be an exaggeration, Rajagopal argues, to say that 'most social movements in India since the 1970s have actively used the courts as part of their struggle, be it the women's movement, the labor movement, the human rights movement, or the environmental movement' (2007: 158). They were, in fact, invited in. Through a unique judicial innovation called the PIL, the Supreme Court sought to democratise access to justice, to become the 'last recourse for the oppressed and the bewildered.'[13]

Through the late 1970s to the mid-1990s, the Court did so, even critics concede, admirably. Judgments expanded the meaning of the Right to Life under Article 21 to include livelihood and the environment; defended the freedom of the press; protected prisoners' rights; addressed sexual harassment at the workplace; argued that basic education was a fundamental right; and guarded the rights of employees (Muralidhar and Desai 2000; Rajagopal 2007; Sathe 2002). Requirements for the filing process were eased to the point that it was commonly said that 'the court treated even a simple letter as a litigation,'[14] taking upon itself the costs of litigation as well as the work of gathering facts and evidence. From the mid-1990s, an early emphasis on civil and political rights broadened to socio-economic rights, distributive justice, and, critically for our narrative, questions of governance, environment and development. Yet within this shift, many claim, the nature of the Court's judgments also changed— an argument that I will return to in the next section.

Sathe argues that the PIL moves the 'character of the judicial process from adversarial to polycentric, and adjudicative to legislative' (2002: 235). It is this polycentric nature of the PIL, where the Court must evaluate competing claims to rights, entitlements and resources in the name of public interest, that critics argue is precisely the work of democratically elected

103

or statutorily appointed institutions of the Executive. Manoj Mate (2013) has noted this in his work as 'the judicialisation of governance'.

As the volume of PILs continues to increase, debates on judicial activism and governance are not just academic or restricted to legal or policy circles—the terms themselves have entered everyday discourse and dominate, for example, media headlines. Rajamani (2007) argues that the Court has emerged as the 'natural choice' not just to seek rights but also to ensure the fulfilment of public duties by the executive arm of the state. Far from being an innovative but marginal part of judicial function senior Supreme Court advocates Muralidhar and Desai (2000) argue that PILs today 'dominate the public perception' of the Judiciary.

How did the PIL become a definitive space for the determination of rights and take on an administrative and legislative character? The PIL is both a substantive as well as technical departure from traditional litigation. Understanding this departure necessitates a return to the site, reason and context of its origin in democracy's darkest hour: the Emergency, 1975–77.

## Public Interest Litigation and the Emergency, 1975–77

The Emergency refers to a two-year period from 1975 to 1977 when a state of national emergency was declared by Prime Minister Indira Gandhi. Basic constitutional freedoms were suspended including the rights to life and liberty as well as to freedom of expression and assembly. The result, as Tarlo argues, was 'press censorship, arrests, torture, the demolition of slums and tales of forcible sterilization' (2001: 2). The official narrative of the Emergency, argues Tarlo, was to protect the nation's security and development. War with Pakistan had just ended, the oil shocks of the early 70s had left the economy in bitter shape, and armed peasant resistance in some parts of the country was growing. 'We are not happy to declare Emergency,' Tarlo quotes Gandhi as saying on Independence Day, 15 August

1975, 'but stringent measures [are] taken as bitter pills [that] have to be administered to a patient in the interest of his health. No one can prevent India marching ahead.'[15]

Other narratives of the Emergency, and indeed the dominant accepted historiography of the event today, is that Gandhi was suppressing the rise of opposition political parties that challenged the Congress party's electoral dominance. The Congress had ruled at the Centre continuously since Independence. Raj Narain accused Gandhi of winning the election by fraud and challenged her victory in the Allahabad high court. On 12 June 1975, the Court declared her election null and void. However, it acquitted her of the much more serious charges of violence, intimidation and fraud levelled by Narain. Trade unions, student movements and opposition parties took to the streets in nation-wide protests. On 25 June 1975, Emergency was declared.

While declaring Emergency, Gandhi's government also enacted the 39th Amendment which retroactively validated Gandhi's election and sought to 'immunize all elections involving the Prime Minister … from judicial review' (Ramachandran 2000: 116). The Supreme Court upheld the amendment and her election. Matters soon worsened. Under Gandhi's control, Parliament made substantive changes to the Constitution including suspending key Fundamental Rights like the freedom of expression, allowing her to arrest anyone who criticised her publicly and censor the press. The notorious Maintenance of Internal Security Act (MISA) essentially suspended the Right to Life by making indefinite preventive detention common practice. As Khanna argues, 'the judiciary bowed to the power of Indira Gandhi' (2012: 150).

The lowest point, argues Khanna, was the *Habeas Corpus case*,[16] where the Supreme Court agreed that *habeas corpus*, the writ that prevents persons from being held without being charged or taken to trial, was suspended as the Right to Life itself was suspended. The case has been described as the Supreme Court's 'contribution to the Emergency' (Muralidhar and Desai 2000). Khanna recounts that his namesake Justice H. R. Khanna, the lone dissenting voice in the case who was later summarily passed over for elevation to Chief Justice, asked the state's Attorney General: 'Life is also mentioned in Article 21 and would the Government argument [suspend] life also?' (Khanna 2012: 150).

The Emergency ended in March 1977, in democracy's 'finest hour', when opposition parties won a landslide election against Indira Gandhi and Morarji Desai became the first non-Congress Prime Minister of India. Yet the Desai government fell in 1979, and in 1980, a mere three years later, Indira Gandhi—no longer democracy's villain—was re-elected as prime minister. In the interim, Khanna argues, 'the Parliament and the Judiciary, now freed of their fetters, had reversed some of the more obviously anti-democratic amendments to the Constitution, the press had returned to its "free" status, and significantly, the Judiciary had begun to make good for the shame of its failure in protecting fundamental rights during the Emergency' (ibid.: 163).

One of the ways of 'making good' was for the Court to aggressively fashion itself not just as the defender of Fundamental Rights but also as the primary agent of their increasingly expansive interpretation and enforcement. The Court declared that the Constitution had a 'basic structure' which included Fundamental Rights and that these could not be violated even by constitutional amendment. It took away, in other words, the Parliament's right to amend the Constitution in any way—even by constitutionally enshrined procedure and an absolute majority—which the Judiciary deemed to violate the Basic Structure of the Constitution. Baxi argues that 'no court in the modern world had gone thus far' (1997: 346). In passing the Basic Structure doctrine, the Court had made itself the ultimate arbiter of the Constitution as well as the protector of fundamental rights.

PILs draw upon Article 32 of the Indian Constitution that give the courts the power to 'issue directions or orders or writs, including writs in the nature of habeas corpus, mandamus, prohibition, quo warranto and certiorari, whichever may be appropriate, for the enforcement of any of the rights conferred.'[17] It is worth quoting at some length how the Court saw its new role as a protector of Fundamental Rights using Article 32:

> Article 32 does not merely confer power on this Court to issue a direction, order or writ for enforcement of the fundamental

rights but also lays down a constitutional obligaticn on this Court to protect the fundamental rights of the peop'e and for that purpose this Ccurt has all incidental and ancillary powers including the power to forge new remedies and fashion new strategies designed tc enforce the fundamental rights.[18]

One of the new remedies was the PIL. How did the Court enable those disadvantaged, poor and marginalised to access the Court for justice? It is here that the technical innovations of legal procedure and the determination of evidence become important. Three main technical aspects are worth noting: (a) ease of rules of standing, i.e. *locus standi*; (b) new administrative and enforcement mechanisms through a *continuing mandamus*; and (c) new techniques of fact-finding and standards of evidence including the formation of Court committees and the recruitment of experts and *amicus curae*. I turn to each of these briefly.

## Procedures within PILs

*Locus standi, or who can speak for the poor?* In a landmark Supreme Court case, *S P Gupta vs Union of India* (1982)[19]— popularly known as the first 'Judges Transfer Case'—Justice Bhagwati eased the rules of locus standi, i.e. the rules that governed who could appear before a court, specifically for the regional high courts and the Supreme Court of India. He did so to enable those in a 'socially and economically disadvantaged position' who were 'unable to approach the court for relief' to access justice through the highest courts of the land. Yet, the Court recognised that the poor themselves often could not do so personally for geographic, financial, linguistic and many other reasons especially if they were in situations (for example in prison where many of the first PILs originated) where their ability to do so was completely restricted.

The Court thus allowed, unlike in traditional legislation, parties not directly affected to speak for and represent the interests of others, presumably the poor. PILs thus opened up the door to 'ordinary citizens' to approach the highest courts of the land in matters of public interest either to 'espouse the cause of the poor and oppressed (representative standing), or to seek enforcement of performance of public duties (citizen standing)' (Rajamani 2007: 1, fn 4). It imagined a range of civil society associations, NGOs and individuals that would speak for the rights of others. Justice Bhagwati argued:

> Where a legal wrong or a legal injury is caused to a person or to a determinate class of persons ... and such a person or determinate class of persons is by reason of poverty, helplessness or disability or socially or economically disadvantaged position, unable to approach the court for relief, any member of the public can maintain an application for appropriate direction, order or writ ... .[20]

As Khanna argues, 'the voice of a "publicly minded", progressive and empathetic civil society came to be formed, both within and outside Court' (2012: 165). The question of who represents this 'voice' and what it asks for will become critical for us to consider when we see how evictions were ordered under PILs.

*The violation of a 'collective right'*: A decision in a landmark case called *Ratlam vs Shri Vardhichand and Ors* (1980)[21] [hereafter, *Ratlam*] further argued that this also meant that petitioners could speak of a 'collective loss of the quality of life' caused, for example, in *Ratlam* by the municipality's failure to provide water and sanitation services. Such 'collective loss' became justiciable. In *Ratlam*, argues Sathe, it was recognised for the first time that 'people could approach the court against violations of their collective rights and that the judicial process could be invoked for the enforcement of the positive obligations that public bodies have under the law' (2002: 214). The shift from adversarial to polycentric jurisprudence was complete. This shift raises an important set of questions that we will return to later in this chapter: How is a 'collective loss' determined? In particular, how are competing rights claims within the determination of what counts towards the 'quality of life' managed within the Court?

*Continuing mandamus*: *Ratlam* was a turning point within PIL that saw courts take 'affirmative action' to 'compel a statutory body to carry out its duty.' In *Ratlam*, that duty was not just to construct sanitation facilities, but to do so 'despite the great cost involved' and to do so in a 'time-bound manner'. The Court's order was a writ of mandamus. Mandamus—literally to 'command' or 'mandate'—refers in common law systems to the Court's directives or orders to a public official, body or a lower court to perform a specified duty in the public interest. As we shall see, however, within PILs the Court often not just ordered public bodies to do their 'statutory duty' but, in fact, also determined what this duty itself entailed.

PILs also represented a further innovation—a *continuing mandamus*. In one of the earliest PILs, *Hussainara Khatoon vs State of Bihar* (1979)[22] [hereafter, *Hussainara*], that concerned under trial prisoners serving extensive pre-trial detention terms, the Supreme Court 'without issuing a *dispositif* judgment ... issued relief in the form of interim orders and directives, thus retaining jurisdiction pending a final ruling' (Mate 2013: 278). In effect, this allows PILs to remain active and alive within the judicial system. Cases are then on-going sites of administration, reporting and action, not just cases that end at the point of a final judgment or Court directive. Another example makes this clear. In *Vineet Narain vs Union of India* (1996) [hereafter, *Vineet Narain*],[23] a PIL was filed relating to the investigation of a corruption scandal by the Central Bureau of Investigation. The court ruled that its orders were to be followed expeditiously not just in the instance but for an unspecified period of time with regular reporting to the court. In *Vineet Narain*, it was clear, argues Muralidhar, that the 'Court controlled the entire investigation' in a manner that was widely reported in the media and publicly lauded, being seen as the only guarantee of a fair process (1998: 8).

In *Vineet Narain*, the judges located the need for *continuing mandamus* in the failure of Executive agencies to be relied upon to follow just a writ of mandamus. Since, the court argued, 'the continuing inertia of the [public] agencies to even commence a proper investigation could not be tolerated any longer' and since 'merely issuance of mandamus directing the agencies to perform their task would be futile,' the Court 'decided to issue directions from time to time and keep the matter pending requiring the agencies to report the progress of the investigation.' Continuing mandamus was a 'new tool', the courts argued, forged because of the 'peculiar needs' of the matter at hand. Yet, in cases hence, it has become a defining feature of PIL jurisprudence, challenging the line between protecting rights and controlling the function of the institutions of the Executive.

*Evidence as expert knowledge, committees and commissioners*: If the Judiciary was willing to treat a letter as litigation, how were judicial proceedings to proceed? What, in other words, was to replace the work that would traditionally be done by a petitioner of a case: framing legal arguments, citing statutes and presenting evidence? Recognising that PIL would need a new technology of fact-finding, gathering and judging evidence, the Supreme Court innovated the procedures of adjudication once again.

Within a PIL, a Court takes on the responsibility of ascertaining the facts. It does so by inviting expert testimony as well as by appointing Court commissioners and committees. These new institutional actors are the 'eyes and ears of the court'. The PIL courtroom is thus populated not just by lawyers but also by 'experts' and fact-finding committees that the Court appoints to gather data, present empirical evidence, and to testify on their subjects of expertise. This knowledge is a critical part and indeed often a basis of the Court's decision-making process in a PIL particularly in adjudicating competing rights claims.

Sharan (2010) argues that the Court thus directly intervenes in knowledge production around each of the issues of public interest raised before it. Citing environmental case law where the courts sought 'scientific truth' about sources of pollution in Delhi, he argues that the courts lose 'their neutrality' because the 'manner in which scientific truths are produced for a legal process' is itself 'embedded in the very practices of the courts though which admissibility of evidence is determined or expertise certified'. Environmental cases are ideal examples of what Sathe calls 'polycentric' issues where competing claims have to be measured against subjective and multiple criteria.

Where do we locate cities and the urban poor within this history? How have they been visible to the Court? In the next section, I briefly trace a particular type of PIL case law—cases related to urban poverty, 'slums' and evictions—identifying a clear shift within this case law from before and after the mid-1990s. This shift, marked most visibly by the rise in evictions that is at the heart of our analysis, sees the claims of the income-poor urban residents steadily excluded, criminalised and read out of a judicial space that was originally created in their name.

## The Urban Poor within Public Interest Litigation: 1980s–2000s

*'The golden triangle'*: Initial post-Emergency PILs predictably centred around prisoners' rights[24] and illegal and preventive detention. Yet from the late 1970s itself, a concern emerged that expanded the Court's purview to look at not just civil and political but also socio-economic rights. The basis of this expansion, Khanna argues, was an expansion in the Court's reading of Article 21, the Right to Life. In *Maneka Gandhi vs Union of India* (1978),[25] the court held that the Right to Life 'attained meaning' in conjunction with Articles 14 and 19, i.e. equality and freedom. The Right to Life, argues Khanna, moved from, 'being simply a right to a bare life, to one of equality, of freedom, and the range of grand notions that the Supreme Court laid out in a flourish.' This expansion was 'the starting point for the glorious expansion of the "Right to Life" as it found its place in a "golden triangle" of fundamental rights' (2012: 163).

Within the expanded Right to Life, Baxi argues, the Court was able to give life to the Directive Principles of State Policy, a chapter about socio-economic ideals in education, health, livelihood, etc. in the Indian Constitution. Directive principles are guidelines for the State but are unenforceable and non-binding unlike fundamental rights.[26] Through the 1980s and early 1990s, in the first phase of PILs, Baxi argues, socio-economic rights enshrined in the directive principles were often read into Fundamental Rights. The Indian courts, he argues, 'have deployed the Directives as a technology of constitutional

111

interpretation: they have favoured interpretation that *fosters*, rather than *frustrates*, the Directives giving them an "indirect" justiciability' (Baxi 2003: 325; emphasis in the original). Early PILs soon took on cases of livelihood, bonded labour,[27] child labour, housing, health, privacy, education, sexual harassment at the workplace,[28] domestic violence and the environment.

This was a time of great optimism about PILs. Baxi, a noted legal scholar and commentator, was moved to describe the period as no less than a 're-democratizing of the processes of governance and the practices of politics' (1997: 351). PILs were seen as filling a democratic vacuum as the 'Supreme Court *of* India' became a 'Supreme Court *for* Indians' in what Baxi called 'chemotherapy for the carcinogenic body politic' (2002: *xvi*). The Court became a site where rights were interpreted, expanded and enforced. The Emergency had, it seems, been well overcome.

Within the city, the effect of this moment was palpable. In 1985, the Supreme Court of India issued a landmark judgment that was to hold precedent over cases regarding evictions and resettlement in cities. In *Olga Tellis vs Bombay Municipal Corporation* (1985),[29] the Supreme Court ruled that, 'the right to livelihood is an important facet of the right to life.' In effect, the court argued that 'the eviction of the [pavement dwellers] will lead to deprivation of their livelihood and consequently to the deprivation of life.' It argued that the urban poor do not 'claim the right to dwell on pavements or in slums for the purpose of pursuing any activity which is illegal, immoral or contrary to public interest. Many of them pursue occupations which are humble but honorable.' Importantly, the Court also acknowledged that it was the state's non-implementation of the master plans of cities that had caused the problem in the first place.[30]

It is important to read the judgment in this case clearly. Though the Court did not stop demolitions, the text of the judgment betrays empathy for the plight of 'pavement dwellers,' a desire to minimise harm caused during the process of resettlement and an acknowledgement of the planning failures of the state. Further, it instructed the government to resettle those that (implicitly) it had failed to house. There were other cases at this time that echoed a similar empathy. In *K Chandru vs State of Tamil Nadu* (1985),[31] the court argued that alternative accommodation must be provided *before* evictions can take place. The judges further hoped that 'the government will continue to evince the same dynamic interest in the welfare of pavement dwellers and slum dwellers.'

In 1989, the Supreme Court went a step further and stated that 'reasonable residence is an indispensable necessity' for human development and the fulfilment of the Right to Life.[32] In another case, the Court held that the 'right to life guaranteed in any civilized society implies the right to food, water, decent environment, education, medical care and shelter.'[33] It went even further a year later and ruled: 'Article 19(1) (e) [of the Indian Constitution] accords right to residence and settlement in any part of India as a fundamental right. Article 25(1) of the Universal Declaration of Human Rights declares that everyone has the right to a standard of living adequate for the health and well-being of himself and his family; it includes food, clothing, housing, medical care and necessary social services.'[34]

*The late 1990s: A paradigm shift?* The shift in discourse within the courts was sudden and palpable. In Delhi, urban scholar Ravi Sundaram marks the beginning of the 'new phase' of PILs with the *Industries Case*[35] in 1996.[36] The case ordered 'hazardous' and 'polluting' industrial units within the city to cease operating and relocate to the peripheries. The impact on livelihoods, argues Nigam (2001), was considered secondary, if at all, to the 'right to fresh air and to live in pollution-free environments.' In a judgement 'widely reported in the Press,' Nigam argues, the Court 'made clear that health is more important than livelihoods, and indeed the health of some are more important than the livelihoods of others.' The drive against 'polluting industries,' he says, 'and the drive against the poor [had] become synonymous.'

As evictions increased through the city, the judgments both followed and furthered their journey. In *Almitra Patel vs the Union of India* (2002),[37] the court opined that Delhi should be the 'showpiece of the country' yet 'no effective initiative of any kind' has been taken for 'cleaning up the city'. Rather than see them as the last resort for shelter, 'slums', the court said, were 'large areas of public land, usurped for private use free of cost.' The slum dweller was named an 'encroacher' and the resettlement that had hitherto been mandatory became, suddenly, a matter of injustice: 'rewarding an encroacher on public land with an alternative free site is like giving a reward to a pickpocket for stealing.'[38]

The courts continued in the 2000s to refuse to hold the Executive responsible for its failure to provide low-income housing and to erode the right to resettlement. When they did acknowledge state failure, they no longer interpreted it to mean that resettlement was therefore due. In *Okhla Factory Owners vs Government of the National Capital Territory of Delhi*[39] (hereafter, *Okhla*) even as the Court said that it was the 'duty of the government to provide shelter for the underprivileged,' it simultaneously argued that the failure to do so does not mean that the state 'take up an arbitrary system of providing alternative sites and land to encroachers on public land.'

The very citizenship of the urban poor began to be called into question. In *Maloy Krishna Dhar vs Government of National Capital Territory of Delhi*, the Court differentiated between the justice deserved by slum dwellers who are 'unscrupulous citizens' versus the 'honest citizens who have to pay for land or a flat.'[40] In *Hemraj*,[41] the rights of 'unscrupulous citizens' were summarily dismissed—'when you are occupying illegal land, you have no legal right, what to talk of fundamental right, to stay there a minute longer'—in the name of order: 'if encroachments on public land are to be allowed, there will be anarchy.'

In its latest order for demolitions in 2006, the Delhi high court refused to stop demolitions even though most households in the settlement did not have any alternative resettlement sites. No more delays were permissible, the judges argued, because the land has 'uses that cannot be denied' and that the more settlements are removed, the 'more they come'. Using language that echoed ideas of epidemics and illness, the judges argued that 'their' numbers were 'growing and growing' and that steps must be taken to 'deal with the problem'. When asked about where the poor were meant to reside in the city if not in informal settlements, the judge said: 'if they cannot afford to live in Delhi, let them not come to Delhi.'

In the section that follows, I look closely at this case law to try and understand this shift. How was this shift made possible within a judicial innovation meant to safeguard the rights of the poor? How was 'public interest' redefined to make such exclusion possible? What new rationalities, technologies and moral forms, to bring back our analytics of government, enabled this new regime of practices?

## The City as Scale: Reframing and Rescaling as Techniques of Government

The construction of scale, argues Neil Smith (1992), is a 'social process, i.e. scale is produced in and through societal activity which in turn produces and is produced by geographical structures of social interaction'. This continual production and reproduction of scale express, argues Smith, 'the social as much as geographical contest to establish boundaries between different places, locations, and sites of experience.' Within the case law on evictions, this production is part of the techniques of government used by the courts. The courts produce the city as the scale at which the 'pressing concerns' of public interest must be diagnosed and defined. Simultaneously, this is then the scale at which interventions, judgments and solutions must be conceptualised and implemented. Two techniques are key to this production, what I am calling *rescaling* and *reframing*.

*Rescaling*: Let us return to the case of *Hemraj*.[42] In this case, the Delhi high court took a local and located problem of the movement of heavy goods traffic on a particular street and argued that the matter of public interest is, in fact, traffic in the city of Delhi per se. Stepping far beyond the single stretch of road that was the focus of the petition, they spoke of how 'with every year the problem of traffic will increase with addition of new vehicles.' They appointed a committee that would report on other obstructions to traffic *anywhere in the city*. The commissioners of the Court—its 'eyes and ears'—thus travel to different parts of the city far beyond Deragaon, the urban village where the petition and Mr Hemraj himself had begun their PIL journey. The committee's reports define and demarcate the problem of 'traffic in the city of Delhi'. As they name streets, roads, neighbourhoods, settlements, fallen trees, narrow interchanges and encroachments, each becomes visible within the Court and is included within the anvil of the petition.

The courts' directions changed appropriately: 'A direction is also issued to Government of Delhi to study the problem of traffic passing through University of Delhi'; or 'a comprehensive travel plan is needed as Pragati Maidan, Zoo, Supreme Court, Patiala House, National Stadium, and other important institutions and buildings fall in this zone and therefore let a comprehensive plan be prepared by the Central Roads Research Institute.'[43] It is a Court committee's report that brings Nangla within the purview of the *Hemraj* judgment and Nangla isn't the only basti to be noticed. In orders passed in another hearing, the Court issues notice on a different basti in yet another corner of the city: 'The Committee has also brought to the notice of this Court that large scale encroachment exists at the road from Nangloi to Mundka Village which is encroached by a large number of fruit/vegetable vendors, timber merchants and building material sellers. The road requires widening. A direction is issued to Municipal Corporation of Delhi to remove all the encroachments from Nangloi to Mundka village on the main road and for the purpose of widening the road.'[44]

*Hemraj* is just one example of how the Court produces the city as the scale of its gaze, diagnosis and intervention. In *Maloy Dhar*,[45] the Delhi high court spoke of waste management and performed a similar shift by saying: 'this is not a problem limited to the petitioners, it is rampant all over Delhi. Therefore, we call upon the local authorities, Municipal Corporation of Delhi, New Delhi Municipal Corporation, Delhi Cantonment Board and the Delhi Development Authority to show cause as to why action should not be taken against them for non-implementation of the provisions for waste management in the city.'[46]

The case that exemplifies the transformation of local petitions into large-scale urban interventions, however, remains *Kalyan Sanstha vs Union of India*[47] [henceforth, *Kalyan Sanstha*]. Infamous as the case in which large-scale 'sealing' drives against unauthorised construction or use were ordered by the Delhi high court as well as the Supreme Court of India, the original petition in *Kalyan Sanstha* seeks only the cancellation of building licenses in Patel Nagar and Karol Bagh, two residential neighbourhoods in central Delhi, that have been heavily commercialised over the past two decades. Yet what is more remarkable is that the petition in *Kalyan Sanstha* reproduces almost entirely and directly quotes at length a previous case filed by a resident of the same neighbourhood. The resident—Kumari Sabharwal—lived in No. 22/66 Patel Nagar. Her neighbour, the owner of No. 22/67–68 Patel Nagar, was building an extra floor in his house contrary to the provisions of the master plan and the building codes for the area. Kumari Sabharwal went to Court and the Kalyan Sanstha Social Welfare Organisation followed her ten years later. The largest drive against unauthorised construction in Delhi that resulted in city-wide demolition drives began as quietly as a petition filed by one neighbour against another.

In hearing the case, however, the Delhi high court argued that the question of public interest in *Kalyan Sanstha* was the 'never-ending drama' of 'illegal encroachment' in 'this capital city of our republic'. All buildings with any unauthorised construction or any unauthorised use are thus implicated in the petition. Critically, the courts' orders are then not limited to the two neighbourhoods that the petition invokes but are city-wide—'to remove all encroachment on public land and demolition of unauthorized construction undertaken after 1.1.2006'—and include instructions to banks (to not extend home loans for illegal construction), to the electricity and water utilities (to not extend connections without verifying the legality of the unit) as well as to the municipal and urban developmental authorities (to demolish unauthorised construction and remove encroachments). The Court is clear that its interventions must reproduce the scale in which it has identified the problem:

'No unauthorized construction can be allowed in any part of Delhi.'

This movement occurs in almost every petition in the case law on evictions. It is the Court, rather than the originating petitions, that produce the city as the scale at which the question of public interest should be determined and where solutions and interventions must be implemented. I call this process *rescaling*. As the Court abstracts particular, located petitions to questions facing the city at large it allows one of the most paradoxical aspects of the PIL: one can be subject to the orders of a litigation of which one wasn't even a part, in which one wasn't consulted or given the opportunity to be heard. The first time that residents of Nangla heard about *Hemraj* was through the courts' order of demolition. This has, as Chapter Four will argue in detail, critical implications for resistance but also effectively erases Nangla's voice and presence in the determination of public interest. It prevents, in other words, any other imagination of Nangla except as an obstruction of the right of way of commuters on the road from Pragati Maidan to Noida. Competing claims to rights are not then deliberated, managed or even adjudicated within the Court—they are foreclosed.

The abstraction that rescaling allows makes the Court's gaze on the City ironically similar to that of a rational, comprehensive master planner—seeing the city in its entirety as a unified object that can be defined, visualised, organised and controlled, just as it reduces different settlements, locations, sites and actors to abstracted units that can be adjusted according to what Tim Mitchell (2002) called 'principles true in every country'. The production of the city as the scale at which public interest is to be determined is not just concerned, however, with the socio-geographical hierarchy of neighbourhood versus city but also with how the question of public interest itself changes through the production of this scale. It is to this question that I now turn.

*Reframing*: The second technique that the Court uses is to cluster a set of different PILs together and determine, or *reframe*,

118

what the substantive, shared question of public interest is. Reframing is thus a process of clustering multiple PILs into a single case that, I argue, substantively changes and at times even radically alters questions of public interest as voiced by individual petitions. In most cases, reframing occurs alongside the rescaling of these petitions from their particular and located claims to the city per se.

In the judgment delivered in *Pitampura Sudhar Samiti vs Government of the National Capital Territory of Delhi*[48] (hereafter, *Pitampura*), for example, the Delhi high court combined 63 different petitions, and argued, 'that the issue involved is about the existence/removal of the jhuggi-jhompri clusters[49] in Delhi.' The argument made was that these PILs raise, more or less, the same substantive question of public interest. Here, again, different local petitions that had a range of relationships to the bastis that appeared in their petitions were reduced to a single, city-scale question of the existence of 'jhuggi-jhompries' in the first place. The court chose three 'lead petitions'—two that represented petitions that 'highlighted the problem of existence of JJ clusters and prayed for their removal' and one that represented petitions that, 'are filed by or on behalf of JJ clusters who either want to continue in the same clusters and demand better facilities or are claiming their rehabilitation.'

Reframing through clustering, just like rescaling, erases the specificity of each petition—of details about claims, prayers, contexts, the petitioner's own perception of the question of public interest she is raising or, indeed, how they argue that they represent a 'public' at all. The two lead petitions mentioned above as the anti-basti position are said to represent a cluster of petitions that 'are mostly filed by various resident associations of colonies alleging that after encroaching the public land, these JJ Clusters have been constructed in an illegal manner and they are causing nuisance of varied kind for the residents of those areas.' Yet even these two lead petitions that are meant to represent, in a sense, the same side of the deliberation on public interest are remarkably different in their contexts, histories and relationship with the bastis that they mention.

In the first of the lead petitions—*K. K. Manchanda vs Union of India* (hereafter, *Manchanda*)[50]—the writ petition had complained of the inaction of the municipal authorities and the DDA in protecting a park in a colony called Ashok Vihar. The petitioner complained against the misuse of 'the green belt as an open public lavatory' by residents of a nearby basti. Yet Mr Manchanda and the residents he represents locate and explain these actions within the petition they file: 'there has been no provision of public toilets for the people residing in these jhuggies as a result these people make use of this green belt for easing themselves throughout the day.' In fact, he goes on to berate the municipal corporation for not constructing these toilets. In his petition, Mr Manchanda is seeking merely a resolution of the restoration of the green space through the construction of public toilets in the basti. He does not, at any time, ask for its eviction.

The second lead petition was *Pitampura* itself. Here, the matter at hand is indeed again the encroachment of an open space within a residential neighbourhood. Like in *Manchanda*, the petitioner in *Pitampura* complains that the 'slum dwellers defecate all around their clusters on the roads and in the parks.' Yet unlike in *Manchanda*, the petitioners in this case argue that 'slum dwellers' do so not because they have no choice but instead are without 'any regard to the safety of the public at large'. The petition speaks of 'bonafide residents' who are living in a 'highly unhealthy, disturbing and insecure atmosphere' because of 'slum dwellers who have no right, title or interest in the said land and are merely trespassers.' The petitioner goes on to describe the 'illegal construction' of the slum dwellers that are 'converting their sheds into concrete structures' along with 'openly stealing electricity from the main transmission lines'. Even the mere presence of the poor—including little children—draws the petitioner's ire: 'many dwellers are sitting or sleeping on the roads most of the time in front of their jhuggies. The children of the jhuggi dwellers have become a nuisance .... They always play on ramps and in front of their houses. They often uproot the plants, scribble obscene words on the gates/walls/

floors of the residents and further harass the residents by pushing their bell buttons.'

The starkest difference in these two petitions that raise the 'same' substantive question of public interest is when, like the petition in *Manchanda* had suggested, the municipality actually begins to build public toilets in the basti in response to the petition in *Pitampura*. The petitioners in *Pitampura*, rather than feeling like their problem may be eased, argue that they are 'shocked to know that the [construction] is being done for the proposed lavatories to be constructed for the jhuggi dwellers.' The petitioners, on seeing this construction, accuse the municipal authorities of 'open discrimination between the law abiding bonafide residents of the area and the encroachers of public land by openly favouring the jhuggi dwellers and depriving the bonafide residents of their essential public civic rights as per the constitution of India.'

Reframing and rescaling together thus produce the city as a scale that distances the Court from the sites, contexts and particularities of actual petitions. In doing so, it is the 'public' itself that gets redefined. The 'public' at hand is not the residents of the colony in *Hemraj*, for example, or Mr Manchanda's neighbours, but the body politic of the city at large. The competing claims to rights, space, needs, resources and entitlements are thus to be evaluated not between the residents of *a* neighbourhood and *a* basti around *a* park, but between the 'poor', 'slum dwellers' and 'jhuggi dwellers' who live in 'bastis' and others— 'bonafide residents' or 'citizens'—at the scale of the city itself. This abstraction allows a particular deliberation of the public interest. Such a process of deliberation invisibilises bastis like Nangla and other settlements that the courts' orders evict— bastis whose literal and discursive absence within the Court marks the exclusions and consequences of how competing rights claims are adjudicated and managed in the name of public interest.

Reframing and rescaling raise a set of questions for our analysis: If the courts determine the substantive question of public interest and do so through the production of the city as a scale at which public interest is to be determined, then how

121

do they see the 'city' they produce? What are the 'discursive fields', in other words, within which the city is produced and understood as an object of government? What is the relationship of production with the 'moral justifications' of government as exercised by the courts? In the next section, I argue that the city is imagined and created within the Court as a site marked by a particular crisis—one marked by the absence of 'planned development' and caused by failure of what the courts call 'Government'.

## The City as Crisis: Encroachment and/as the Failure of 'Government'

In PILs that led to evictions between 1990 and 2007, the city is repeatedly described and created as a site of crisis. In this section, I argue that this crisis is part of a judicial governmental rationality. In other words, it is a basis on which government is, to use Rose's (1999) phrase, 'legitimized in relation to truth'. Rationalities, Rose reminds us, have an epistemological character, i.e. they are 'articulated in relation to some understanding of the spaces, persons, problems, and objects to be governed' (ibid.: 26). The crisis is part of creating such an 'understanding' of the city as such an object. It embodies the city as it is made visible within the Court and becomes the context in which the courts' intervention into the city are understood and legitimised.

How do we understand the crisis *of*, *in*, and even *as* the city? Within the case law on evictions, the crisis of the city is repeatedly defined as a failure—pressing, immediate and urgent—of what the courts call 'planned development'. This failure, they argue, is the primary question of public interest, one that forecloses other claims, narratives and contestations. What is this 'failure'? Two intertwined elements form the answer: (a) what the courts term as 'encroachment'; and (b) the failure of what the courts call the 'Government', i.e. the world of policy, institutions of representative and electoral politics, and statutory public bodies including city utilities, municipal authorities and developmental authorities. For the rest of this chapter, I refer to this particular notion of 'Government' in quotation marks to distinguish it from my use of government as an analytical concept defined earlier.

'Encroachment'—the 'illegal' and 'unauthorised' occupation of land, unauthorised construction in individual building units, and the violation of permitted land use especially within residential colonies—is, for the courts, the most visible symptom of the failure of planned development. It is what separates the complexities of the real city from the imagination of the planned city. It is the multiple disjunctures between the city and its Plan. The courts perform a particular reading of these disjunctures— one that marks them as scars, gaps to be filled, violations that must be undone.

Vyjayanthi Rao has argued that in thinking about 'slum as theory', one must challenge the reduction of the 'slum' to a 'spatial and demographic form' by thinking instead of it more as a construct that 'straddles the conceptual and material forms of city-making' (2006: 231). Both the 'slum' and 'encroachment' perform the work of city-making within the Court. When the Court argues that the failure of planned development through encroachment turns the city into a 'slum', it creates the slum as a shorthand of what Rao calls 'the distortion of urban substance'—of all that is not planned, not orderly and, therefore, neither legitimate nor desirable. The problem that the slum represents then shifts. It no longer represents the vulnerability of its residents. It no longer marks poverty. It no longer marks the history of a failure to build adequate low-income housing. Its residents, their lives and histories, stand reconfigured and reduced to the land the settlement sits on, the zone it occupies in the Plan, and the colour of that zone on the master plan. From a basti, it becomes a slum—something whose erasure is an act of 'good governance', of order and of public interest.

Like the negative of a photograph, it is through encroachment then that planned development itself is defined—as that which stands undone. What the Delhi high court in *Maloy Dhar* calls the 'menace of encroachment' figures as a central and pressing concern in the case law on evictions. The encroachment of public land 'acquired for the planned development of Delhi,' argues the Delhi high court in *Okhla*,[51] is 'the very anti-thesis of the concept of planned development'. The 'whole concept of urbanized development in land has almost collapsed' in Delhi, says the Court. It is almost as if, they say, 'any person can sit where he wants'.

The city, in judgment after judgment, appears as a site marked and threatened by this sense of collapse at a time of great transition. 'No doubt,' the court argues in *Pitampura*, the 'city is growing at an unprecedented pace.' This pace, however, is marked by the 'haphazard development' and 'irrational policies' described in *Okhla* that stand alongside the 'totally haphazard and unplanned growth' in *Joginder Kumar Singla vs Municipal Corporation of Delhi*[52] (hereafter, *Joginder Singla*) to together diagnose the 'complete breakdown' (*Kalyan Sanstha*) and the 'degeneration' and 'decay' (*Pitampura*) of the city. The city, the Court argues in *Kalyan Sanstha*, has itself been 'turned into a slum'.

*The failure of 'government'*: In *Hemraj*, the Court, frustrated with its orders not being implemented speedily enough, says: 'the drama of encroachment goes on unabated. Our direction in this regard for the removal of the jhuggies has been flouted with impunity as detailed in our order dated 12.12.05. We had earlier issued notice to Special Secretary (Power) and the Commissioner of Police, but the main culprit seems to be the Additional Commissioner (Slum and JJ Dept) of the MCD.'[53] It is this, most often, how authorities and members of the 'Government' appear within the Court—as 'culprits', the subjects of notices, summons and, as was the case in the order cited above, accusations of contempt of the Court. Municipal and development authorities, public utilities and the police appear, both in the petitions from the litigants and the judgments by the judges, somewhere between incompetence, at best, and malfeasance, at worst. Elected representatives of the city and central Legislatures are rarely directly mentioned by the courts although I will argue in the next section that the courts' dismissal of 'policy' is directed precisely at them. Petitions and orders alike are underscored by the failure of municipal and developmental authorities to deliver basic services, implement policies and plans, and deliver what different residents see as their rights.

Petitioners for and against eviction are unflinching in their mistrust and dismissal of the Municipal Corporation of Delhi, the New Delhi Municipal Corporation as well as the DDA even as they continue to direct their demands to them in a parallel to what Blom Hansen and Stepputat (2001) have called a 'paradox of the inadequacy and indispensability' that defines many post-colonial states. While petitions representing the poor accuse the authorities of failing their constitutional and statutory obligations to build housing for the poor and anticipate migration and development, other petitions accuse the authorities of being inaccessible and unresponsive, at best, and corrupt and criminal, at worst. In *Pitampura*, petitioners seeking the removal of bastis accuse the authorities of 'sleeping over the various representations of residents' but soon go further and allege them of possessing both 'political reasons and malafide considerations' to avoid fulfilling their 'statutory duty'. In *Jagdish and Anr vs Delhi Development Authority*[54] (hereafter, *Jagdish*), the petitioners seeking the prevention of eviction claim that the DDA 'in abdication of its statutory functions under the Delhi Development Act has not provided for housing for low-income/city service personnel families.'

The judgments are, if anything, harsher and, more importantly, particular in locating the failure of 'Government' as the origin of encroachment as well as the mechanism of its reproduction. In *Pitampura*, the judges argue that 'it does not require any great intelligence to know that it is because of the negligence, carelessness or rather active connivance of the officials of these departments as well as others at the helm of affairs that these encroachments take place and slums are created.' In *Hemraj*, the courts argue that encroachments occur 'as a result of the passing the buck from one government agency to another.' As the agencies 'squabbled', they argued, 'this gave ample time to the encroachers who further proliferated on the said land unchecked by any agency as if it was no man's land.' It seems, the courts argue, 'that the Delhi Development Authority itself does not have a plan.'

In *Joginder Singla*, the court reminds the senior officials of the DDA and the MCD, which it has summoned, that the constituent

Acts that made each of them into statutory bodies contain provisions for the protection of lands from enforcement and give both agencies wide powers of demolition and enforcement. After several pages of citing each of these sections and sub-sections of the DDA and MCD Acts, the court asks: 'how is it, when the aforesaid provisions are on the statute books' that 'such encroachments and huge unauthorized construction' have taken place?

If encroachment is the most visible manifestation of the crisis of the city for the courts, then the failure of 'Government' is both its cause and the agent of its reproduction and expansion. What then is to be done? It is here also that the courts see their own emerging role. In *Joginder Singla*, the judges within the Delhi high court argue: 'it is observed that action is normally taken by these authorities only when such petitions are filed and the court issues directions. It is only then that the administrative machinery of the Municipal Corporation of Delhi and the Delhi Development Authority is activated.' What happens, the Supreme Court asks in *M C Mehta*,[55] 'when violators and/or abettors of the violations are those, who have been entrusted by law with a duty to protect these rights?' The task, they answer, 'becomes difficult' but, more importantly, 'requires urgent intervention by the court so that the rule of law is preserved and people may not lose faith in it finding violations at the hands of supposed implementers.' The Court, the judges argue, 'cannot remain a mute spectator'—the 'enormity of the problem' does not mean that a 'beginning should not be made to set things right'.

The Court thus legitimises its interventions into the city precisely through a narrative of failure, i.e. the failure of 'Government' to manage and control the city and protect it against the threat and reality of encroachment. This failure allows the Court to position itself as a powerful urban actor, legitimising its interventions within the city and its attempts to actively subject the Executive to its power. In fact, this subjection becomes framed as inevitable and necessary precisely because of the portrayal of an inefficient, corrupt and unreliable 'Government'. This shift marks a clear break from PILs in the 1980s, where—as scholars have noted (Sundaram 2009;

126

Sathe 2002; Muralidhar and Desai 2000)—the courts may have held the 'Government' responsible for failing to do its duty but they saw their role as being limited to the determination of this failure. Redressal and further response remained the responsibility of executive authorities—the work of policies and programmes, the work of 'Government'.

From the mid-1990s within PILs in general and within case law on evictions in particular, the courts emerge as a site of intervention, administration and decision-making in and of themselves. I described earlier the courts' innovation of *continuing mandamus* within PILs—the system of regular reporting on the implementation of the orders of the Court often for indefinite periods of time. There, as within case law on evictions, judicial legitimacy was built on the failure of 'Government'. Merely issuing orders to the governmental agencies, the court argued, would be 'futile'.

It is in *Kalyan Sanstha* that the 'Government' first objects to the courts creating what it calls 'a parallel administration'. The MCD files applications against the court's orders in the case.[56] It argues that:

By order dated 23rd March, 2006, this Court appointed Court Commissioners giving direction to the Commissioner of MCD to take immediate action on the receipt of the report of the court commissioners and further giving an authority to the court commissioners to directly inform the Commissioner of Police. It is, thus, submitted that what has been put in place by these orders is virtually a parallel administration.

The court rejects MCD's argument, responding swiftly:

Various proceedings/orders passed by this Court in this very case from 23rd July, 2003 will show that those who are responsible to comply with the statutory provisions of the Act have not only failed to perform their duties but were found to be indulging in permitting illegal and unauthorized construction and commercialization of residential properties. It has become apparent that there has been a complete breakdown of municipal administration.[57]

*The efficiency of contempt*: The Court's narrative of the failure of 'Government' is given legitimacy precisely by the efficiency of its own urban interventions. What makes this implementation possible? I am not suggesting here that the Court orders don't get flouted or delayed. Yet Rajamani (2007) reminds us that PILs are popular precisely because of the perception that 'things get done' within the Court. This chapter began with a series of urban interventions—from the conversion of public transport into CNG, the relocation of industries, the evictions of 'slums'—that are a transcript of the Court's ability to carry out their intentions. Indeed, looking at PIL cases with respect to the environment, Rajamani argues that, 'judicial intervention resulted in improved governance and delivery of public services, and enhanced accountability of public servants.' It is 'little wonder' then, she argues, 'that the courts are the natural choice for individuals who wish to direct the executive to perform its duties' (ibid.: 319).

The debate on why judicial orders enjoy such legitimacy is a complex one. For our purposes here, however, on understanding the failure of 'Government' in the context of evictions, I want to point out one key judicial tool that ensured the implementation of evictions that, once again as Chapter Four will argue, has critical consequences for anti-eviction movements and resistance. This instrument is the threat of contempt. An anecdote yet again from *Hemraj* will make the role of this instrument in producing, exemplifying and reproducing the failure of 'Government' clear.

The first time that the Delhi high court ordered the eviction of 'the encroachment on the left side of Bhairon Marg on the way to Noida', or Nangla, was on 21 January 2001, nearly four years before evictions at Nangla actually took place. In a hearing in December 2005, the court returned its attention to Nangla. 'Even after four years of the passing of the said order', the judges argued, 'no actions have been taken in spite of the fact that the Court on several other occasions have passed directions.' The judges say that their last reminder was when 'we issued directions to the Engineer in Chief, Public Works Department, to identify as to who was to take action for removal and report to the Court.' That direction, they argue, 'has fallen on deaf ears'. This 'non-compliance of the directions for removing the encroachments in this area', the Court argued, 'amounts to a willful disobedience of the orders passed by this Court.'

The court's response is swift:

> We issue notice of contempt to Commissioner of Police, Engineer in Chief of PWD as well as Special Secretary (Power), GNCTD, as to why action for committing contempt of the orders passed in this court should not be initiated against them.[58]

On the next hearing, they issue another notice to who they determine is the real 'culprit'—the Additional Commissioner of the Slum and JJ Department of the Municipal Corporation of Delhi. They summon him: 'We make it clear that on the next date of hearing if the orders passed by this Court are not complied with by the MCD, the Additional Commissioner, Slum and JJ Wing, shall remain present in the Court.'[59] Importantly, notices of contempt are not issued to institutions but to particular holders of public office. The notice is often used alongside the power of the Court to summon the physical presence of these senior officials of 'Government'. It is a powerful set of techniques: evictions at Nangla are completed three months after the notice of contempt is issued and the additional commissioner is summoned to appear in person in the court. The court withdraws the contempt charge saying that, 'it is accepted that no willful disobedience has been committed by the officers in relation to which contempt notice was issued.'

I cite this story not to indicate that Court orders are implemented solely because of their disciplinary and punitive power. Instead, I suggest that the idea of practice of contempt plays an additional role in our analytics of government. The physical summoning of senior officials of 'Government', often from across different institutions and agencies, is part of the process by which the Court performs its legitimacy as an authority powerful enough to ensure implementation—to overcome, in other words, the very root of the urban crisis it has diagnosed. The discursive fields created by the Court—of the twin failures of planned development and 'Government'—stand performed, reified and legitimised. When Sathe (2002) argues that there are few complaints about 'judicial governance' among 'people', it is this ability to hold 'Government' accountable that he is primarily referring to.

The crisis of the city—visibilised by encroachment and understood as the failure of planned development and 'Government'—legitimises judicial urban interventions. The need to address these intertwined failures, to restore order, and to intervene in the idiom and temporality of crisis becomes not only the primary meaning of public interest but also an ethico-moral imperative, what Rose might term the moral form of the rationality of judicial government. This imperative reads the judicial action and the rule of law itself as an act of restoring order and governance to a city in crisis. It is not coincidental that, as they order evictions, the courts argue, as they do in *Pitampura*, that, 'no city, no democracy can survive without law and order. Public interest requires the promotion of law and order, not its degeneration and decay.'

Yet even if the courts see themselves as legitimate urban actors and create a governmental rationality that allows them to intervene into the city, what is the basis by which the Court decides what to do? If encroachment is the anti-thesis of planned development, what is the latter meant to be? It is here that the final component of an emerging governmental rationality falls into place: an epistemological shift that represents and reframes the planned development of the city in terms of what they call 'the legal position' of the master plan.

The problem is not 'the absence of law', argues the Delhi high court, 'but its implementation'. In *Joginder Singla*, they argue that the crisis of the city occurs despite 'Master Plans prepared for the city and in existence for last more than (*sic*) 40 years wherein the planners have envisioned planned growth with [a] beautiful city in mind.' The law in question then is the MPD. The beautiful city is the planned city, the city of order, the city that looks like its master plan—the city without encroachment. Having rescaled the determination of public interest to the city and argued that they are the legitimate actors of urban government, the Court constructs the basis of a regime of rule:

the master plan. To do so, however, they must transform the master plan itself.

## The City as Governable Space: The 'Legal Position' of the Master Plan

*It is because of the Courts that people finally know that the Plan is like law. It is because of them that it has some respect.*

—A. K. Jain[60]

To govern, argues Nikolas Rose, it is necessary to 'render visible the space over which government is to be exercised' (1999: 36). Acts of mapping, drawing, scaling and rendering visual, therefore, are particular acts that spatialise government. Within case law on evictions, the Court privileges a particular representation of the city: the city's three master plans. Yet how does the Court use documents produced by the one of the authorities of the very 'Government' that it accused of failure? What is the life of the Plan, in other words, within the courtroom?

*The legal position of the plan:* In a series of judgments within the Delhi high court as well as the Supreme Court of India, the master plan attains a legal, enforceable and statutory character. The Supreme Court judgment most commonly cited as precedence for treating the Plan as statutory law is *M C Mehta vs Union of India*.[61] The judgment indicts—in the strongest terms—the 'Government' for its failure to implement the master plan. The representatives of the 'Government' protest and argue that the Plan is 'only regulatory in nature'. Being unable to implement regulatory aspects of policy, they argue, is not a violation of law. The courts respond sharply:

[T]he provisions may be regulatory but all the same, they are mandatory and binding. In fact, almost all the planning provisions are regulatory. The violations of the regulatory provisions on massive scale can result in plans becoming merely scraps of papers. That is the ground reality in the country. *None has any right, human or fundamental, to violate the law with immunity* and claim any right to use a building for a purpose other than authorized.[62]

131

Further, the Delhi high court argued, an argument that plans are only 'broad guidelines and cannot be taken as specifics' is 'clearly misconceived and not based on a correct understanding of the legal position of the Plan.'[63] The legal position of the Plan has become common sense. From *Jagdish*: 'it is now well settled that a plan prepared in terms of statute concerning the planned development of a city attains a statutory character and is enforceable as such.' What does it mean for the Plan, an instrument of policy, to become 'law'? What is, in other words, the 'legal position' of the Plan?

The Plan in its legal position inhabits a different life from the document produced by the DDA. Here, it is understood as static; a final, codified document stripped of its own internal mechanisms of review and change, removed from its relationship with the city as it actually exists, and erased of its history of implementation and its undemocratic and opaque drafting process. It must be implemented, *as it is*, despite any impact on 'any right—human or fundamental' even if its provisions may violate precisely these very human or fundamental rights, especially of the poor. Indeed, in *Joginder Singla*, the Delhi high court reversed a common fundamental rights claim made by the urban poor, i.e. the evocation of Article 21 and the right to life and livelihood. In the landmark *Olga Tellis* case in 1985, the Supreme Court had argued that displacing pavement dwellers violated their Right to Life since life could not be read without livelihood. The pavement, the Supreme Court had argued, was both life and livelihood for those who lived and survived on it. Nearly two decades later, the Delhi high court argued that it was, in fact, 'any act of attempt which amounts to nothing but mischief with the Development Plan' that was 'in itself vocative of Article 21 of the Constitution of India.'

In its legal position, the Plan's boundaries both create and bind the city as a governable space. The master plan spatialises governmental thought. Its categories of land use and ownership—in their visual, literal, two-dimensional allocations—reduce the complexity of the city to a neat binary of all that *does* or *does not* ally with the Plan at any given point of time. It becomes the framework, in other words, of the legal and the illegal. In the previous chapter, I used a history of housing in Delhi to show that neat separation of legal and illegal housing in Delhi was itself one of the planning's foundationalist fictions. I argued that it was within illegalities that planning theory must understand the urbanism of Indian cities. Within the Court, however, this history stands erased. Repeatedly, when the history of other existing and older failures of the implementation of the Plan are brought to the Court's attention—say, for example, the failure of the Executive to build adequate low-income housing—the Court repeats a singular refrain: 'that is not our concern.'

The 'legal position' of the Plan is what James Scott describes as a 'simplification'—a 'synoptic view' that uses a 'narrowness of a field of vision' to impart a logic on reality as it is observed. Simplifications, he argues, 'collapse or ignore distinctions that might otherwise be relevant'. They reduce an 'exceptionally complex and poorly understood set of relations and processes' to 'a single element of instrumental value' (1998: 77–81). The Plan as seen by the Court is reduced to the spatial order it represents—a two-dimensional system of classification of land use. Perhaps more importantly, it is simplified to what this spatial order represents within the crisis of planned development in the city: a legible, enforceable sense of order. The Court, Sundaram (2009) has argued, seeks the 'the phantasm of control' typified in Delhi's very first master plan and its vision of the city as an urban machine whose parts, movements and intentions could be controlled by the techno-modernist master planner.

This simplification of both the Plan and planned development is evident, ironically, through what I described earlier as a rare 'victory' for social movements representing basti residents: *Jagdish*. In *Jagdish*, the eviction of the basti has already occurred. The 'victory' is that the courts award the right of resettlement to the residents. In *Jagdish*, the judges argue, as in other cases, that 'adherence to planned development is unexceptionable.' The court argues that the petitions filed by evicted members of the basti 'raise significant questions concerning the implementation of the Master Plan for Delhi and their entitlements to Low income housing in terms thereof.' In response, the Court determines that 'the broad issue which arises for consideration in the present petition is a consequence of the failure of the respondent to develop adequate LIG/Janta housing in colonies or in peripheral areas which has also resulted in encroachment of public land.' It is important to read this judgment clearly. While it acknowledges the rights of the poor to resettlement, it does not question or seek to reverse the act of eviction. Further, it still determines public interest as an adherence to 'planned development'. It is in its nuanced, historical, aspatial reading of planned development that it departs from the body of PIL case law emerging from the Delhi high court. Justice Mudgal, in writing the judgment, notes the exceptional status of the judgment himself. He is aware that he is writing against the hava of the Court. 'This court', he argues, 'is aware that on several earlier occasions different benches of this court have deprecated the conduct of the DDA in allowing slums to mushroom on public land.' Writing against this body of work, he suggests only, and perhaps as a minder to future challenges to eviction case law within the Court that 'perhaps the attention of the court was not drawn to nor did the court deal with the detailed provisions of the [Delhi master plan] set out hereinabove.'

*Plans, not policies:* The Plan allows the Court to position itself clearly against the failure of 'Government'. The Court's reliance on the master plan is explicitly placed against their ire at 'arbitrary' policy regimes, selective 'regularization', the non-implementation of the master plan, and the lack of action against 'slums'.[64] Implicit in their turning to the Plan is their desire for a regime of urban governance that can be read against an explicit and codified order that can result in a visible and enforceable spatial transformation. Unlike the Executive, the courts need not contend with the democratic aspirations and needs of the citizens of Delhi. When they say that, 'a populist measure need not be a legal one',[65] it is important to also unearth the embedded reversal of the same thought: a legal measure need not be a popular one.

The Plan stands both as law and as ideal, the singular basis and legitimacy of the Court's intervention into the city. It becomes the benchmark of how the city must be ruled in order to escape the crises of infrastructural decay, the breakdown of order, the lack of housing, increasing migration and the proliferation of 'slums'. Within the Court, an ordinary land-use plan becomes a mark of a spatial, aesthetic, social and political urban order that must be attained. The implementation of the Plan becomes not just the mechanism of government but its rationality, a defining component of public interest.

Policy, in fact, is no longer the dominant domain and mechanism of government in the Court's eyes. In *Ambedkar Slum Utthan Sangathan vs Municipal Corporation of Delhi*,[66] it denies petitioners the right to use existing and previous Executive policies as any kind of precedence: 'the Government comes out with schemes of rehabilitation from time to time. Merely because on earlier occasions some of the slum dwellers at the some other place, on their eviction from those slums, were given a particular kind of flat, is by no means an assurance to all other slum dwellers that they would also be allotted same type of flats when they are evicted from the accommodation under their occupation.'

The emergence of the Plan as the desired order of the city and of 'planned development' as a rationality of government is highlighted perhaps most starkly by the Court's ire at 'regularisation'. In Chapter One, I argued that unauthorised colonies were often 'regularised', i.e. made legal post-facto, often decades after they had been established. Regularised colonies accounted for 13 per cent of the city's population in 2000. This process of entering into the Plan and legality long after the occupation and the building of settlements is one, as I have shown in Chapter One, that defines how rich and poor alike settle the city. Yet it is precisely this process that the Court's emergence into planning and urban governance breaks—the Plan in its 'legal position' cannot tolerate regularisation. The seeds of this conflict are seen clearly within PILs. When petitioners in *Welfare Association of Majlis Park vs Municipal Corporation of Delhi*[67] argue within the Court that the Executive has just announced the regularisation of their homes and hence they are no longer within the Court's jurisdiction as violators of the master plan, the Court argues, 'the petitioners argument that

135

the matter is beyond the scrutiny of the Court since the action has been regularized by the MCD is untenable.' Their views on regularisation are clearly expressed in *Kalyan Sanstha*: 'Already there are enormous difficulties for Delhiites are facing on account of mushrooming of unauthorized colonies and the process of regularization of the same by the state.' The time has come, argue the courts, 'for the Delhi Government to ... [prevent] ... unauthorized, unplanned, and hazardous structures thereby making Delhi a complete slum.'

## Two Readings of 'Good Governance'

*A welfare state is expected to care for its citizens from cradle to grave. This concept has to change. The role of the State, in today's world, has to be one of regulator. The state has to create an environment of growth and equal opportunity. Thereafter it is for each to prosper or perish.*

—Supreme Court, *Pitampura*

In this chapter, I have argued the Judiciary—particularly through the body of judgments within PILs—has been under analysed for its impact on understandings of urban governance in the contemporary Indian city. Urban case law within PILs has not been sufficiently seen as a site where a set of 'active processes' (L. Fernandes 2004) both produce the city as a scale and object of government as well as fashion a set of altered governmental rationalities. Using an archive of PILs that resulted in evictions in Delhi from 1990 to 2007, I have shown one set of such rationalities. I argued that the courts construct—through techniques I have described as rescaling and reframing—the city as an object and scale of intervention. The city appears within the Court, however, as a site of a crisis of planned development marked by encroachment and caused by the failure of what the Court calls 'Government'—the institutions of the Executive. The failure of 'Government' thus acts as an 'ethico-moral imperative' to govern and a basis for judicial intervention. To obey this imperative, an alternate rationality emerges: the restoration of planned development as represented and understood by what the courts call the master plan in its 'legal position'.

In the concluding section of this chapter, I perform two intertwined readings of the narratives within the courtroom against the two particular debates on urban governance 'outside' it: discourses and practices of reform, on the one hand, and of neoliberal urbanism, on the other. I do this as a reminder that the walls of the Judiciary and the law are porous. While it is beyond the scope of this chapter (and this book) to delve the strategic and critical juxtaposition that follows, it serves as a useful reminder that notions and practices of urban governance are formed in what Swyngedouw (2005) calls a 'polycentric ensemble' that occurs across public and private institutions and, certainly in this case, both within and outside the courtroom.

*'Good governance' as reform:* The court's construction of the city in a crisis caused by the failure of 'Government' echoes a broader narrative of failure and reform in India. On the scale of the city, this narrative is perhaps best symbolised by India's largest urban programme in its history: the JNNURM.

Planned through the early 2000s and officially launched in 2005, the JNNURM is a $2bn urban policy intervention that is a flagship programme of the Government of India. It has a particularly and clearly stated urban vision—it seeks to build 'world-class cities'. The mission statement of the JNNURM is well worth quoting in its entirety: 'The aim is to encourage reforms and fast track planned development of identified cities. Focus is to be on efficiency in urban infrastructure and service delivery mechanisms, community participation, and accountability of urban local bodies and para-statal agencies towards citizens.' The keywords of the mission—'reform', 'efficiency' and 'service delivery'—are premised on a new imagination of the role of the state as well as an increasing role for the private sector in urban development in India—a new model of urban governance itself.[68]

JNNURM parallels the World Bank's evolving focus on 'good governance' and indeed the programme has significant World Bank funding. Coelho, Kamath and Vijaybaskar (2011) argue that the Bank's focus on 'good governance' can be read through their own 1997 report—*State in a Changing World*. In it, they argue, the Bank crafts a shift from the minimal state that structural adjustment demanded to an 'effective state' that can promote both growth as well as the democratic participation that can legitimise it. Such participation, however, is 'pinned within a paradigm of reforms which aim to procure autonomy from the political sphere' in order to '[steer] economic reforms and facilitate markets' (Coelho, Kamath and Vijaybaskar 2011: 14).

Creating an effective, leaner state requires the displacement of an older developmental imagination of a welfare state. As the courts argue for the failure of 'Government', this narrative finds its echo (and perhaps its origin) outside the courtroom as well. Two examples of highly influential and oft-cited urban documents will make this clear—the McKinsey Global Institute (2010) report on urbanisation in India and the Government of India commissioned High Powered Expert Committee report on Urban Infrastructure (HPEC 2011; hereafter, HPEC report). In both reports, key challenges facing India's urbanisation—and the possibilities of what the reports call 'inclusive and sustained growth'—prominently feature 'governance' as a critical obstacle. For McKinsey, urban governance is one of the five missing elements that are preventing India from building 'thriving cities'. The HPEC report is just as categorical: 'governance is the weakest and most crucial link which needs to be repaired to bring about the urban transformation so urgently needed in India.' The prognosis is dire: 'a radical change is needed if cities are to provide a socio-economic environment that will be inclusive, contribute to a better quality of life, and sustain rapid growth.' (HPEC 2011: *xxv*).

In both the reports, the recommendations for improved urban governance are strikingly similar: corporatisation of service delivery institutions, extensive private sector involvement, deregulation of distorted land markets, and the creation of fiscally and politically empowered and accountable urban local bodies within a new framework of 'city management'. Governance is to be efficient, transparent and accountable, and built on an entirely new institutional foundation. Citizen participation and 'third sector' involvement are repeatedly mentioned yet even their agenda is to fix institutional failure: '[Citizens] need to stop asking their political leaders to "fix the roads" and instead also ask them to "fix the institutions that fix the roads,"' argues the McKinsey report. The HPEC report momentarily acknowledges the possibility of fixing the existing system but then summarily moves on: 'Cities could, in principle, improve their management skills and deliver better quality of services, but given the complex web of relationships, often infusion of a new organisation or private participation tends to catalyse success' (2011: 64). The HPEC makes these recommendations as an explicit basis for the 'New Improved JNNURM' widely believed to be the blueprint for the second phase of the mission slated to cover the coming decade and extend the mission to many more Indian cities, particularly second tier settlements currently not included in the JNNURM.

Coelho, Kamath and Vijaybaskar (2011) have described this new governance paradigm as an 'impatient pragmatism' dominated by 'the imperatives of getting things done, of "fast-tracking" India's cities into a post-Third World regime of global cities' (ibid.: 9). Sunila Kale (2006) argues privatisation and institutional change are examples of 'second generation reforms'—those that often have 'welfare losses' attached to them and carry the possibility of protest and opposition. Second generation reforms, argues Robert Jenkins (2004), writing about labour policy in India, are often passed in a process he describes as 'reform by stealth'.

Do evictions ordered in the public interest by the Judiciary—an arm of the state partially insulated from democratic opposition—represent 'reforms by stealth'? The case law on evictions certainly suggests that governmental rationalities underlying eviction are both shaped by as well as shape in turn prevailing narratives of the need for 'radical change' and 'reform' in the functioning of 'Government'. In doing so, as I have argued in this chapter, they actively create and reproduce this failure. The reframing of the public interest arguably reflects a particular conception of 'reform' read at the scale of the city through the idea of planned development. The macro-narrative of failure and reform and the imperatives of 'good governance' are then created, urbanised and legitimised within the courts. It is here that what Rose calls the moral forms of governmental rationalities within and outside the courts align to shape contemporary urban governance—ideas of order, efficiency and transparency inform the urbanisation of a macro-narrative of 'good governance' and, critically, come to determine conceptions and politics of the city itself.

*The political economy of 'good governance', Accumulation with legitimation*: 'The developmental ideology', argues Partha Chatterjee, 'was a constituent part of the self-definition of the post-colonial state in India' (1997: 277). The state's claim to legitimate rule was based not just on electoral representation but on 'directing a program of economic development on behalf of the nation' (ibid.).[69] It was in framing 'the administration of development' as the 'universal goals of the nation' that post-colonial development broke with colonialism. These two foundations of post-colonial legitimacy—democracy and development—as well as their often conflicting demands were linked, Chatterjee argues, to what is arguably still the post-colonial state's central problematic: 'accumulation with legitimation' (ibid.: 277–79).

While many would argue that both the moment and model of development that Chatterjee is referring to may have passed, the central problematics of his analysis—democracy's entanglement with development, accumulation's with legitimation—and his insistence on the relevance of the state remain, I argue, critically relevant in contemporary India. Scholars of the post-colonial state and of the urban global South have, therefore, rightly criticised what Aihwa Ong (2006) calls 'Neoliberalism writ large' and its attendant dismissal of the state. This critique is not to deny that shifts in political economic systems are not indeed happening, but to shift the question and locate its inquiry. What are the actually existing 'processes and effects of neoliberal governmentalization in the post-colonial world?' (Gupta and Sharma 2006). The state, as Jessop (1999) argues, is neither bypassed nor excluded in the new global economy. It is actively involved 'in developing new accumulation strategies' that are accompanied, he reminds us by the 'new governmental rationalities' that are required to sustain 'changed articulations of government and governance' (ibid.: 399).

It is here, then, that a second reading is possible. In this reading, the Court's reading of the Plan acts as a mechanism, in a Lefebvrian sense, of abstraction—it makes space appear homogenous by depriving it of content and stripping it of representations other than those of the Plan itself. It 'destroys (historical) conditions, its own (internal) differences, and any (emergent) differences, in order to impose an abstract homogeneity'[70] on the city as a space. For Lefebvre, abstract space, as 'a political product of state spatial strategies', has a particular function: it makes a rational, economic calculation of value and exchange possible, allowing space to act as a circuit of capital accumulation. It is central, in other words, to regimes of accumulation. It does so not just through state strategy, however, but also through shifting political imaginaries, what Brenner and Elden describe as 'new ways of envisioning, conceiving, and representing the spaces within which everyday life, capital accumulation, and state action are to unfold' (2009: 359).

The Court's invocation of planned development, therefore, enables the navigation of a particular conjuncture: the deregulation of the urban land market, the restructuring of the Indian economy after liberal reforms in 1991, and rise of a new political imaginary of the transformation of the capital into a 'world-class city'. This imagination centres on a new paradigm of urban development, one typified within the JNNURM as an infrastructural transformation of the city and a new model of urban management based on corporatised institutions. The failure of the 'Government' is then rewritten as the failure to enable this transformation, to remove the blockade to a new regime of accumulation.

In this reading, governance is, as De Angelis argues, a central mechanism that enables the 'social stability fundamental for capital's accumulation' (2005: 229). De Angelis reminds us that global discourses on 'good governance' emerged during the period of structural adjustment and are tied with particular notions of the role of a state that best enables the markets to function. The JNNURM is significantly supported and partially funded by the World Bank and many of its reforms are precipitated on, for example, the repeal of all rent control and urban land ceiling regulations within Indian cities. Its very *raison d'etre*, as described in the mission statement, is to recognise that Indian cities will drive 'up to 65% of the national GDP by 2025.'

Evictions then are markers of the emergence of a new regime of accumulation, one legitimised through a new articulation of government that is built, as argued above, through the narrative of good governance within and beyond the JNNURM in a moment of political and economic transformation in Indian cities. The Court's reframing of the public interest as planned development then represents a process of commodification, of paradigms of urban development built on new conceptions of value and particularly the value of public land. New urban political economies require new legitimacies, as Jessop reminds us. As in the first reading, the emerging rationalities of the Court are not then just the result of the failure of 'Government'— they are also the sites of the production of this failure. The ends, however, differ. The production of failure, in this reading, enables 'reform' in a manner that allows the circulation of new registers of value and creates new frontiers of capital accumulation.

## Notes

1. From orders of 3 March 2003.
2. See http://nangla.freeflux.net/ (accessed 22 September 2011). Nangla's Delhi is a blog run as part of the Cybermohalla programme at SARAI, a media research initiative. For more information, see sarai.net (accessed October 2015).
3. For my use of the word basti, see note 2 in Introduction, this volume.
4. *Hemraj vs Commissioner of Police and Ors*, CWP 3419 of 1999 (hereafter, *Hemraj*).
5. All citations that follow in this paragraph are from orders of 14 December 2005.
6. For many basti households, producing paper documentation is extremely difficult. Documents are hard won in lives that are predominantly informal and if any family has moved locations within the city, documents are rarely transferred from older addresses to

newer ones, thus making proving continuous stay extremely difficult. Gender concerns, lack of access to local bureaucracies, and accidents like fire or even cases of theft are other reasons why producing acceptable documentation is difficult. I will take this issue on in more detail in Chapter Three, this volume, as documentation becomes a barrier to accessing the courts as well.

7. Personal interviews with Dunu Roy, 1 October 2010, and Kalyani Menon-Sen, 12 February 2011. See also Bhan and Menon-Sen (2008) and Nigam (2001).

8. *M C Mehta vs Union of India*, CWP 4677 of 1985 (hereafter, *M C Mehta*, CWP 4677).

9. *M C Mehta vs Union of India*, CWP 13029 of 1985 (hereafter, *M C Mehta*, CWP 13029).

10. *Almitra Patel vs Union of India*, CWP 888 of 1996 (hereafter, *Almitra Patel*, CWP 888).

11. *Kalyan Sanstha Social Welfare Organisation vs Union of India and Ors*, CWP 4582 of 2003 (hereafter, *Kalyan Sanstha*).

12. Initial orders of this cancellation have just begun to be reported in the media at the time of writing. See http://articles.timesofindia. indiatimes.com/2011-07-07/india/29746406_1_builders-land-acquisition-shahberi-village (accessed 19 April 2012).

13. Justice Goswami in *State of Rajasthan*.

14. See note 6 in Introduction, this volume.

15. Speech from Red Fort, 15 August 1975, as cited in Tarlo (2001: 25).

16. *ADM Jabalpur vs Shivkant Shukla* (1976) AIR SC 1207. Habeas Corpus—literally 'you shall have the body'—is a writ that insists that a person must be brought in front of the law if held. As Khanna (2012) argues: 'It is most often used in cases of illegal detention by the state, but also in the context of confinement by non-state actors.' It is important to note, as Mate argues, that this ruling also overturned the actions of many high courts in the country that were entertaining habeas corpus applications despite the declaration of Emergency rule (Mate 2013).

17. For the full text of Article 32, see http://indiankanoon.org/doc/981147/ (accessed 19 April 2012).

18. *M C Mehta vs Union of India* (1987) 1 SCC 395 (hereafter, *M C Mehta*).

19. *S P Gupta vs Union of India* (1982) AIR SC 149 (hereafter, *S P Gupta*). In this case, the matter of judicial accountability and the system of appointment of judges—a critical post-Emergency topic—was brought to the Court by lawyers, not judges themselves.

The lawyers for the Union of India argued that the lawyers had no *locus standi*, i.e. they weren't affected parties since their own appointments were not the matter in question. The court argued that the lawyers had a right to raise an issue of substantive public interest.

20. As cited in Khanna (2012: 215).
21. *Ratlam vs Shri Vardhichand and Ors* (1980) AIR 1622.
22. *Hussainara Khatoon vs State of Bihar* (1980) 1 SCC 81.
23. *Vineet Narain vs Union of India* (1996) AIR SC 3386.
24. See, for example, *Sunil Batra*.
25. *Maneka Gandhi vs Union of India* (1978) 1 SCC 248.
26. For a more detailed description of the Constituent Assembly debates on fundamental rights versus directive principles, see Chapter Three, this volume.
27. *Bandhua Mukti Morcha vs Union of India* (1984) AIR 802.
28. *Vishaka vs State of Rajasthan* (1997) AIR SC 3011.
29. *Olga Tellis vs Bombay Municipal Corporation and Anr* (1986) AIR 180.
30. A recent report by the National Planning Commission found that 90 per cent of the shortfall in public housing units to be built under the MPD was in low-income housing targets. See Government of India (2006).
31. *K Chandru vs State of Tamil Nadu* (1986) AIR 204.
32. *Shantistar Builders vs Narayan Khimalal Totame* (1990) AIR SC 630.
33. *Chameli Singh vs State of Uttar Pradesh* (1996) 2 SCC 549.
34. *Ahmedabad Municipal Corporation vs Nawab Khan Gulab Khan and Others* (1997) 11 SCC 123.
35. *M C Mehta*, CWP 4677.
36. Personal Interview, dated 9 November 2010.
37. *Almitra Patel vs Union of India* (2002) 2 SCC 679 (hereafter, *Almitra Patel*).
38. Orders dated 15 February 2000, *Amrita Patel*.
39. *Okhla*; judgment recorded at 108 (2002) DLT 517.
40. Orders of 21 September 2005, *Maloy*.
41. *Hemraj*.
42. *Hemraj*.
43. Orders of 21 December 2001.
44. Orders of 1 March 2006.
45. Orders of 21 September 2005, *Maloy*.
46. Orders of 21 April 2004.
47. *Kalyan Sanstha*.

48. Petition was filed as CWP 4215 of 1995. Judgment was delivered along with multiple other PILs on 27 September 2002. All citations are from final orders of that day.
49. See note 11 in Chapter One, this volume, on jhuggi-jhompri clusters. Also, see Chapter One, this volume, for a detailed analysis of the housing typologies in Delhi.
50. *K K Manchanda vs Union of India*, CWP 531 of 1990 (hereafter, *Manchanda*). Final orders were given in the petition along with *Pitampura* on 27 September 2002.
51. See note 39 above.
52. The petition was filed as CWP 1397 of 2001. Final orders were delivered on 29 August 2002.
53. Orders of 1 February 2006.
54. *Jagdish and Anr vs Delhi Development Authority*, CWP 5009 of 2002. Final orders were given on 14 July 2006.
55. From final orders of 16 February 2006, *M C Mehta*, CWP 4677.
56. CM 1238/2007 and 239/2007 in *Kalyan Sanstha*. 'CM' indicates that the petition was filed as an interim application within an existing PIL, namely *Kalyan Sanstha*.
57. Orders of 10 September 2008.
58. Orders of 14 December 2005.
59. Orders of 26 July 2006.
60. Personal interview with A. K. Jain, former director of planning, DDA, 2 January 2011.
61. *M C Mehta*, CWP 4677.
62. From orders of 16 February 2006, emphasis added.
63. From final orders of 14 July 2006, *Jagdish*.
64. See Chapter One, this volume, in particular.
65. *Okhla*; judgment recorded at 108 (2002) DLT 517.
66. *Ambedkar Slum Utthan Sangathan vs Municipal Corporation of Delhi*, CWP 6981 of 2002 (hereafter, *Ambedkar*). Final orders on 20 December 2002.
67. *Welfare Association of Majlis Park vs Municipal Corporation of Delhi*, CWP 7758 of 2007.
68. See jnnurm.nic.in (accessed 19 April 2012).
69. On this point, see also Ludden (1992).
70. Lefebvre, quoted in Brenner and Elden (2009: 358).

# 3

# Unmaking Citizens

*Spatial Illegality, Urban Citizenship and
the Challenges for Inclusive Politics**

I n the northern part of Delhi lies one of its origins. It is called
'the city' by those who live within it and the 'Walled City'
or 'Old Delhi' by those who live in what came to be known,
from the early twentieth century, as New Delhi. It houses nearly
half a million people in an incredibly dense built environment
that has both symbolised historical urban form in India as well
as challenged modern planning. As a result, for much of the
last three decades, it has alternatively been classified as a 'slum'
under the 1956 Slum Areas Act, a protected heritage zone, or,
most recently, a Special Development Area. For nearly a decade,
it was all three at once.

In 1982, a redevelopment scheme was announced for parts
of Old Delhi, including a neighbourhood within it called Kali

* An earlier version of this chapter appeared as 'The Impoverishment
of Poverty: Reflections on Urban Citizenship and Inequality in
Contemporary Delhi' in *Environment & Urbanization* 26, October
(2014): 547–60. The article has since been revised.

Masjid. The scheme made residents of Kali Masjid an offer: those who 'voluntary surrendered' their houses would be given expedited resettlement into permanent alternate accommodation of 60–70 sq m area in Kali Masjid itself or a nearby location within two to three years. In the interim, they would be given transitional accommodation on near Minto Road. A set of about forty households—who would come to be described by the Delhi high court as 'slum dwellers'—surrendered their properties. Nineteen years passed in the 'transitional accommodation'. The promised resettlement never came.

A generation came of age in Minto Road. In 2001, the households received another eviction notice informing them that they were—once again—to be shifted into 'transitory accommodations' pending resettlement. No details about the time, nature or location of the resettlement were given. These households, now organised as the Ambedkar Slum Utthan Sangathan (the Ambedkar Slum Empowerment Coalition;[1] hereafter, ASUS), approached the Delhi high court in July 2001. They filed a PIL that came to be known as *Ambedkar Slum Utthan Sangathan vs Municipal Corporation of Delhi* (hereafter, *Ambedkar*).[2] They argued that they had built their lives and those of their children in Minto Road and did not want to move—'our children study in local schools, everyone we know is here.' In August, the Court refused to halt their eviction but argued that they must be given permanent accommodation immediately. In October 2002, the MCD sent a second notice to the households. Permanent alternate accommodation had been found for them. The flats were, ironically, in the Kali Masjid area, the original home of the households from where they had been evicted twenty years earlier. The caveat was that these flats were only 24 sq m in area. The ASUS went back to the Delhi high court arguing that the flats on offer were too small, citing the promise made to them in 1982 of 60 sq m flats.

The ASUS argued that they represented a vulnerable community. They were an association committed 'to look after the welfare of the people belonging to the scheduled castes[3] in Delhi living in the slum area.' They argued that the resettlement on offer ignored the fact that as members of lower castes they

147

have 'their own community life and their own traditional lifestyle and social customs' and therefore 'the alternative accommodation to which they are to be rehabilitated has to be one compact area' which the housing on offer was not. They accused the MCD of being 'totally blind to the needs of this particular class unfortunately having born in scheduled caste families.' At one point in the legal petition, breaking with standard legal form, the members of the ASUS seem to address the municipal officials directly: 'the size of the flat to which you are forcing us to shift is so small that the very right of decent living in healthy and congenial environment is being denied to us.' They argued that as people from the 'lower strata of life' they are entitled to protection from a state that 'boasts and rather loudly speaks of being a welfare state'. It is 'strange', they argued, that such a state would 'crush' the rights of the poor. The last line of the petition is this: 'We request you kindly not to crush us but to rehabilitate us as per assurances.'

The claims of the ASUS are familiar ones within Indian politics. Poverty and vulnerability, defined both by a lack of income as well as social marginalisation (in this case embodied through caste) as the basis of political claims to protection, rights and entitlements from the state. Yet the Delhi high court refused this claim. Summarily refusing to halt eviction, the court argued, rather curiously, that the members of the ASUS had 'no right to remain in transit accommodation' despite the fact that these households had been 'in transit' for twenty years. A court-appointed commissioner examined the resettlement options offered to the households and argued that the 'flats in question are commensurate with the status of persons sought to be shifted.' In reply to the ASUS's claim that they had been assured of flats of a certain size and that the new flats amounted to 'hostile discrimination' against them, the court replied that the concept of discrimination under Article 14 of the Indian Constitution 'cannot be stretched so far.'

The court reasoned thus: 'We are not convinced that by offering flats in question to the members of the petitioner society, any discrimination is meted out to them. We cannot turn a blind eye on the fact that the members of the petitioner society are, after all, encroachers who created slums by encroaching upon public land in the first place. We, therefore agree with the local commissioner, that the flats in question are commensurate with the status of the persons sought to be shifted.' Their shifting, the court said, cannot be delayed because the site was 'urgently needed' to build a new station for the expanding Delhi Metro as well as a new Civic Centre that was to be the new headquarters of the MCD. In all its orders leading up to its final judgment, the judges never once referred to, or acknowledged as relevant, the caste of its petitioners.

★ ★ ★

Thus far, I have shown how the courts justified evictions in the name of public interest in part by reframing the latter as the failure of 'planned development'. Within case law on evictions, this failure was most visibly marked by the distance between the city and its master plan—what the courts termed as 'encroachment'. Evictions, rather than being acts of exclusion and violence, corrected encroachment. They became acts of a return to order, to planning and to 'good governance'. In this chapter, I return to the case law on evictions with a different inquiry—to ask what evictions tell us about the possibilities of urban citizenship in Indian cities.

Why citizenship? Recent writing suggests that cities of the global South could be sites of a more egalitarian politics, be it through Arjun Appadurai's (2002) notion of a 'deep democracy' that represents efforts to 'reconstitute citizenship in cities', or James Holston's writing on the possibility of insurgence that he describes as 'a counter-politics that destabilizes the dominant regime of citizenship and renders it vulnerable' (2009: 245). Urban citizens, Holston argues, see the city rather than the nation as the 'primary community of reference' (2008: 23) for claims to rights and belonging. This claim is particularly important, argue Holston and Appadurai, in post-colonial societies where a 'new generation has arisen to create urban cultures severed from both colonial memories and nationalist fictions' (1999: 3).

Has Lefebvre's oft-quoted 'right to the city' indeed 'moved South, so to speak' (Holston 2009: 245)? There is no doubt that the urban has emerged both as a site and context in an India that was long meant to have lived in its villages, as Gandhi once put it. Yet the 'urban turn' that Gyan Prakash (2002) heralded over a decade ago remains immensely debated. Many scholars have argued that the dominant discourses of citizenship in urban India reflect, in fact, the rise of a new growth coalition that sees cities as the 'engines of national development' (HPEC 2011: *xxi*). In the speech that launched the ambitious JNNURM in 2005, then Prime Minister Manmohan Singh said: 'We must plan big, think big and have a new vision for the future of urban India,' realising that 'our urban economy has become an important driver of economic growth' that is a 'bridge between the domestic and global economy.'[4] The JNNURM, argues Om Mathur (2009), marks 'one of the most extraordinary shifts in thinking in India about cities and urbanization' that realigns 'urban sector policies to the emerging macro-economic context in the post-1991 period.'

Others describe this moment as a 'post-development social formation' within which even the 'nominal ethical relationship' between the 'state, elite and the poor of a previous developmentalism stands fractured'(Gidwani and Reddy 2011: 1640). As a self-fashioned 'middle class citizen' becomes the object of what Deshpande (1993) once eloquently called the 'imagined economy' at the heart of any developmental imagination, Drèze and Sen (2013) argue that this citizen becomes the new aam aadmi in our cities—not necessarily elite but certainly not poor given the demographic realities of both poverty and destitution in Indian cities. Indian cities, to twist an older argument from Partha Chatterjee (2004a), seem indeed to have become bourgeoisie at last.

Delhi captures several of these dynamics. Beyond the evictions that are the subject of this book, it is marked by a rapidly changing economic landscape with altered patterns and possibilities of employment, consumption, production and work.[5] It is home to what has, in recent years, begun to settle into a contested yet undeniably coherent discursive and aesthetic form in the idea of a 'world-class city' with particular imaginations of emergence, transformation and renewal (Baviskar 2007, 2011;

D. A. Ghertner 2011b; Bhan 2009; Dupont 2011). It has seen significant shifts in the sites and mechanisms of governance and new forms of political participation by residents both poor and privileged that arguably respond to new expectations and practices of state-citizen relations (Ghertner 2011a, 2012; Lama-Rewal 2011; Mehra 2013).

What do these dynamics tell us about the nature and possibilities of urban citizenship in Indian cities? I argue that while the power of the claims of the 'middle class' and the emergence of a new urban political economy are well documented, the specificity of how subaltern urban residents have been displaced from a developmental imagination remains relatively understudied. Put simply: How have the claims, presence and resistance of a significant proportion of urban residents been managed and even evaded within urban politics? Negotiating the claims of differentiated citizens takes particular forms in different citizenship regimes, places and times. To explain and challenge what Satish Deshpande describes as the 'elusiveness of counter-hegemonic politics in urban spaces' (2013: 39) in India today, understanding this particularity matters.

To do so, I utilise a second analytical category: impoverishment. Upendra Baxi (1988) has argued that, 'people are not naturally poor, but are made poor.' He argues that 'poverty' and the 'poor' are passive words that invisibilise the processes by which poverty is produced and reproduced. He argues instead for a perspective based on 'impoverishment'—'a dynamic process of public decision-making in which it is considered just, right and fair that some people may become or stay poor' (ibid.: *viii*). In this chapter, I trace processes of impoverishment through looking at evictions. I show that the principle mechanism of impoverishment that evictions make visible is how more familiar loci for accessing citizenship in India—for example, caste and poverty as in the case that began this chapter—can be rendered ineffective within the urban through the rising salience of a third: spatial illegality. In earlier chapters, I have shown the relational nature of this illegality and argued that its correction was a cornerstone of planned development and good governance. In this chapter, I take spatial illegality seriously as a logic that mediates contemporary urban citizenship—impacting not just the legal status of settlement forms such as the basti but the conditions of possibility for politics for the residents within them.

To do so, I return to the case law that formed the main archive of the previous chapter. I argue that this case law makes evident three distinct processes of impoverishment: (a) the displacement of the basti from the imagined economy that marked the developmental nation-state as it has been re-articulated at the scale of the city; (b) an altered representation of basti residents through an erasure of their vulnerability amidst a broader criminalisation that legitimises a disavowal of their substantive rights; and (c) the emergence of an elite insurgent urban citizenship that claims the city as its primary community of belonging. Understanding these processes of impoverishment, I argue, is a critical part of formulating different urban futures.

The chapter itself is divided into four parts. The first locates my argument within two theoretical fields: (a) a history of the configurations of citizenship within Indian constitutionalism, and (b) a shift of its determination from the scale of the nation to city. The second then turns to the case law on evictions to detail the three processes of impoverishment described above. The third juxtaposes the arguments of the judges within the courtroom against broader political, economic and aesthetic shifts in the city, arguing that the processes of impoverishment that evictions make visible both originate and extend beyond the courtroom. The fourth and final part then draws out implications for inclusive urban politics.

## Citizenship and/in the Post-Colonial City

*On 26th of January 1950, we are going to enter into a life of contradictions. In politics we will have equality and in social and economic life we will have inequalities. In politics we will be recognising the principles of one man one vote and one vote one value. In our social and economic life, we shall, by reason of our social and economic structure, continue to deny the*

*principle of one man one value. How long shall we continue to
live this life of contradictions?*

—B. R. Ambedkar[6]

Citizenship, Etienne Balibar argues, is a concept 'as old as
politics itself' (1988: 723). Indeed, since the eighteenth century,
say Holston and Appadurai, two linked concepts have been
'the defining marks of modernity' in the establishment of
'the meaning of full membership in society'—citizenship and
nationality (1996: 187). The nation-state—with its attendant
promises of freedom, equality and sovereignty—is where 'the
universal ideals of modern citizenship were expected to be
realized' (Chatterjee 2004b: 30).

Within the nation-state, each person is meant to take the
identity of a citizen above and beyond any other. It is this move,
argues Menon (1998), 'from particularity to universality' that
allows citizenship to bear the possibility of a politics of equality.
An 'unmarked' citizen carries the potential of justice through the
'winning, granting and protecting' of rights precisely because
such unmarking allows the individual to be part of a modern
public sphere solely as a rights-bearing citizen (ibid.: PE3–PE4).
This is why, Balibar argues, the dimension of equality—with 'all
the problems of definition it poses and the mystifications it may
conceal'—is always present in the constitution of a concept of
citizenship (1988: 723).

My interest is not in seeing citizenship in this assumed
republican ideal. The citizen, as post-colonial and feminist
scholars both remind us, has never been 'unmarked', especially
in a context where neither nationality nor modernity can be
understood outside the encounter with colonialism. Marshall's
(1977 [1964]) classic formulation[7] of the linear and steady
progress of civil, political and social rights, argues Chatterjee,
doesn't translate 'here' in the post-colony. The ideals of 'republican
citizenship', he argues, were overtaken 'by the developmental
state' precisely because it was in framing 'the administration
of development' as the 'universal goals of the nation' that
post-colonial development broke with colonialism. These
two foundations of post-colonial legitimacy—democracy and

development—as well as their 'often conflicting demands' are then 'the context for the determination of citizenship' (Chatterjee 1997: 277).

The management of the conflicting demands of political and social equality—outlined so precisely above by Ambedkar—does indeed lie at the heart of the history of Indian citizenship in the twentieth century. If equality was, as Niraja Gopal Jayal (2013) argues, both the 'the premise and promise' of the constitutional moment, how was it to be instantiated in a context marked both by diverse inequalities and an inheritance of colonial forms of rule? Jayal argues that three key arenas of contestation have particularly shaped citizenship in India: (a) citizenship as legal status, (b) as a bundle of rights and entitlements, and (c) as a form of identity. Two of these—rights and identity—are central to our concerns in this chapter.

Let us take identity first. Within theories of citizenship, one of the most enduring debates is between its universalist and differentiated forms. The former posits that since all citizens are individuals of equal moral worth, they should—at least formally—enjoy equal (read, same) rights and treatment before law. Critics argue that such formal equality masks and even perpetuates inequality precisely because it does not recognise social, cultural and economic differences among citizens. Iris Marion Young's (1990) seminal formulation of differentiated citizenship argues that 'effective representation and recognition' of groups, especially 'those opressed or disadvantaged', required acknowledging their distinction instead of treating them the same. These are broad debates whose key words are familiar ones not just in academic writing but in daily newspapers around the world—think of multi-culturalism (Banting and Kymlicka 2006), language rights, the rights of immigrants, or affirmative action, to name just a few. Across these debates, what's at stake is the distribution of rights, resources and entitlements that are both material as well as symbolic. Yet there is one other key aspect especially for our analysis: difference is often acknowledged here by speaking not just of individuals but of groups, communities and collectivities. Young's formulation is, in fact, often described as 'group-differentiated citizenship'.

The ink had hardly dried on the Indian Constitution, argues Upendra Baxi (2003), when the first amendment to the Indian Constitution enshrined affirmative action—colloquially called 'reservation'—in employment, education and electoral representation for historically disadvantaged communities. It is a framework that continues to this day. In line with Young's argument, in other words, the Indian Constitution used group-differentiated citizenship from the very beginning as a strategy of inclusion. Such a strategy, Jayal argues, 'created new categories of exceptions to equality (as sameness of treatment) as a way to tackle inequality' (2013: 18). The naming of inequality, she argued, was considered a predecessor to addressing it even at the risk that such naming could entrench difference rather then gradually erase it.

Jayal marks two key originary lines of differentiation: 'the provision of cultural rights for religious minorities and positive discrimination for historically disadvantaged and "backward" caste and tribal groups' (ibid.: 21). In the lexicon of everyday life in India, the categories of 'Scheduled Caste', 'Scheduled Tribe' or 'Other Backward Castes' have becomes ordinary utterances associated with quotas in public employment, admission into universities or budget provisions in local, state and central government on the basis of caste. Over time, they have been subject to both vigorous defence and just as stringent critiques, not just within the state but in public protests, media campaigns, public discourse and even within intimate conversations and debates among friends. Long before debates on multicultural citizenship, argues Baxi, the Indian Constitution authorised 'exacting solicitude for group/collective rights' (2003: 326) in, as Jayal reminds us, significant continuities as well as differences with colonial practice.

It is beyond the scope of this chapter to debate whether such differentiation aided equality or entrenched the exclusions they sought to address. For this chapter, I seek only to mark that group differentiation remains an important mediator in the relationship between the individual and the state. The criteria of what defines a group, therefore, is an important site for the politics of citizenship as categories old and new, established and emergent, seek to access rights, resources and entitlements.

The second key facet of Indian constitutionalism is its resolution of rights, i.e. what individuals and groups are entitled to and fighting for. While it was remarkably progressive in its imagination of civil and political rights, a keen contest in constituent assembly debates on socio-economic rights resulted in a foundational split in the rights framework of the Indian Constitution. Civil and political rights were framed as Fundamental Rights. All citizens were thus guaranteed the rights to life, liberty, equality and the freedom of expression, among others. These were justiciable though exceptions on the lines of group differentiation discussed above already marked their form. Socio-economic rights (education and health, for example) were relegated to another chapter termed the Directive Principles of State Policy. Familiar debates on the capacity of the state, availability of resources as well as the need to prioritise and progressively realise rights, implied that socio-economic entitlements are neither guaranteed nor binding within the Indian Constitution. This, Jayal argues, made 'economic and social rights the eternal desiderata, forever compromised by considerations of what was legally feasible, politically expedient, and financially viable' (2013: 21).

Separating Directive Principles from Fundamental Rights allowed a key differentiation in post-colonial development. As Chatterjee (2004b) has argued, it allowed welfare to be linked to ideas of need and charity as opposed to being seen as an entitlement of citizenship. Welfare, agrees Jayal, was 'not subject to the rule of formal equality that obtained in the political and civic spheres.' On the contrary, 'the absence of rights implied the absence of obligations, and a predominance of the language of relief, charity, and alleviation' (2013: 169).

The organisation of such forms of 'poverty alleviation' defined the post-colonial developmentalism of the Indian state in its initial decades. Programmes, policies and interventions became discrete, sectoral and often ad-hoc in a techno-managerial frame that sought to manage populations further categorised into different kinds of 'beneficiaries' for different kinds of welfare programmes. A new set of categories and differentiated social groups emerged that drew not just from identities such as caste or religion but more empirical and technical criteria such as income poverty. Thus social policies in India have consistently targeted, for example, households 'Below the Poverty Line'. These different markers—lower caste, Muslim, poor—often, of course, fell upon the same bodies yet these intersections co-existed without acknowledgment as different programmes in different government ministries sought particularly marked beneficiaries instead of unmarked citizens.

It is in this context that Partha Chatterjee (2004b) draws his now well-known distinction between 'civil society' and 'political society'. 'Most Indian citizens,' he argues, 'are only tenuously, and even then ambiguously and contextually, rights-bearing citizens in the sense imagined by the constitution.' They are 'populations' to be governed, objects of welfare—subjects, not citizens. They exist, for Chatterjee, as 'political society'. Unlike citizenship, he argues, which 'carries the moral connotation of sharing in the sovereignty of the state' and 'of claiming rights in relation to the state,' members of political society 'do not bear any inherent moral claim' (ibid.: 136). Political society instead, he argues, must be situated in the 'constant tussles of different population groups with the authorities over the distribution of governmental services' (Chatterjee 2012: 47). The modes of engagement with rights and the state thus shift. To take one aspect of this distinction: members of civil society— citizens—speak of rights, use institutions of the state, invoke constitutional protections and access law. Members of political society—subjects—use patronage, electoral sway, negotiations, violence, informal workarounds and popular politics.

Contemporary India both continues and breaks with the debates of the constituent assembly of 1950. Social rights have certainly expanded and done so in the name not of welfare-as-charity but as entitlement-centred rights. Baxi (2003) reminds us that the Indian Judiciary has often read Directive Principles into Fundamental Rights, for example, expanding social rights such as the Right to Education. The Indian courts 'have deployed the Directives as a technology of constitutional interpretation: they have favoured interpretation that *fosters*, rather than *frustrates*, the Directives giving them an "indirect" justiciability' (Baxi 2003: 325; emphasis in the original). More often, however, the agents of change have been social movements that have struggled to expand right-based entitlements such as the rights to information and food though they have remained frustrated on other accounts such as land, health and housing. Jayal (2013) agrees that social rights have expanded in recent decades in India but points to a curious contradiction: right-claims have grown precisely as the state withdraws from its commitment to welfare and an altered political economy 'privileges unrestrained economic growth with little evidence of pro-poor policy concern' (ibid.: 176). This, she argues, puts contemporary India squarely in danger of what Marshall (1977 [1964]) described as 'class abatement'—the expansion of rights-talk and formal rights without substantive changes in the outcomes of inequality.

The contemporary expansion of rights provokes new questions: Who is claiming these rights, on what basis, and from whom? While group differentiation endures in contemporary India, it stands significantly transformed. Changing terms of classification abound as older categories are redrawn and newer ones emerge. Separately, the salience of group membership is itself changing. Universalising public food distribution systems in some states, for example, has rendered the distinction between Below Poverty Line and Above Poverty Line less relevant in some contexts. Increasing privatisation of basic services—formally and informally—makes consumption demand a stronger determinant of access to entitlements rather than state patronage or rights. As political economies shift, particularly in urban areas, the curious case of 'middle-caste' group such as the Gujjars of Haryana in northern India seeking a technical 'downgrade' in status to be declared 'backward' seems rather less ironical than at first glance.

The complexity of these new negotiations suggests, Nivedita Menon (2010) argues, that Chatterjee's distinction requires modification. He errs, she argues, in seeing political and civil society as 'empirical spaces'. A neat distinction between 'civil society consisting of citizens with rights; the zone of corporate capital' and political society made up of 'populations which are the object of development policies, people with no legal rights; the zone of non-corporate capital,' flounders on empirical examination. Citizens of civil society groups can just as well be treated as populations and the objects of welfare and development, and people in political society often make rights-claims using the institutions of the state that Chatterjee describes as the domain of civil society. Menon argues that the two terms should be understood as 'conceptual distinctions' rather than as empirical groupings. There is, therefore, not 'political society' or 'civil society' to be found, but 'two styles of political engagement' that are available to all people (ibid.: xx).

Menon is arguing that what Chatterjee calls the 'thicket of contestations' in describing political society is, in fact, the dominant space within which all citizens negotiate for substantive rights using a range of strategies though always with differentiated power. The terms of this negotiation, or even this contestation, are precisely how the 'dimension of equality' (Balibar 1988: 723) within citizenship is determined though never settled. Conceptually, citizenship allows us to assess these negotiations because it has always been, argues Holston, 'both subversive and reactionary, inclusionary and exclusionary, a project of equalization and one of maintaining inequality' (2008: 21). It is the terms of these disjunctions that are of interest to us. Yet before we return to the case law on evictions to see what they tell us about contemporary negotiations of citizenship in India, we must make one additional move: from the nation to the city.

*Urban citizenship*: Contemporary scholarship on citizenship increasingly contests the very notion of the 'nation-state' as the appropriate scale or site of citizenship. A diverse range of critiques across disciplines argue that the nation can no longer be understood in the same way in a global age, making a case for denationalised understandings of citizenship and belonging (Ferguson 2006; Ong 1999; Sassen 2006); unpacking the easy equation of nationhood and territorial sovereignty (Ong 2000); looking at emerging institutions and sites of global governance

ranging from international instutions and corporations to discourses of universal rights; citing the rise of new transnational and
non-governmental politics as more powerful sites of rights-
claims (Appadurai 2002; Keck and Sikkink 1999); and engaging
with the emergence of inter-connected global cities that inter-
reference each other through the 'casing' of the nation-state and
are perhaps the relevant 'political community' within which to
gauge and assess citizenship (Held 1999; Held and McGrew
2007; Zhang 2001).

Of interest to our analysis is a particular scalar shift in
thinking about citizenship: from the nation to the city. Arguing
that 'formal membership in the nation-state is increasingly
neither a necessary nor a sufficient condition for substantive
citizenship,' Holston suggests instead that it is cities that
are 'especially privileged sites for considering the current
renegotiations of citizenship' (1999b: 168). For Saskia Sassen
(2003), cities are 'foremost in a new geography' formed because
'the national as a container for social process and power [has]
cracked' just as there has been a 're-articulation of the political-
economic system' at the scale of the city. The question that arises,
she says, is 'how and whether we shall see the formation of new
types of politics that localize in cities.' Cities are 'key sites for
this type of political work,' she argues, and indeed are 'partly
constituted through these dynamics themselves' (ibid.: 58).

Claims to the right to the city have become powerful discourses
both in theory as well as the practices of social movements
worldwide. Henri Lefebvre's (2003 [1970]) call for the right
to the city as *oeuvre* sought to democratise the production of
the city as social as well as economic space. The neo-Marxist
urban theorists it inspired such as Manuel Castells and David
Harvey located the struggle for the right to the city in a series of
changes in urban political economies, the most recent marked
by what Harvey (2005, 2008) described as 'accumulation by
dispossession'. For Harvey, the questions of citizenship and
belonging in the city had to be understood as a struggle over the
'democratization of the right to the city' as a 'working slogan
and political ideal' precisely in its focus on 'the question of who

commands the necessary connection between urbanization and surplus production and use' (Harvey 2008).

In recent and influential work, James Holston (2008, 2009, among others) suggests that it has not been, as Lefebvre expected, the working classes of the cities of the North Atlantic that brought about the right to the city. Holston, writing about citizenship claims to and through rights to the city in the peripheries of São Paulo, sees the city through the possibility of insurgence: 'of a counter-politics that destabilizes the dominant regime of citizenship, renders it vulnerable, and defamiliarizes the coherence with which it usually presents itself to us' (Holston 2009). He gives us a compelling definition of what he calls an *urban citizenship*:

> ... where urban residence is the basis for mobilization, rights claims addressing the urban experience compose their agenda, the city is the primary community of reference for these developments, and residents legitimate this agenda of rights and participatory practices on the basis of their contributions to the city itself. (2008: 23)

How does a conception of urban citizenship align with a history of claims built on group membership and identity—caste, religion, or poverty, for example—that has marked the history and contemporary configurations of Indian citizenship in the twentieth century? What do evictions tell us about the nature and possibilities of urban citizenship in the Indian city? How do they relate to shifts in imaginations of development and democracy as both are not just altered but reproduced in and through the 'urban turn' (Prakash 2002) in contemporary India? It is to these questions that I now turn.

## Making and Unmaking Citizens

### Of Citizens and Their Rights

Rights, argues Nivedita Menon, 'come into being within specific sets of shared norms of justice and equality' (2004: 26). Writing about attempts by women's movements in India to instantiate rights through the law, she argues that, in contradiction to this contextual specificity of rights, appeals to the law are usually made on 'the assumption that rights are self-evident, universally comprehended and universally applicable.' It is this tension, in part, that makes the 'language of rights no longer unproblematically available to an emancipatory politics' (Menon 2004: 2). In this section, I describe what Menon calls 'diverse discourses of rights' as they emerge in the case law on eviction, arguing that they signal the emergence of a new 'set of shared norms of justice and equality' that I will return to in more detail later in this chapter. Three aspects of right-claims within case law on evictions are striking: (a) a conscious and particular use of the word 'citizen' as a primary identity and descriptor by both petitioners and judges; (b) the articulation of this citizenship within the city rather than the nation; and (c) a shift in these claims towards articulations of the right to a certain quality of life, or as some authors have termed it, a 'lifestyle' (L. Fernandes 2004) as opposed to basic needs in the determination of the meaning and bounds of the constitutionally guaranteed Right to Life.[8]

Petitions filed by residents as well as business and trade associations represent the majority of petitioners in PILs that have led to evictions. These petitioners describe themselves repeatedly as 'citizens'. This citizenship is articulated, however, not as a national but a local, city-centric identity. In multiple petitions, such petitioners describe themselves as 'citizens of Delhi'. They emphasise residence. They use terms like 'locality' or 'colony' that are colloquially used in Indian cities to indicate what I have described earlier in this book as legitimate housing—neighbourhoods that, whether, legal or not, enjoy a certain de facto security of tenure.[9] The word 'citizen' in many petitions is used interchangeably with 'resident'. Petitioners describe themselves, for example, in *Manchanda*, 'as an association of residents of a posh colony in Delhi', or, in *Pitampura*, as the 'residents of a locality'. In the petition filed by the Delhi Builders and Promoters Association,[10] even an association of business owners and self-described 'trade representatives' emphasise that they 'speak for the public' as they are also 'residents of the locality' in question.

The emphasis on residence, I argue, produces the city as the scale for the determination of citizenship. The city, to paraphrase Holston (2008), is the primary political community of reference and belonging. 'Urban residence' is indeed 'the basis for mobilization' (ibid.: 21). Within case law on eviction, 'residence' is based on a particular claim: belonging to a legitimate colony. One of the primary markers of legitimacy then is the formal purchase of property. These are 'formal' if not necessarily 'legal' transactions—documented transactions of sale and purchase of property or built housing whether or not the resultant titles are legally recognised.[11] The idea of the 'resident' and the 'locality' both underscore therefore not just an urban location, but a claim to a certain regime of legality and property. In *Pitampura*, the petitioners thus argue that they are 'a voluntary association of law abiding, peace loving bonafide residents' who have 'purchased the plots and constructed their respective houses from their hard earned money'. In *Wazirpur*, petitioners describe themselves as 'citizens who have paid for the land'.

A particular set of rights claims emerge from this location. What is it that 'citizens of Delhi' want? The demands of petitioners from resident and trade associations interpret the Right to Life to imply a certain quality of life understood through the environment, infrastructure, leisure and consumption.[12] A new set of rights claims thus emerge: 'right to passage and to enjoy good environment of the user of a main arterial road'[13]; 'right of citizens for a peaceful and decent living'; multiple claims to 'healthy-living and a good environment'; the 'statutory duty of the state' to provide 'law-abiding citizens with a shopping centre and well-maintained park';[14] 'rights of the people of Delhi to clean potable water from the River Yamuna'; and, finally, the right to planned orderliness. It has to be remembered, argued petitioners in the *Delhi Builders* case, that a 'residential area means planned orderliness in accordance with the requirements of the residents.'

Lawyers and advocates for the urban poor offer a different conception of residence in both scale and content. They use the

163

word 'citizen' largely in a national context—the poor are, as they are described repeatedly in petitions filed against evictions, 'citizens of India'. Their claims to rights and entitlements are based largely on an emphasis on their economic, social and cultural vulnerability, often presented as inextricably intertwined. They are 'members of the scheduled caste community'; 'landless dalit labourers'[15]; 'poor' or 'hapless slum dwellers'[16]. Here we see a pattern that will echo through the cases and that I will return to in my conclusion: the unsettled juxtaposition of identity-based claims (on caste), status-based claims (work, poverty) against what I will argue is the increasing salience of *spatial* claims (resident of a locality, slum dweller, migrant, owner of property).

In most of the cases, basti residents are portrayed as migrants to the city despite having lived in the city for decades. In *Dev Chand and Ors vs Union of India*,[17] for example, the petitioners remind the court that residents have lived in the basti since 1978. Yet a description of the petitioner still emphasises a tale of rural-urban migration, even twenty-five years later:

> Applicant No 1 is 53 years old and came from Bihar in search of employment as a daily wage labourer. His family income is Rs 1800 per month. He has a family of five members who survive on such a meagre income. He does not own any land or house and therefore, demolition will definitely render him and his family homeless as he cannot even afford any rented house or room in a city like Delhi.

The city thus appears ambiguously in petitions arguing for the rights of basti[18] residents. Unlike in petitions by residents, the claim to the city is tenuous. Where it is strongest is in claims of economic contribution. Several petitions do emphasise the poor's economic contribution and often specifically within the city. In *Dev Chand*, the narrative of vulnerability is buttressed by a claim that basti residents are 'an essential element in the city's overall life' that 'supply a major work force' and 'make a significant contribution to the economic life of the city.' Yet these are rarely either the primary identification of the poor within petitions or the basis of rights-claims. The primary basis of the rights-claims remains the recognition of vulnerability and need within the broader context of formal national citizenship. Here, the Right to Life is articulated in terms of basic needs and particularly of the imperatives of shelter and housing. As demonstrated in *Ambedkar* at the start of this chapter, these claims are premised on a right to protection that is demanded not from the city but from the nation-state which remains the primary political community in question.

It is from these differentiated subject positions and through divergent sets of rights-claims that the city and questions of citizenship appear within the Court. How do the courts respond to these claims? Who are understood to be 'citizens' and on what basis? How are those not considered 'citizens' excluded from claims to belonging and citizenship?

## Illegality as Personhood:
## From Encroachment to Encroacher

I argued in Chapter Two that encroachment—the 'illegal' and 'unauthorised' occupation of land, unauthorised construction in individual building units, and the violation of permitted land use especially within residential colonies—is, for the courts, the most visible symptom of the failure of planned development. It is what separates the complexities of the real city from the imagination of the planned city. It is the multiple disjunctures between the city and its Plan. The courts perform a particular reading of these disjunctures—one that marks them as scars, gaps to be filled, violations that must be undone. Restoring 'planned development' in Delhi is one of the rationalities of judicial interventions into urban governance, ranging from evictions to the attempts to 'seal' thousands of unauthorised commercial establishments running in neighbourhoods zoned residential under the Plan.

During 2006–08, 'sealing drives' ordered by the courts led to the demolition and closure of hundreds of unauthorised commercial units in neighbourhoods across the city, ranging from small workshops to large high-end showrooms. This is another form of 'illegality' within planning—the violation of

165

zoning laws that determine appropriate use in different streets and neighbourhoods. Commercial shops and offices in residential zones violate norms of use under the master plan which imagines single uses for most of its zones—either residential *or* commercial. Under judicial orders, municipal officials padlocked illegal shops and a red municipal 'seal' was placed on the shutters hence creating the popularity of the term 'sealing'. Unlike with evictions, however, strong trader action, a supportive Executive, a legislative intervention and, finally, a new master plan with new zoning regulations altogether, cut short the courts' efforts to take these drives further and most shops re-opened.[19]

The courts described both unauthorised shops and bastis as 'encroachments' and ordered their sealing or demolition. Yet one important difference remained. It is only in case law on evictions that the courts refer, as Ramanathan (2004) has argued, not just to 'encroachment', but also to the figure of the 'encroacher'. To use the term 'encroacher' is to characterise personhood. It describes not an *act* of occupation but the *identity* of the basti resident. The courts perform this shift repeatedly. In *Kalyan Sanstha*, the central case that began the sealing drives, the judges at one point consider a basti that a court commissioner has brought to their attention. They argue: 'occupants *who are themselves unauthorized* cannot be permitted to raise unauthorized, unplanned, and hazardous structures thereby making Delhi a complete slum' (emphasis added). It is in the distinction between acts that are unauthorised and 'persons who are themselves unauthorized' that encroachment translates into personhood for the residents of the basti in a way that it does not for the trader or shop owner.

Building on Usha Ramanathan's argument, I argue that an 'encroacher' is the antithesis of the 'citizen' (Bhan 2012). Each is produced in contradistinction to the other as the judges differentiate between 'unscrupulous elements in society' and 'honest citizens who have to pay for a land or a flat';[20] or argue, when basti residents demand justice, that they 'cannot forget' that they are, after all, 'encroachers on public land'.[21] As an identity, 'encroacher' performs exactly the same function as 'citizen'—it supersedes other claims and sites of belonging.

Within the Court, it becomes the primary and often the only identity of a certain set of urban residents.

This is a critical move because it unsettles previous terms in which citizenship entitlements have been negotiated. As I argued earlier in this chapter, group-differentiated citizenship has been the norm in Indian constitutionalism and caste has been one of the central and abiding categories of group membership. Yet as the case that began this chapter—*Ambedkar*—illustrates, judges often refused to acknowledge either the poverty or the caste of basti residents by privileging the identity of the 'encroacher', a spatial category that signals a different mediation in the relationship between the individual and the state.

In a city where the majority of the population has produced and claimed urban space illegally in some form or other (Bhan 2013),[22] the differentiated consequences and approaches to two forms of illegality tell a broader story. Vyjayanthi Rao (2006) has argued that the 'slum' stands as a shorthand for 'a distorted urban substance'—of all that is not planned, not orderly and, therefore, neither legitimate nor desirable. The use of the identity of the 'encroacher' reduces the basti resident to the slum. It is not just the encroachment that is the distorted urban substance, it is the encroacher himself that is no longer legitimate nor desirable. Personifying illegality, the encroacher becomes unworthy of rights. He cannot possess what Chatterjee calls, 'the moral connotation of sharing in the sovereignty of the state' that is implied within citizenship (2004b: 136).

It is thus that the courts can argue that even small, dilapidated resettlement flats are 'commensurate to the status of persons'[23] to whom they are being offered, or petitioners can claim that public authorities must act to protect public land that has 'been encroached by slum dwellers who have no right, title or interest in the said land and are merely trespassers.' It is thus that the Court dismissed the very right of basti residents to seek rehabilitation after being evicted by saying that, 'since [slum dwellers] are encroachers of public land and are unauthorized occupants of public spaces, they have no legal right to maintain a petition [demanding resettlement].'[24] Any possible relief to basti residents thus shifts from a question of rights to an action that is at best discretionary but, at worst, unjust. Humanitarianism, the Court cautions in *Satbeer*, must not be confused with 'a miscarriage of justice'. The last line of the judgment is terse: 'Temporary inconvenience has to be suffered. Rehabilitation of slum dwellers is a colossal task. Respondents have adopted a benevolent and sympathetic policy. The land is required for public purpose. No malice is alleged. The petitioners must meet the inevitable fate.'

It is within the separation of eviction and resettlement, though, that the use of encroachment as the basis of the disavowal of rights becomes most evident. In *Okhla*, the Delhi high court deliberated on the right of those evicted from slums to get resettlement or rehabilitation. They argued: 'If a scheme were to be devised for the economically weaker sections of society based on rational criteria, it would achieve a social objective. The basis cannot be encroachment on public land; such a basis, in our considered view, would be arbitrary and illegal on the face of it.' One cannot help, they said further, 'to use the expression as stated in the Supreme Court judgment[25] which best describes this position as "giving a reward to a pickpocket".' A few sentences later, the court issued orders that made resettlement post-eviction discretionary, and arguably, even illegal: 'No alternative sites are to be provided in future for removal of persons who are squatting on public land.' The parting words of their judgment yet again invoked what I will argue later in this chapter is an emergent and aspirational urban public in contemporary Indian cities:

> We part with this judgment with the hope and desire that it would help to make Delhi a more liveable place and ease the problems of the residents of this town who undoubtedly suffer and are harassed as a consequence of this encroachment on public land.

Historically, bastis represented not just an acknowledgment of state failure to provide promised housing, they were also a visual and spatial marker of the vulnerability of the poor who were still, crucially, democratically empowered through their vote. Their illegality was understood within the imperatives of this vulnerability—as a last resort to shelter. Such an exception is well recognised within imaginations of welfare within post-colonial development. Claims arising from need and vulnerability have long played a central role in framing citizenship claims to a state that drew its legitimacy from managing the promises of development. How then were these claims so evident in the history and presence of the basti evaded in the moment of its eviction?

## Two Tales of Victimhood

*The improper citizen*: In interim orders passed in *Kalyan Sanstha*, the Delhi high court ordered the eviction of 'encroachments' in the vicinity of the Wazirpur Industrial Estate in the western part of Delhi. The 'encroachment' was, in fact, a basti named 'Ambedkar Park Colony'. Faced with the notice of eviction in a case that they did not even know was going on within the courts, residents of the basti scrambled. One of the things they tried was to get a temporary injunction on the eviction. Their lawyer filed an application under Section 151 of the Civil Procedure Code which allows a court to pass an injunction against its own orders in a proceeding legislation.

The petition argued that basti residents were 'landless dalit labourers'. It described them as 'daily wage workers' whose monthly income was 'about Rs 1500–2500' and who 'on such a meagre income' supported a family of five members. 'Other members of the community,' the petition argued, 'include women and children who were totally dependent on the meagre income of their husbands.' The petitioners 'just cannot afford any house or room on rent in a city like Delhi, and have no option but to live' in bastis. The petitioners, it was stated, 'are living well below the poverty line' and 'throwing poor people along with their families along with the old, infirm and young children on the roads without shelter is definitely against the basic tenets of a democracy and therefore permitting the same to happen in a democratic country like India is absolutely unacceptable.'

The petition makes a familiar political argument: the poor are vulnerable and dependent. They have meagre resources.

Their vulnerability is the responsibility of the state. In a 'democratic country like India', the vulnerable poor cannot be evicted without mercy. This is a historically recognised claim within Indian constitutionalism. Indeed, the same residents would use Below Poverty Line cards, or certifications of lower caste status, to rightfully gain entitlements from the state. In the petition, two forms of group-differentiated claims are simultaneously being made: identity-based claims on caste and status-based claims on poverty. Yet the Delhi high court refused the petition. In its response, after arguing that the basti residents were 'encroachers' without rights, the Court made an additional observation. Citing the report of one of its monitoring committees, it suggested, in fact, that the basti was not what the petitioners claimed it to be.

'JJ Clusters',[26] they argue, 'have undergone sea change inasmuch as three to four storey buildings have come up in place of *jhuggis* and several industrial and commercial establishments are running therefrom [sic].' Our attention, they argue, is 'drawn to the Wazirpur Industrial Area' where 'there are huge encroachments on Delhi Development Authority land measuring about 17 acres spread in nine pockets where *pucca* residential structures including 2–3 storey buildings are existing and even factories are being run apart from commercial use.' *Pucca* is a colloquial Hindi term that refers to being built of permanent materials like brick or concrete rather than temporary or fragile materials like sheets, bamboo or tarpaulin. The latter are known as *kuccha*, which literally means 'raw' or 'unmade'. The narrative of development, in other words, is the movement from kuccha to pucca—a movement that literally and metaphorically maps the possibility of moving out of the rawness of poverty into a pucca, fully formed life. When the courts argue that bastis are now dominated by pucca housing, therefore, they are arguing that they are no longer kuccha, raw, or unmade and, critically, no longer impoverished and vulnerable. By re-configuring the content of the spatial category, they are indirectly refusing the eligibility of residents to make status-based claims on poverty or vulnerability.

In a last effort to prevent eviction, the residents of the basti then are forced to try a peculiar legal strategy: to convince the Court of their poverty. They argue that the comissioners are mistaken—'these *jhuggis* and slum clusters consist of *kuccha*, one storied, temporary mud-mortar structures only. Some people have built such roofs on their jhuggies where they can put temporary beds to sleep on at night to beat the summer heat or build a temporary shelter for temporary storage. It is submitted here that the 8th Monitoring Committee Report with regard to the Wazirpur Industrial Area wrongly submitted that *pucca* residential structures including 2–3 storied buildings were in existence.' The court remained unconvinced and the evictions proceeded.

There is a critical move here. The distinction between pucca and kuccha is a metaphorical measure of the vulnerability of the basti residents themselves. The pucca construction of a house that, in any other context, would translate into desirable indication of a marginal but important rise in the economic security is interpreted instead as a sign of diminished vulnerability. This interpretation is performed repeatedly by the courts. In *Hemraj*, the case that began Chapter Two and led to evictions at Nangla Machi, the court repeated, in no less than five different interim orders, that 'unauthorized occupants' were using the 'encroachment not for shelter but for commercial activities'. The accusation that residents of bastis use them for commercial gain rather than shelter serves a dual function: it makes them appear pucca, i.e. less economically deprived just as it implicitly suggests an ironic but useful possibility—perhaps that the poor don't live in bastis at all.

Who is running these commercial activities from the pucca structures? In many judgments, courts often point out, as they did in *Okhla*, that older resettlement colonies, some of which face a repeated risk of eviction, are in fact not the homes of original evictees: 'an extremely important and relevant data given is that about 50% of the slum dwellers have sold away or transferred the land and no action has been taken against them though plots were allotted only on license basis.' The basti is thus emptied.

It is seen instead as a site of illegal gain and commercial profit rather than of vulnerability. It is reduced to an image—flattened of the people who live within it, erased from its historical origins and its structural location within the political economy of the production of space in the city.

The courts make one final move. In *Okhla*, basti residents are compared to an originary displacement within which the authentic victim of urbanisation is located: the farmer. As the judges ruled that resettlement was to be delinked from eviction, they argued that if farmers had no absolute right to rural land then the question of basti residents having rights simply did not arise. Speaking of farmers, they argue, 'that on the one hand persons who are displaced by acquisition of their land for planned development of Delhi are held to have no absolute right for allotment of plot yet on the other hand the same very land is being utilized to give largesse to encroachers who have settled on the land from which farmers were ousted in the name of planned development of Delhi.' Once land is acquired from farmers, they ask 'can such land be utilized for the purposes of providing accommodation to persons who have encroached on public land? Our answer to this question is in the negative.'

*The miniscule taxpayer*: Even as the vulnerability of the poor is denied and erased, the resident-citizen suffers. In some cases, quite literally. In the petition filed by Mr K. K. Manchanda, he described his neighbourhood as 'one of the posh localities of Delhi' but argued, still, that he and his fellow petitioners belonged to the 'Ashok Vihar Residents Sufferers Association'.[27] The construction of the victimhood of the resident-citizen is the counter-narrative of the erasure of the vulnerability of the poor. It is, however, similar in form if not content. A spatial claim simultaneously wields a status-based claim. These are residents of a colony as opposed to a basti, yet they appeal to the Court as 'sufferers', i.e., a group that is vulnerable or oppressed. Several different discursive shifts allow these intertwined moves. In *Satbeer Singh*, the judges represent the resident-citizen as 'a miniscule taxpayer' who, in echoes of their argument about the failure of institutions of government that I detailed in

Chapter Two, is 'being made to pay for a corrupt and inefficient political apparatus'. Indeed, part of this political apparatus is the politics of patronage and vote banks that the courts argue are the root cause of 'slums'. These are what the court describes in *Pitampura* as the 'vested interests of certain sections of society' that compound urban problems. The 'citizens of Delhi', the Court argues in *Court in its Own Motion*, 'are silent spectators to this state of affairs' just as it argues the 'residents of this town undoubtedly suffer and are harassed as a consequence of this encroachment on public land.'

In the framing of self-proclaimed elite 'residents' as the 'citizens of Delhi', the Court performs an inversion of the traditional politics of welfare: it stakes an implicit claim to representing a majority—the 'public'—when it speaks of the 'miniscule taxpayer'. The erasure of the vulnerability of the poor is thus completed by a counter claim—it is the resident-as-citizen and the miniscule taxpayers that represent those that suffer and are vulnerable. It is they that are entitled to the protection and attention of the Court as it seeks to determine public interest. Even purely within a calculus of needs, therefore, it is the resident-citizen that claims priority. It is thus that the judges argue, in *Pitampura*, that, 'residential colonies were developed first. The slums have been created afterwards which is the cause of nuisance and breeding ground of so many ills. The welfare, health, maintenance of law and order, safety and sanitation of these residents cannot be sacrificed. Their right under Article 21 [the Right to Life] is [being] violated in the name of social justice to the slum dwellers.'

## From The Courtroom to the City: Two Juxtapositions

The processes of impoverishment I have been describing above are made visible through the case law on eviction but they originate and extend beyond them. In this section, I juxtapose the arguments of the judges against two sites beyond the courtroom. I do so in order to trace how discourses and imaginations of poverty, vulnerability and inequality move between the courtroom and the city. I am particularly interested in showing how these discourses shape who can be an urban citizen, what kind of claims different citizens can make, and what they are entitled to. These sites are: (a) emergence of new urban aesthetic regimes of poverty and the city itself; and (b) emergent discourses and institutionalised policy directives on 'citizen participation'.

## One: The Aesthetics of Poverty

The State Bank of India (SBI) is India's largest public bank, one of the many nationalised by Indira Gandhi in the 1970s. Its current advertising campaign is seen in Figure 3.1. It's a campaign that seems appropriate for a bank that introduced rural banking to much of the country and perhaps best exemplified what public banks could be made to do: open branches that were low or even non-remunerative in the name of financial inclusion rather than being dictated by purely financial bottom lines. As much of India's state-run economic structures have been disinvested and privatised, the banking sector, though it has been significantly deregulated and opened up to foreign banks, is arguably a sector where public performance has been the least criticised. India's central bank, the Reserve Bank of India, has been praised for its strong regulatory controls. Public banks have remained robust and competitive even after the entry of private retail banks.

The SBI campaign shows a typical urban street scene in an Indian city—a street hawker is selling a snack to an office-going professional. Their dress and appearance immediately mark their socio-economic origins: the vendor wears a slightly worn shirt, tucked out of his pants, while the office-goer wears a cleaner, bright striped shirt typical of a white collar desk job. It is, following propriety, tucked in. Above both of them, the caption reads: 'SBI Customer'. The advertisement claims that as a national, public bank, it is the SBI that is the bank of the rich and the poor. The marketing strategy thus emphasises access to the bank and plays upon a common perception in urban India that private banks are 'fancy', English-speaking and meant for the rich. The tagline was apt: 'Banker to every Indian'.

### Figure 3.1: Banker to Every Indian

*Source*: Courtesy of State Bank of India.

In a series of print and television advertisements in 2006, the SBI announced its new debit card. The print advertisement is shown in Figure 3.2. It shows a once iconic image of Mumbai—the *dhobi ghat*s, basins made in stone where clothes are hand-washed, bleached, laundered, dried and ironed before being distributed back to households. *Dhobi*s, or washermen, are common to all Indian cities but the ghats in Mumbai have long represented both a built environment and an iconic urban site associated with the workers of the city that has been

Figure 3.2: Welcome to a Cashless World

*Source*: Courtesy of State Bank of India.

immortalised in cinema, literature and photography on the city. In the advertisement, however, the workers' face is hidden. Above his body, a text reads: 'Raghu'—he is only given a first name. Underneath his name, it says 'Ex-Pickpocket'. In a world where customers carry the SBI debit card, the poor can no longer do what they usually do: steal. They must, instead, work and labour. Within the city, they must return to the dhobighats where they belong. The tagline of the country's largest public bank meant to be the 'Banker to every Indian' is 'Welcome to a Cashless World'.

The debit card advertisement was ultimately removed at the order of the Advertising Standards Council of India. Yet the reason for the complaint was not the outrage of many writing about its depictions of the poor but a formal complaint received by the Council that the advertisement would 'incite pickpockets' by 'conveying that the advantage of being a pickpocket far outweighs the hardships of physical work'.[28]

I argued in this chapter that the basti residents are reduced to 'encroachers' just as the basti is reduced from being a community that provides shelter and marks vulnerability to an 'encroachment'. This reduction is, in part, an aestheticisation. Ananya Roy (2003) defines aestheticisation as a simplification that changes the relationship between the 'viewer and the viewed' to one of 'aesthetics rather than politics'. The SBI advertisements are part of a visual landscape of Indian cities that Leela Fernandes has called an attempt to create 'an urban aesthetic of class purity' within which the poor are invisibilised, at best, and criminalised, at worst. The SBI debit card advertisements create income-poor urban residents as improper citizens rightly excluded from the imagination of the city marked by an upward financial mobility into a cashless world. It is ironic but instructive that the advertisement does not even consider Raghu as a possible consumer of its product even though the 'bottom of the pyramid' is arguably an acknowledged target market for a nationalised, public bank. As basti residents are reduced to the spatial illegality of the basti within the courtroom, they are similarly reduced to criminality outside it. They are hypervisible and invisible, seen in flattened images emptied of identity, personality, context, structural exclusion, history or location— Raghu, the ex-pickpocket, does not get a last name.

It is not just poverty that is aestheticised, however, but the city itself. A second image is then pertinent. The *Times of India*, the country's largest English language newspaper, began a campaign in its daily supplement printed only in Delhi called the *Delhi Times* right as evictions were underway at Nangla Machi whose narrative began the previous chapter. The campaign championed the city's 'urban transformation', highlighting infrastructural improvements and development projects. Its headline read: '*Chalo, Dilli!* From Walled City to World City'. Its flagship image (see Figure 3.3) was painted on the walls of the newspapers' headquarters in Delhi and carried in its city supplement every week for a period of nearly six months. In this image, the city stood both emptied and recreated. The familiar chaos of the Indian city is replaced by a set of upwardly

177

**Figure 3.3: From Walled City to World City**

mobile citizens in a hyper-modernity. The illustrations in the background show skyscrapers, an elevated highway, super-fast trains and cell phones: all flowing smoothly, uninterrupted. The 'citizens' lie in postures of leisure: all are dressed in 'modern' Western clothing. Importantly, three of the four are women: tradition and hyper-modernity will both, it seems, be written on and through the bodies of women.[29]

The image creates Delhi as a city of consumption and leisure, a city of an emboldened, modern and global citizen. Extensive daily searches of the newspaper's English and Hindi editions for a month before and after the evictions at Nangla Manchi showed that the newspaper did not carry even a single report of the evictions that occurred just as this campaign started.

Asher Ghertner has argued that evictions in Delhi make visible an 'aesthetic governmentality' where 'the visuality of urban space itself is a way of knowing its essential features and natural standing' within what he calls a 'grid of norms'—aesthetic norms that determine legality as well as status (2011b: 281). These norms, he argues, are determined by perceptions of a 'world-class aesthetic' in Delhi, one that is both a site of elite attempts to 'advance new norms and forms of the urban' as well as their subversion, resistance and evasion by the poor.

The reduction of the basti to the 'slum', therefore, and of the slum to the image of its built environment, must be seen alongside the aestheticisation of city space itself as the city itself is turned into an image, a commodity called the 'world-class city'. Most recently in Delhi, the Commonwealth Games 2010 made clearly visible the importance of how this image of the city is to be consumed by a global audience. Amita Baviskar (2007) describes the Games as 'a grand vision to make Delhi a "world-class city", words that have been repeated so often that they have become Harry Potter-esque incantations, charms endowed with magical powers. Say "world-class" and you conjure up a gleaming cityscape of skyscrapers, fast-flowing traffic, and neon-lit branded shops and restaurants, with unlimited power and water. The Games offer an opportunity to fast forward into this future.' Within this imagination, Leela Fernandes (2004) has argued that Indian cities are being reconstituted through a set of 'aggressive claims to public space and cultural discourse.' Spaces of entertainment and leisure, she says, are 'the new dams of modern India.'

## Two: Citizen Participation

In December 1998, the then newly-elected Chief Minister Sheila Dixit announced a new programme of 'city-wide changes' that would institute new forms of 'citizen-government partnerships'. The programme was called *Bhagidari*, which in Hindi means 'partnership', or literally, to 'have a stake in something'. Dixit was, until 2014, Delhi's most successful chief minister, serving three consecutive terms and celebrating over a decade of Bhagidari as her administration's most definitive and well-known policy framework. Through its existence from 1998 to 2014, the programme won her national and international recognition and was awarded, for example, with the United Nations award for innovations in public service. Bhagidari's aim was to address the 'simple and common issues that impact on a citizen's everyday life'. It claimed to draw 'from the ideological heritage' of Gandhi and his attempt to 'involve the common man in governance' by giving 'power to the people'. For responsive and participative governance, it argued, 'citizens must feel that successful and meaningful governance cannot be achieved without their involvement and without their role.'[30]

Who did Bhagidari imagine to be 'citizens'? The *bhagidars*—or participants—were represented by registered neighbourhood associations that are limited to legal and legitimate neighbourhoods, or colonies as they are colloquially known. Initial programme statements presented this as a 'temporary' phase in the programme that would gradually expand to 'all residents' in the city. Fourteen years after the programme's initiation, however, 'slum clusters, resettlement colonies and the unauthorised areas [sic]' remain excluded.

The 'citizen' here is institutionally defined within the bounds of a spatial legality. Access to participation in governance, in other words, remained premised on a legal presence within the master plan. This exclusion of a majority of the city's residents from being 'citizens' was embodied in the nature of the programme's objectives itself. The programme imagined specific activities to be shared between resident associations and different urban authorities. It is here that a familiar conception re-enters the discourse: encroachment. In the imagined partnership between the Delhi Police and resident associations, 'prevention of encroachment' was listed as one of three main foci. With the DDA, 'solutions to prevent encroachment' was listed; with the Department of Industries, the focus is even more explicit: 'clearance of encroachments in parks, and on roadsides and pavements within industrial area/estates' stands alongside 'removal of Slums/JJ clusters, encroachments on approach roads and pavements'. Bhagidari as a whole listed the 'prevention of encroachment', in fact, as one of the markers of its success, of what it called the 'changes observed' in the city since its initiation.

The 'citizen', the 'encroacher' and the idea of 'encroachment' thus travel. They are produced and reproduced between the courtroom and the city, simultaneously institutionalised in judicial verdicts in the name of public interest just as they are codified in the city's largest policy paradigm on governance and embedded in the language of everyday life. As the city is produced as a site of politics, a particular referent—a housing typology of legality and legitimacy—thus stands transformed into a socio-spatial foundation of what Holston (2008) has called a differentiated citizenship, where the 'emphasis is on differentiating and not equating kinds of citizens' as a result of which inequality stands institutionalised and justified. It was thus within the context of Bhagidari that the Court moves from the 'residents of a locality' to the 'residents of Delhi' to the 'citizens of Delhi', redefining both the imagination of the urban citizen as well as laying claim to the constitution of the 'public'. Claims to welfare within a national discourse of development in India have long been based on the idea that the income-poor represent a majority of Indians—the sheer demography of poverty commanded priority in the allocation of resources. At the very least, accumulation had to be legitimised by its direct and indirect impact on poverty as part of the narrative of national development. As development rearticulates itself within and through the contemporary Indian city, evictions remind us that it now must cater to a new set of elite 'citizens'—arguably insurgent and undeniably urban.[31]

## Spatial Illegality and Challenges to an Inclusive Urban Politics

I opened this chapter intending to take seriously spatial illegality as a logic that mediates contemporary urban citizenship. I have done so by showing how spatial illegality was used to undermine a set of historical and recognised negotiations that have shaped the functioning of the state-citizen relations in India. In the move from nation to city, and from national to urban development, evictions make visible how status categories based on the production of space and spatial location foreclosed claims to citizenship based on more familiar loci of economic and social marginalisation such as caste or poverty. Spatial forms of group differentiation, in other words, act precisely as modes and processes of what Baxi described as impoverishment.

This impoverishment marks both the basti and its residents. As land markets shift, city aesthetics change, developmental aspirations alter and urban governance bends in order to enable cities to become engines of growth, case law on evictions shows how the basti stands displaced from the imagined economy that marked the developmental nation-state as it has been re-articulated at the scale of the city. Stripped of a history of state failure to build housing, a socio-spatial marker of the promised welfare state yet to come, or as a site of the survival practices of the income poor, it stands re-signified as an 'encroachment', a site of spatial illegality that is emptied of all other meanings and histories.

This displacement then enables an altered representation of basti residents that erases their vulnerability amidst a broader criminalisation that further legitimises a disavowal of their substantive rights. Chatterjee has argued that for the state to recognise claims made by citizens as valid, they must be seen to possess what he calls 'the moral attributes of community' (2004b: 57). Spatial illegality makes it impossible for basti residents to do so by inextricably tying their personhood to an act of illegal occupation and foreclosing more familiar claims to community such as caste, religion or work. As basti residents are reduced to being simply and only 'encroachers' within the 'slum', and the slum itself is flattened and emptied into the 'encroachment', an eviction can be re-framed as an act of public interest. As ideas of the 'encroacher' and 'encroachment' travel between the courtroom and the city by entering aesthetic regimes and governance programmes, negotiations of citizenship further deepen and legitimise inequality.

Seen from here, urban citizenship in contemporary Delhi appears to be a site and a moment not of equity and insurgence, but of inequality, impoverishment and differentiation. Claims to the city are, in fact, being made not by basti residents but by an elite insurgent urban citizen that sees the city as a primary community of belonging. Crucially, this figure lays a claim to both a newer political mode of aspiration as well as an older discourse of vulnerability. He is thus both the city's aam aadmi as well as its aspirational citizen-subject of a new developmental regime. This does indeed suggest the presence of what Jayal (2013) described as an 'unsocial compact', and what Gidwani and Reddy (2011) suggested was a 'post-development social formation' at the heart of urban development in India today.

How can a more inclusive urban politics then be imagined? While the arguments of this chapter have made visible multiple and particular processes of impoverishment, they have sought to do so as part of a praxis that seeks to formulate effective resistance and imagine different urban futures. This resistance is already at play. It is not my intention to argue that the trends I have outlined in this chapter are not being countered, both within and outside the Court. There are, for example, judgments that emphatically underline the citizenship of basti residents and that protect their rights to work and be in the city[32] though most analysts agree that these are a small minority. Evictions are fought and, at times, successfully resisted by communities and basti residents themselves, many of whom explicitly refuse the language of 'encroachment' and 'encroacher' used to describe them. I have not engaged here with how basti residents themselves receive, perceive and engage with narratives and practices of impoverishment and that work must be done.[33] Yet it is difficult not to agree with Deshpande when he describes an 'elusiveness of counter-hegemonic politics in urban spaces' (2013: 46) that is appropriate to the scale of the exclusion it seeks to resist.

A new and more inclusive politics for the city must take seriously the role that spatial illegality plays as a mode of impoverishment. In moving from the nation to the city, it must look beyond familiar categories of identity and status such as labour, caste and poverty to new locations for insurgent urban politics that take seriously the urban not just as a location but a context for the determination of citizenship. In doing so, it must begin, following Richard Pithouse (2014), to see the basti as a 'site for and of politics' in order to re-configure how it is viewed, valued and imagined. It must follow Vinay Gidwani in asking: What is an urban politics that 'pivots around the waste-picker, the shack-dweller and the informal vendor'[34] so that a new political personhood can be framed that is spatial as well as economic, cultural and political, and emerges from the realities of fighting for substantive citizenship within auto-constructed cities.

One possible site of such resistance is the urban welfare state. Historically, the Indian welfare state has largely been rurally imagined. Programmes of social security in India—ranging from enabling and rights-based entitlements to basic transfers seeking to prevent destitution—have been and remain focused on rural poverty and vulnerability. Recently, however, the makings of an urban welfare state have begun to emerge. While still fragmented, a framework for social security—from principles and entitlements to policies and programmes—is beginning to take shape in urban areas. The list of its possible components is substantial: from the proposed urban livelihood mission to the already won Right to Education; social security for unorganised sector workers to entitlements to housing; expansion of basic environmental services to universal health insurance; as well as the initiation of cash and direct transfer programmes. Together, this range of urban interventions could potentially see the emergence, for the first time, of an integrated urban welfare regime that defines rights and entitlements for urban residents. It will be, therefore, a crucial battleground where growth-centred paradigms of urban development will negotiate questions of equity, welfare, redistribution and rights.

Many have argued that the delay in setting up urban welfare programmes stems in part precisely from an unsaid belief that the poor should claim rights either 'where they are' or 'where they came from', i.e. their imagined rural origins and anchors. Could the fear of expanded welfare rights giving the urban poor a greater claim to the city (and a greater reason come to it) be, paradoxically, an encouraging sign for inclusive politics? In other words: Could an emergent welfare regime be a site that makes re-articulations of urban citizenship possible as an expanded set of social rights for subaltern urban residents offer new locations, claims and identities that offset their spatial illegality?

Will the recent success of the Food Security Bill or the expansion of the Right to Education, for example, temper

184

our claims of impoverishment based on spatial illegality by opening up other rights to urban residents? Alternatively, does this new regime of rights make visible its own processes of impoverishment so that urban residents can make some claims but not others—to food but not, for example, to shelter, land or work—in a system of divided entitlements that is precisely one way in which they are 'managed' and inequality reproduced? Close readings of specific processes of impoverishment across different urban developmental policies and domains is essential especially if they play out within what Menon (1998) once called 'diverse discourses of rights'. Within such readings, evictions are a sobering reminder that a new welfare regime will be able to engender a more egalitarian urban citizenship only if it can acknowledge and counter the realities of spatial illegality in auto-constructed cities.

# Notes

1. The word 'Slum' is used in the organisation's name as an English word.
2. *Ambedkar*, final orders on 20 December 2002. All subsequent quotes in the paragraph are from this petition.
3. Scheduled Caste is the official term used by public agencies to refer to a set of lower caste groups identified in a Schedule of the Constitution that entitles them to protections and privileges from the state. Members of these castes take the name '*dalit*', a word meaning the 'oppressed', to refer to themselves following its reported first use by dalit leader and activist Jyotirao Phule in the nineteenth century.
4. See http://jnnurm.nic.in/wp-content/uploads/2011/01/Prime-Ministers-Office.htm (accessed 12 September 2013).
5. See, for example, the trends between the 2006 and 2009 economic surveys (Government of Delhi 2006, 2009).
6. *Constituent Assembly Debates* 11, 25 November 1949, pp. 972–81.
7. It is worth noting that Holston (2008) argues that it doesn't, in fact, hold true in 'established' democracies either. 'All democracies—emerging and established,' he argues, 'are normally disjunctive in their realization of citizenship—they expand and erode, progress and regress in complex ways' (ibid.: 14, 317).

In the Public's Interest

8. For a more detailed history of interpretations of the Right to Life under PIL in India, see Chapter Two, this volume.
9. See Chapter One, this volume, for a discussion on the use of the word 'colony' to indicate legitimate housing.
10. *Delhi Builders and Promoters Association vs Municipal Corporation of Delhi*, CWP 4980 of 2001 (hereafter, *Delhi Builders*).
11. See Chapter One, this volume, for a detailed discussion on my use of the terms 'formal', 'legal' and 'legitimate'.
12. See also V. Dupont (2011), Baviskar (2003), A. Ghertner (2011b) and L. Fernandes (2004).
13. *Delhi Builders*
14. *Pitampura*
15. *Ambedkar*
16. *Dev Chand and Ors vs Union of India*, CM 6982 of 2007 in *Kalyan Sanstha*.
17. The CM was filed against orders for eviction of Sanjay Camp passed in *Kalyan Sanstha* on 14 February 2007.
18. For my use of the term 'basti', see note 2 in Introduction, this volume.
19. For a chronology of events, see Jain (2010).
20. *Maloy*
21. *Satbeer*
22. Also see Chapter One, this volume.
23. *Ambedkar*
24. *Court in its Own Motion vs Union of India*, CWP 689 of 2004.
25. The Delhi high court here is referring to *Almitra Patel*, in which the Supreme Court justice likened giving resettlement to evicted basti residents as 'rewarding a pickpocket for stealing'.
26. See note 11, Chapter One, this volume, on JJ clusters. Also, see Chapter One, this volume, for a detailed explanation of planning categories in Delhi.
27. *Manchanda*, see note 50 in Chapter Two, this volume.
28. See http://www.thehindubusinessline.in/2006/09/24/stories/2006092403470500.htm (accessed 10 November 2011).
29. On women as repositories of tradition in Indian politics and history, see Butalia (2000) and Das (1990).
30. See delhigovt.nic.in/bhagi.asp (accessed 19 April 2012).
31. In the final phase of writing and editing this manuscript, Bhagidari came to an end as the Aam Aadmi Party (AAP) won elections in Delhi in 2014, and then again in February 2015. The party has focused on *mohalla sabhas* (neighbourhood assemblies) as their

technology of participatory governance. It is too early to be able to say how these sabhas will function vis-à-vis the Resident Welfare Associations (RWAs). I address AAP's election in the last chapter.

32. *Sudama Singh and Others vs Government of Delhi and Anr*, CWP 8904 of 2009.
33. See Datta (2012).
34. Remarks made at the inaugural meeting of the Urban Poverty and Inequality Collective at the University of California, Berkeley, August 2014.

# 4

# 'You Can't Just Walk into a Court'

## Notes on the Judicialisation of Resistance

The notice came six days before the eviction. It was the end of April 2006, and Vikaspuri—a basti[1] in Delhi that had been settled in 1984—faced the threat of demolition. The West Zone Deputy Director of the DDA had come to meet representatives of the Delhi Shramik Sangathan (literally 'Delhi Residents Coalition'; hereafter, DSS), a federation of basti-based groups that has a presence in over a hundred bastis in the city and had worked, at that point, in Vikaspuri for nearly a decade. He met Ramendra, one of the founding members of the DSS. His presence, Ramendra said, 'was the result of years of work—at least the government now knew who we were.'[2] Ramendra was under little illusion about the DDA officer's intentions—'he wants to do this without any trouble.' Ramendra recalled the officer being straightforward with him: 'You tell me how we should proceed. I need three days to write the report. Let's get together and do this.' The 'report' was a compliance report to be filed not with the director's superiors in the DDA or to any member of the Delhi government. The report was due to the Delhi high court on whose directions the deputy director had come personally to evict Vikaspuri—it had to be filed by the tenth of May. The date for the demolition was set for the fourth of May at 10:30 AM. Ramendra recounted the details: how many buses would come, how people would have time to pack their belongings, how it would all be peaceful. 'It was a strange conversation,' he remembers, 'how calmly we discussed all this.'

Neither the residents of Vikaspuri nor the activists involved with the DSS had known that a case involving their settlement was being heard in the court. Vikaspuri had existed for over two decades. 'There was so much government investment in the colony,' said Ramendra, 'we had gone to the local magistrate's court ourselves to force the government to put a primary school in the area. We sat with the Delhi Jal Board[3] to get water hydrants. All the toilets in the slum are built by the Slum and JJ Department.' For Ramendra and the DSS, the strategy had been to seek legitimacy for the settlement through maximising public investment by what he called the sarkar—a term often translated and used as 'the state' but one that refers, as I have argued in this book, specifically to institutions of the Executive including elected representatives and counsellors, urban authorities like the DDA and the MCD and public utilities like the Delhi Jal Board. It had seemed to be working. According to Ramendra, the DSS had been in talks with the DDA to 'regularise' (to post-facto make legal and legitimate[4]) the JJ cluster through an in situ up-gradation process—'We were almost there. We thought it was just a matter of time.'

When the notice came, the DSS scrambled. It approached a well known senior lawyer of the Supreme Court who had a history of taking on PILs for basti residents and who Ramendra happened to know personally from when they were both part of the National Alliance of People's Movements (NAPM).[5] One team from DSS thus started working on an emergency petition in the Supreme Court looking for a 'stay'—a temporary injunction on the eviction orders pending further deliberations and hearings. Another team went to meet senior officials of the DDA, trying to get them to intervene or at least to get allotment letters for resettlement sites in case the eviction proved unstoppable. The emergency petition was filed literally overnight and asked for

189

an urgent hearing on the fourth of May—the same day that the demolition had been planned. As the petition was being filed, a third team from the DSS pressured authorities as they surveyed residents of Vikaspuri to determine who would be eligible for resettlement sites. The initial DDA survey had identified only 293 households out of 1100—the DSS pressure increased the number to 700.

On the fourth of May, despite all the agreements with the DDA on the process and schedule of resettlement, the demolition bulldozers came at 7:00 AM—three and a half hours early and well before the Court could hear the emergency petition. The team was led by an Additional Commissioner of Police who arrived armed with orders from the court. The commissioner was willing to listen to no reason. 'Many people were still asleep when they heard the trucks,' said Ramendra, 'few could save their belongings in time.' There was a 'back-story' here: the Commissioner was 'angry at us', said Ramendra. A few months earlier, the DSS had exposed corruption in the local food distribution centre through a series of public hearings. The commissioner had been made to publicly apologise for letting the theft of subsidised food grains go unnoticed. 'He just wanted to get even', said Ramendra. The director of the DDA with whom the agreements had been negotiated was immediately called to the site. He came but professed helplessness: 'the commissioner has orders from the Court, what can I do now?'

An application under the Right to Information (RTI) Act[6] later found that 1040 police officers had been put on duty that day—nearly one per household. Ramendra claims that activists of the DSS were held under virtual house arrest though he said that the police later denied this in the media. Vikaspuri was demolished. Eligible evictees were sent to Bawana, nearly 40 km away on the northwestern periphery of the city, where households from multiple eviction sites in the city had been continuously sent since 2003. Facilities were minimal and conditions abhorrent. Moreover, most families from Vikaspuri had still not been assigned plot numbers. They encamped on the edges of the resettlement colony, living in temporary shelters for nearly a year. This time, the DSS took a different tack. They sat on an indefinite day-and-night *dharna* (protest) at the offices of the DDA itself, living on the pavement outside the office and refusing to move. 'Nearly 400 people came and camped outside the DDA,' remembered Ramendra. Supporters came from all over the city and slept anywhere between one and three nights with DSS members. They demanded that their plot numbers be assigned immediately through an unbiased draw of lots that took place in front of them. On the twentieth day, the director of the DDA emerged, first to threaten and then to negotiate. At the end of that dharna, Ramendra said he had a realisation: 'I thought back to the eviction and it seemed to me that we should have fought like this then—we should have stayed and refused to move. We didn't realise what resettlement would be like.'

★ ★ ★

This chapter follows Ramendra's musing. It asks: Why didn't an activist institution like DSS, well capable of protesting against the DDA as they later did, not take direct public action against the Court-ordered eviction?

Thus far, I have described the logics of Court-ordered evictions in millennial Delhi by asking what the framing of these evictions as acts within the public interest tells us about the politics of governance and citizenship in the contemporary Indian city. This final chapter shifts focus from the court's rulings to the impact that these judicial orders have on resistance within the basti. It asks: How did social movements react to and resist evictions? What were the sites and forms of their struggle? What strategies did they employ and what claims to rights, relief or resources were embedded within these strategies? Particularly, it asks: How, if at all, did the fact that these evictions were ordered by the Delhi high court and the Supreme Court of India rather than the sarkar impact resistance?

Drawing upon a series of interviews conducted with activists who are members of urban social movements resisting evictions in Delhi from the late 1990s, this chapter argues that Court-ordered evictions in Delhi make visible what I am calling a *judicialisation of resistance*—changes in the claims, sites and strategies of urban social movements in advocating for the rights

191

and citizenship of the basti residents. Specifically, the chapter argues that the emergence of the Court as what Colin McFarlane (2004) has described as a 'space of political engagement' impacts resistance in three ways: (a) it shapes the choice of strategies used by urban social movements; (b) it introduces new actors and decision-making processes into movement spaces; and (c) it alters the content of rights-claims and forecloses certain kinds of claimants just as it shapes the political identity, narratives and history of bastis and basti residents themselves.

The chapter is organised in four main parts. The first locates the main argument in a set of theoretical debates on rights to and in the city and the role of resistance within attempts to realise these rights, as well as within a history of engagements between social activism and the law in the post-colony. The second then describes and assesses the multiple strategies of resistance used by activists to resist Court-ordered evictions in Delhi over the past decade. The third explores the dynamics of the Court as a site of resistance particularly looking at challenges it poses to conceptions and practices of rights-based approaches. The fourth and final part outlines the judicialisation of resistance and draws out its implications for thinking about the rights and citizenship of the urban poor.

## Rights In and To the City

How does one think about the conceptions and practices of rights in an urban context? For many urban social movements, within the academic literature and in policy and practice,[7] the Right to the City is an emergent framework within which to advance an agenda of urban inclusion and social justice. French philosopher Henri Lefebvre wrote about the Right to the City in the 1960s when he argued that the urban was becoming the primary mechanism of capital accumulation replacing the industrial mode of production. The city would soon be, he predicted, dominated by exchange value rather than use value. It was in response to this shift in the mode of production and accumulation that Lefebvre wrote about the 'the right to *oeuvre* (the city as a work of art), to participation and to appropriation (clearly distinct from the right to property)' as a claim to the city (Lefebvre 2002 [1968]). As David Harvey describes it: 'The right to the city is far more than the individual liberty to access urban resources. ... It is, moreover, a common rather than an individual right since this transformation inevitably depends upon the exercise of a collective power to reshape the processes of urbanization' (2008: 23). For Harvey, the right to the city must be adopted 'as both working slogan and political ideal precisely because it focuses on the question of who commands the necessary connection between urbanization and surplus production and use' (ibid.: 40).

Yet how is this 'political ideal' to be operationalised and how are urban social movements meant to act upon and towards it? Peter Marcuse argues that it is necessary to explore 'the question of whose right is involved, who the potential actors, the "agents of change", are and what moves them either to propose or to oppose basic change' (2009: 189). He asks: 'who is likely to lead the fight, who will be most likely to support it, what will their reasons be?' There are few obvious answers. Harvey (2009) concedes that it is difficult to 'define who the agents of change will be in the present conjuncture' and adds that it will 'vary from one part of the world to another'.

In recent and influential work, James Holston (2008, 2009, among others) suggests that it has not been, as Lefebvre expected, the working classes of the cities of the North Atlantic that brought about the Right to the City. The 'foundations of this right,' argues Holston, 'moved south, so to speak' (2009: 247). For Holston, it is within the contemporary moment of extraordinary urbanism in cities of the South that the Right to the City finds some realisation. It is precisely in the 'peripheries of these cities,' he argues, 'that residents organize movements of insurgent citizenship to confront the entrenched regimes of citizen inequality that the urban centers use to segregate them' (ibid.: 245). In writing about São Paulo, Holston (2008) argues for an 'insurgent citizenship'. Urban insurgence of home-owners and other actors in the peripheries, he argues, has generated a 'national transformation of citizenship' where the 'current of change went from the local to the national' and created 'new conceptions and practices of rights and citizenship, along with new processes of participatory planning and democratic governance' (Holston 2008: 252).

Susan Parnell and Edgar Pieterse disagree. They argue, in fact, that 'the absence of an articulated rights-based agenda for cities of the South' indicates that notions of urban citizenship have found little resonance within debates on urban development in cities of the South (Parnell and Pieterse 2010: 148) though they mark Brazil as a strong exception. For them, the challenge is instead to bring 'the developmental state to the city scale' (ibid.: 146). Zerah, Lama-Rewal, et al. describe this approach as a more 'reformist' take on the Right to the City, which they call 'rights *in* the city'. Rights in the city are a bundle of rights that can be obtained 'only by engaging with the institutions of the developmental state' (Zerah, Lama-Rewal, et al. 2012: 2).

For Parnell and Pieterse, it is socio-economic rights like service provision, housing, livelihoods and shelter that particularly need this engagement. These require 'bringing the state back into development debates' in a manner that 'tackles the appropriate scale at which government can act to support rights realization' (2010: 150). Parnell and Pieterse are writing against what they see as the marginalisation of the state as a development actor through the undifferentiated charge of 'neoliberalism'. For our purposes in this chapter, however, it is also their understanding of the nature of engagement with the state that deserves close attention. They argue that

> citizen action that relies exclusively on an oppositional logic or a political stance of perpetual resistance is unlikely to achieve reforms in the mundane functioning of the state, which we have shown from the Cape Town experience to be a precondition for cumulative changes that can transform the political economy of opportunity and provide institutional access to resources. (ibid.: 158)

Colin McFarlane (2004) describes this relationship with the developmental state using the idea of 'spaces of political engagement'. Writing about the Mumbai-based Alliance—the network of SPARC, the National Slum Dwellers Federation and Mahila Milan—praised internationally for their role in community-led resettlement, precedent setting as well as in the self-provision of services like toilets and sanitation (Appadurai 2002; Burra, Patel and Kerr 2003; Patel, D'Cruz and Burra 2002), McFarlane argues that these spaces 'refer to spaces of struggle and negotiation' between the Alliance and 'authorities' which are 'not just particular meetings or events' but 'on-going attempts to frame relations between the Alliance and authorities' (2004: 894). For some, like Margit Mayer, such engagement may represent some improvements for the marginalised but they lose the Right to the City. 'Unlike the Lefebvrian notion of the right to the city,' she argues, 'this institutionalized set of rights boils down to claims for inclusion in the current system as it exists. It does not aim at transforming the existing system" (Mayer 2009: 369). At stake here are questions of the role and form of resistance: can systemic change occur from within through an inclusion that nevertheless challenges structures of power, or must what Mayer calls 'transformation' occur outside the system in which case inclusion is closer to co-optation than a spark of change?

The tensions between rights to and in the city came to a fore in Indian cities in 2005. In that year, Mumbai witnessed a series of brutal evictions of informal settlements and pavement dwellers that displaced nearly 300,000 people. The Alliance famously, and to much public criticism, did not mount a campaign of public resistance. It said instead that, 'our experiences in the past and the outlook of the poor communities that we work with have propelled us to eschew the path of righteous indignation and protest' (Mitlin and Patel 2005: 3–4). The Alliance, as Sheela Patel recounts, argued that:

> we have learnt from these communities that the only way, at present, that the poor get housing entitlements regardless of international covenants and national policies is to survive the evictions and demolitions until such time that the state concedes and enacts first, protective legislation, and, later, legal entitlements. However irrational this might sound, this is the real insight into the process—the subtext to the on-going war of attrition between the poor and the state. (2005: 2–3)

Ananya Roy (2009b), however, argues that the work of the Alliance—with its focus on dialogue and negotiation in what Appadurai (2002) calls the 'politics of patience'—can also be read as a 'politics of compensation' that creates a 'distinctive political subjectivity'. This politics, she argues, is steeped in the 'morality of collaboration, participation and mediation. To protest, to confront, is to stand outside the parameters of citizenship' (2009a: 173).

This tension, or perhaps more accurately this calculus, between negotiation and confrontation as modes of engagement, as well as the relationship of this calculus to rights to and in the city, lie at the heart of this chapter. Yet it asks the question in the particular context provoked by Delhi's evictions. It asks: How does the relationship between negotiation and confrontation as strategies for activists change when they respond not to the sarkar but to the Court? The question shifts. The authors above assess the nature and scale of either negotiation or confrontation with the 'state' when the latter is understood largely and implicitly to be the institutions of representative government and urban authorities—what Ramendra called the sarkar. Yet can one enter into a 'war of attrition' with the Judiciary? What does it mean to 'negotiate' or 'confront' a Judiciary? Is such a politics possible? What is, in other words, the nature of the space of political engagement when the 'authorities' are not the institutions of representative government but the Judiciary?

## Social Movements and the Law in the Post-Colony

The space of law as a site for social activism is a deeply contested and complex terrain especially in post-colonial societies. Narrain and Thiruvengadam (2013), in writing a history of the Alternative Law Forum—an important site of human rights lawyering based in Bangalore—argue that often the debate skews to a 'law or nothing' stand-off between either a dismissal of the law as a site where sustainable social change can be realised or an uncritical appreciation of the law's role in social transformation for 'those who see it as a blunt instrument of social engineering' (ibid.: 563). In between, they argue, lie a range of outcomes and, importantly, different strategic pathways for social movements to engage with the law.

Nandini Sundar (2011) describes three such pathways, arguing that each is based on a different notion of citizenship. Writing about adivasi and tribal movements in central India, she argues that three different kinds of engagement with the rule of law emerged: (a) to 'try to transform the legal framework of governance by exploiting democratic spaces within the state and within law' (ibid.: 423) by seeking rights in the Court and later the Legislature to pass a new forest rights act; (b) to use the technicalities and details of the procedures of law *against* the state (such as the demand for public consultations and acquiring consent to stall land acquisition); or (c) to 'secede from the law and set up parallel judicial mechanisms as in the case of Maoist groups' (ibid.: 424).

Narrain and Thiruvengadam (2013) add two further possible uses of the law for social activism. The first, they argue, is to gain immediate relief from the threat and possibility of rights violations by using either process or rights as a shield against excesses by the state or by citizens against each other. This is particularly relevant for us in studying activist responses to the threat of evictions and will be examined in detail later in the chapter. The second is that the process of going to the Court and demanding rights has gains for social movements regardless of whether victories or losses result. Using the examples of cases on caste, religious freedom and sexual orientation, they argue that going to Court allowed the 'greater effect of shifting the signposts of the debate and taking the discussion to a public level,' and had a 'radiating effect ... on developing a culture of constitutionalism and human rights.' 'The law,' they argue, 'is a potential tool for all those interested in a politics of social transformation ... either from a direct impact arising from the coercive power associated with the law [or as] one of the tools through which wider and deeper shifts in public opinion can be created' (ibid.: 564). In this, they write alongside schools of thought that speak of 'legal mobilization' (McCann 2006) or 'legalism from below' (Eckert 2006).

Yet all three authors acknowledge that social movements are not the only ones using the law's force to direct change. Sundar points out a 'growing middle-class emphasis on the rule of law and procedure, especially when it is subverted by the bureaucracy or the rich' (2011: 423) that Comaroff and Comaroff described as a generalised condition in the post-colony they termed 'lawfare': 'the law's use of its own rules—of its duly enacted penal codes, administrative law, states of emergency, charters and mandates and warrants, norms of engagement— to impose a sense of order upon its subordinates by means of violence rendered legible, legal, and legitimate by its own sovereign word' (2008: 30).

Comaroff and Comaroff go further. They argue that the law is becoming the primary site of political engagement particularly in post-colonial contexts. Using a range of examples from illegal drug trade to real estate, generic drugs to evictions, they describe a judicialisation of politics. Politics itself, they argue, is 'migrating to the Courts. Conflicts once joined in parliament, by means of street protests, mass demonstrations, and media campaigns, through labour boycotts, and other instruments of assertion, to name a few—now tend more and more to head to the Courts' (ibid.: 27). To engage with the law, they argue, is no longer a choice but an inevitability, making the terms of such engagement a critical question for politics.

To think of law, especially in the case of social activism, in a positivist or procedural sense has limited purchase in most post-colonial contexts, particularly given the continuing legacies of colonial penal codes and the fashioning of law in a context of domination and colonial subjection. In India, argues Balakrishnan Rajagopal (2007), the most promising space for the more substantive and justice-oriented aspects of law and social transformation was, as this book has argued at length, the rise of public interest litigation. While it will 'not be an exaggeration,' Rajagopal argues, that 'most social movements in India have actively used the Courts as part of their struggles since the 1970s,' it is by now clear that the ability to reach desired normative and equity-oriented ends within the Indian Judiciary has serious limits and varies widely across the nature of rights being sought as well as across time and sites. As Baxi writes almost ruefully after initially optimistic writings on what he called social action litigation: 'judicial activism is at once a peril and a promise, an assurance of solidarity for the depressed classes of Indian society as well as a site of betrayal' (2000: 161).

As strategy or as a last resort, as substantive struggle or a procedural wrench, as shield of protection or a hammer of violence, social movements continue to engage the law necessitating a constant reflexivity at different times of the outcomes of such engagement. Viewed from the basti on the specific issue for struggles on tenure, services and eviction, uncertainties and ambiguities in judicial outcomes persist and do so beyond Delhi and, indeed, beyond India. Richard Pithouse writing about slum- and shack-dwellers movements in Durban describes a range of outcomes from engagements between slum dwellers and the law. In the case of the Marakana land occupations in 2012, a series of legal victories and guarantees could not prevent violent Executive- and police-led action resulting in displacement. Yet, Pithouse concedes, 'historically one of the primary continuities between every major upsurge of successful organization by shack dwellers in South Africa has been an enthusiastic embrace of the courts as a platform from which to engage both the state and private interests' (2014: 196).

The basti's engagement with the law then reflects a range of possibilities across sites and time. While Holston's description of the insurgent citizens using the law to 'legalise the illegal' that has been frequently cited in this book suggests emancipatory possibilities, the Murambatsvina campaign under Mugabe in Zimbabwe[8] stands in contrast as a classic example of lawfare. Echoing the legal justifications for evictions in Delhi described in earlier chapters of this book, the mass evictions of informal settlements in Harare occurred precisely under the law's ability to cast them as illegal spatial forms.

The remainder of this chapter grounds these debates, as have other chapters in this book, within millennial evictions in Delhi. In doing so, it focuses on a particular kind of engagement between the basti and the law: to assess the possibilities of actions, practices and politics in the case of Court-ordered evictions, where the law and legal institutions are the agents of displacement itself.

## On Archives and Activism

This chapter draws from three key archives. The first is a set of fourteen interviews conducted in 2010–11 with key figures within a significant site of organising and resistance against evictions in Delhi—Sajha Manch. Literally 'Our Joint Platform', Sajha Manch is a coalition of nearly forty non-governmental organizations, voluntary associations, individuals, resident associations, basti-based groups and worker organisations including trade unions. It was formed in 1999 with the aim of bringing together interconnected issues that affect the urban poor—livelihood, housing, shelter and safety. The DSS was an active part of Sajha Manch until about 2005–06, after which they parted ways.

Each of the interviewees self-identifies as a *karyakarta* (activist) both as part of the Sajha Manch as well as of their individual organisation within the coalition. All the interviews were bilingual and conducted in a mix of Hindi and English, with the degree of each language varying across subjects. About half the interviewees are activists who are relatively privileged and live outside bastis, though they have been working within them for many years. The others are activists in the coalition and also basti residents themselves. Excerpts from interviews used in the text of the chapter are written in English using my own translations though original Hindi text has been retained as far as possible to indicate particular translation choices as well reflect the body of interviews that were largely conducted in Hindi.

What marks the choice of this set of interviewees is their understanding of themselves as 'activists'. Each was actively engaged through their membership in Sajha Manch in attempting to respond to multiple evictions throughout the city and not just, for those who lived in bastis, in their own settlements. What this archive does not represent is interviews of basti residents

200

who fought the evictions of their own homes outside organised platforms or the forms of resistance in everyday life that basti residents employ just to survive.[9] This is, therefore, an analysis of (even if often loosely) institutionalised activism rather than a broader narrative of resistance within the basti.

The second archive is a set of interviews with lawyers involved in filing legal petitions on behalf of basti residents. Lawyers representing bastis in five of the petitions studied in this book were interviewed. Two of the lawyers are eminent senior lawyers[10] practicing in the Delhi high court and the Supreme Court of India, and are widely known as public figures associated with human rights causes. The first, Prashant Bhushan, heads the Campaign for Judicial Accountability while the latter, Colin Gonsalves, heads the HRLN. The other three lawyers are both junior and younger to the two above but also have a history of being involved in activism beyond the law. All the lawyers are Delhi-based. It is important to note that the Sajha Manch never filed a legal petition in court as a coalition, though individual member organisations (like the DSS) within it did.

The third archive the chapter draws upon are the numerous single page pamphlets—called *parchas*—released and authored by Sajha Manch that are printed for mass distribution at its various political actions and demonstrations. Parchas are a staple of public events organised by social movements across India. Usually printed on brightly coloured recycled paper, they are printed in the thousands and handed out not just to those who attend political rallies but to people walking on the street, officials and curious onlookers. Their aim is to summarise the key messages of a public event or protest from the perspective of the organisers and to communicate this not to fellow protestors but precisely to what is often referred to as the *janta* or the 'public'. Parchas are then moments when movements present themselves and their political mandate making them an ideal complement to interviews with activists and ethnographic artefacts in their own right.

Vikaspuri is a JJ cluster. Within bastis, as I argued in detail in Chapter One, JJ clusters are illegal, informal, unplanned and

201

illegitimate, implying that they possess little to no legal claim to tenure vis-à-vis land and planning laws. This is not the case for two other forms of settlement also known as bastis— Slum Designated Areas (also called 'notified slums') and Resettlement Colonies—both of which have some degree of legality and legitimacy when faced with the threat of eviction. The conceptions and practices of resistance in these latter settlement types, therefore, could be considerably different from those within JJ clusters. In this chapter, therefore, my analysis refers specifically to the conditions within JJ clusters.

## Strategies and Narratives of Resistance

*Of multiple fault lines*: 'I remember,' said Kalyani Menon-Sen to me one afternoon as we sat in a café in south Delhi far from either the bastis of Yamuna Pushta or the resettlement colony of Bawana where we had worked together, 'more than anything else the suddenness of it all. Everybody was so stunned. The first day I don't think people even got their breath back.'[11] Kalyani was describing the evictions at Yamuna Pushta, the first of a series of large-scale evictions that have scarred Delhi's landscape in the first decade of the millennium. Over 150,000 people were evicted over four months from the banks of the River Yamuna in the northern part of the city—less than 30 per cent received any resettlement (Bhan [2009] among others; Bhan and Menon-Sen [2008]; Dupont [2008]; see Ramanathan [2004]).

At the time of the evictions, Kalyani was co-ordinator of Jagori, a feminist NGO that is one of the oldest womens' organisations in the city.[12] Jagori, especially through the personal involvement of Kalyani and her colleague named Sreerekha, was an active part of Sajha Manch which itself had a significant presence in Pushta at the time of evictions. 'Nothing was very clear. Everybody was doing what they could. The night before the demolitions there was a huge protest at ITO.[13] The cops were there in full force and the pradhan[14] came back and said "*baat ho gayi hai, kal toh nahi tootega* (there have been discussions and at least there won't be demolitions tomorrow)." It gave everyone a false sense of security,' she recounted.

The pradhan was wrong. The demolitions did take place the next day and continued on for weeks as the legal petition filed in the Supreme Court seeking a 'stay'—a temporary injunction pending further hearing—failed to move the court. 'At that time, quite a few people in Sajha Manch were quite confident that the court plea would work because it seemed like such a strong case. I never imagined that cases would be swept out quite so summarily. It was quite a revelation. Ruma Pal's[15] bench was churning out judgment after judgment in those days, and suddenly the eviction just happened.' She said further: 'I kept thinking how could this happen to people who have been there for so long? Also people like Colin and all ... they were really very, very sure about the case. This was seen as a landmark case—it would give the BJP a slap in the face.[16] There was this huge confidence. Now I think back and wonder how we could have been so foolish but there was this sense that the Supreme Court was like this benign Uncle—if nothing else, *stay toh de hi dega* (at least we'll get a "stay").'

There is never a consensus within movements on how to respond to the threat of eviction, argues Kalyani. For her, the fault lines of the division in the case of the Pushta evictions were between what she called 'institutional groups' on the one hand and 'residents', 'workers' and 'community groups', on the other. The divisions grew, she said, once the orders for evictions came. Community groups felt that they were the ones who had the most to lose. 'People whose homes were being broken pulled out—they said you guys will keep fighting [in court] and prove your constitutional point and all but *humko jo milega woh bhi chhoot jayega* (what we can salvage we will lose that as well).' There are others, she says, who wanted to fight, who said 'whatever the order *hum nahi maanenge* (we won't agree).' But still others and particularly the lawyers, she says, couldn't think of how to fight. 'There is such a strong segment of legal types within the urban movements ... I mean, they are lawyers themselves ... they can't set aside the system.'

'In all the evictions I have seen,' argues Kalyani, 'it very soon fragments out into those who feel they have a better chance to claim under resettlement and those who know instinctively that they have very weak footing there and so they try to fight with what they have. *Bahut jaldi ho jata hai* (it happens very quickly).' In one sense, this desire not to 'fight' but to try and secure some form of resettlement and benefits is the argument made by the Alliance. Yet Sheela Patel and the Alliance make a clear argument that this desire not to fight but to negotiate, to go 'beyond eviction', is primarily a gendered order that emerges from women's groups within the Alliance. The desire to negotiate, rather than confront, is presented as a call from Mahila Milan, the part of the Alliance composed of women's federations and associations. In the case of evictions of pavement dwellers, the Alliance argued that it was the women who argued for negotiations with the state rather than protest: 'The women said "... we don't want to fight and we don't want to stay on the pavements either! Go and speak to the municipality and to the state government and see if you can explain to them our situation"' (Mitlin and Patel 2005). As Roy has noted, 'negotiated development is presented not as SPARC's mandate but rather as a strategy of citizenship emerging from the experience of poor women' (2009a: 164).

Activist perceptions of responses to eviction in Delhi suggest a different division—one determined by the capacity of different residents within the basti to negotiate in the first instance. In the case of Vikaspuri that began this chapter, Ramendra echoed Kalyani's narrative of Pushta. '*Log unity me nahi rahe* (people did not stay united),' he said, 'struggle-based *route hum nahi jaa sake* (we could not take a struggle-based route).' He described the division thus:

> There was a split between the 'trading community',[17] you could call them, who owned small shops, *chai* shops,[18] *redis*[19] and the daily workers—construction, domestic workers. The traders wanted to get as much resettlement as possible. The daily workers wanted to fight (*laddna chahte the*). The traders tried to reconcile and say lets challenge it in the Supreme Court, but the workers wanted to fight right there.

For Ramendra and Kalyani, the calculus between negotiating for better resettlement versus trying to resist eviction, as well as the strategies to be used ('lets challenge it in the Supreme Court' vs 'lets fight right there') is not just a gendered order. Instead, it is one significantly determined by layers of security and vulnerability *within* the residents. It is determined by one's location as a 'trader' or 'daily worker', proxies perhaps of the ability to recover from an eviction, to have assets and resources that could be damaged or lost during the process of eviction, to have the savings or safety net to begin again in a resettlement site as well as to have the ability to negotiate with 'authorities' to ensure resettlement. Spaces of political engagement, therefore, are accessed differently by different groups within the 'poor' along a series of fault lines that eviction both exposes and exacerbates.

Yet there is a second layer of complexity that we must note: the fact that the eviction order has come from the Court. Ishwar Singh is a member of the Nirmaan *Mazdoor Panchayat* (Nirmaan Workers Council). Nirmaan is also a member of Sajha Manch but in its individual capacity, it is an association for construction workers seeking to further their social security, minimum wages and workplace safety.[20] Speaking of an eviction in 2006 in Banuwal Nagar,[21] Singh recounted a story of negotiated resettlement that aligns with the narratives and strategies of the Alliance. The residents of Banuwal Nagar negotiated with the DDA and the police to voluntarily break their own homes. Singh recounted it with some pride:

> We wanted, like human beings (*insaan ki tarah*), to leave our place and go to another. We didn't want the police force to come after us, or that the police would create such terror (*aatank*) that someone will get beaten, fires will get lit, or some people will die. We wanted to be given a slip [for the resettlement plot]. We get the slip in one hand, we break our own homes with another.

Singh remarked that the JJ cluster was made almost entirely of people who were eligible for resettlement. A pre-eviction survey included nearly everyone—'95 per cent *logon ko parchi milee* (95 per cent of the people got slips).' There were very few people living on rent, he said, and almost everyone had been there for long enough to be eligible for resettlement. Another part of the calculus thus emerges: the quantum of residents in a JJ cluster that are eligible for resettlement. As I shall argue later in the chapter, when this quantum is lower it can rapidly turn into yet another fault line on which divisions emerge.

Yet there is a preceding question to ask: How and why did activists in Nirmaan decide to enter into such a negotiation to 'break their own homes'—one so similar to Ramendra's narrative of Vikaspuri that began this chapter? Singh was categorical that resettlement was a terrible outcome for the residents of Banuwal Nagar. He spoke about the distance to the resettlement colony in Bawana, of the difficulty of life there, the loss of assets that the community suffered, children who had dropped out of school and the paucity of work. Most people, he said, 'don't even live in Bawana because they cannot afford the transportation. They come to the city, work here, sleep on the pavement, and go home once in a two weeks, once in a month.'

I asked him then if people in the Banuwal Nagar had discussed refusing to move rather than negotiating resettlement. Our exchange is below with my questions in italics:

*Was there any discussion in the basti to oppose the eviction entirely?*

It wasn't our emphasis.

*Why do you think that was so?*

Kyunki court ka aadesh tha jhuggi hatane ke liye. Order ka palan toh karna hi tha. (Because it was the court's order to remove the huts. The order had to be obeyed.)

Singh's statement suggests that the fact that the eviction was seen to be ordered by the court, rather than the DDA or another part of the sarkar, impacted the perception of the very possibility of choosing one within different modes of engagement in the first place. The court order 'had to be obeyed' so the emphasis of Nirmaan's response was at least partially influenced to move from confrontation to negotiation. Ramendra echoed a similar sentiment: 'When an order comes from the court, we know that

206

it is very difficult to stop it.' It is not just activists who feel this way, he said. He reminded me of the DDA officer's account of evictions in Vikaspuri—once the Commissioner of Police arrived with the court order, the DDA's own West Zone Deputy Director threw up his hands.

Unlike the narrative offered by Mitlin and Patel (2005) and the Alliance, Solomon Benjamin and Bhuvana Raman have argued that the 'paradoxical situation' where 'poor groups' agree to forms of resettlement must be seen in the context of what they call 'the new political and reforms milieu' where 'a climate of fear of eviction and the trauma of resettlement' curtails the choices of the poor (Benjamin and Raman 2012: 71). The narratives presented in this section add to Benjamin and Raman's analysis. They suggest first that multiple axes of vulnerability—relative resource privilege, location within the basti, or within/outside 'institutionalised groups' as well as degrees of tenurial security measured particularly in terms of eligibility of resettlement—determine the calculus between confrontation and negotiation at the time of an eviction. Ramendra and Ishwar Singh's accounts then suggest a further complexity to how residents in JJ clusters decide the multiple ways in which they respond to the threat of eviction: where the eviction notice is seen to originate. Court-ordered evictions also seem, to twist Benjamin and Raman's phrase, to curtail the choices of activists.

## The Court as a Site of Resistance

How is resisting the sarkar different from resisting a court? Activist narratives of resistance highlight a sense of *distance* from the Court. This distance is one that is both a literal expression of barriers to access to the legal process as well as a metaphor for the relationship that activists in urban social movements feel they share with the Court as a site of protest. Key in the former is the role played by the nature of Court proceedings—of lawyers, petitions, hearings and dates—while the latter is based on a differentiation between the sarkar and the Court as institutions within the state that occupy different political locations in the lives of basti residents and that thus allow for different spaces of political engagement.

## The Right to Fight a Court

In the history of Sajha Manch, it demonstrated against government institutions and urban authorities like the DDA and the MCD numerous times. Yet even through a decade of Court-ordered evictions, it demonstrated against the Supreme Court only once and against the Delhi high court on only two occasions. The most significant demonstration was outside the Supreme Court in March 2007. It was titled *Samvidhaan ko Yaad Karo* (Remember the Constitution). A comment by a sitting judge that giving resettlement sites to 'slum dwellers' was like 'rewarding pickpockets for stealing' had been reported widely in the media and there was an uproar within Sajha Manch.[22]

People felt, Ishwar Singh recounted, angry enough to do what they would not normally do—to protest in front of the court itself. I asked him why protesting in front of the court was seen to be so different from protesting in front of the DDA. He replied it had been 'very difficult' to mobilise people to agree to protest outside the court. He reasoned:

> *Sarkar se ladna humara hak hai. Court ke khilaaf pradarshan karna ... uska koi right nahi banta hai. Court ek aisi cheez hai ... kissi bhi violence ke khilaaf court jayega aadmi ... court ke khilaaf demonstration karein toh court ki tauheen hoti hai ... iss vajah se aam aadmi hai ya jo budhjeevi bhi hain, yeh leke jaate hain ki Supreme Court hai ... usse manniniye Supreme Court karaar diya gaya hai ... uske khilaaf tab hi hum jaayen jab bahut bada ati hua ho ... yeh ati hua isliye hum gaye.*

> (It is our right to fight the Executive. There isn't a right to demonstrate against the Court. The Court is a kind of thing ... you go to court against any kind of violence ... if you protest against the Court, then the Court is humiliated (*tauheen*) ... this is why the common man and even the wise people in society don't ... they take it as a given that the Supreme Court is ... it is declared as the Honourable Supreme Court. ... You can only go against it if you have been very seriously wronged ... this time we had been wronged that way so we went.)[23]

Over five thousand were expected at the protest. A year earlier, under the leadership of V. P. Singh, a former prime minister, nearly 40,000 people had marched against the sarkar to protest against homelessness, eviction, unemployment and inflation. Sajha Manch had accounted for many thousands of people who were at that rally.[24] On the day of the protest outside the Supreme Court, however, only a few hundred people appeared. I asked Singh if people were scared to protest in front of the court. He said: 'see, revolutionary anger (*aakrosh*) does not fear anything. But there is the question of respect (*maryada*).' He differentiated, again, between protesting in front of the court and the sarkar: 'it is the responsibility of the government to provide facilities for the public. If they don't do so, it is the public's right to protest and fight against the government.' He paused and then said, 'but it is true that people also had some fear. They wondered what will happen to us if we go in front of the court? The comrades (*saathi*) who were lawyers were also afraid of contempt … .'

Dunu Roy—founder of Hazards Centre, a people's resource and advocacy centre on urban issues, and one of the founding members of Sajha Manch—had a different perspective on the protest that March outside the court. He argued that the low numbers did not arise out of fear of the Court but out of divisions within Sajha Manch itself. Recalling Ramendra and Kalyani's accounts of fault lines within social movements, Roy argued that Sajha Manch was divided internally between 'funded NGOs' and the 'people'.[25] The key issue, Roy said, was the emergence of the 'committee' within the forum as a form of politics. 'Middle class individuals', said Roy, 'argued that we must have a small sub-committee to take decisions quickly; otherwise we can never respond to evictions.' Community-based groups and people living in the basti, he said, did not like the idea of 'committees' that took discussions 'amongst themselves' as opposed to open, public discussions that took place at Sajha Manch meetings. The logistics of the protest were handled by one such 'committee'. Dunu recounted:

Email had suddenly entered the working of the Manch and people in the basti had a sense that these 'emails' were being

sent back and forth with decisions taken without them. One of
these had been to do the protest under the banner of 'Stop
Evictions'. This is not our demand, people said. When I asked
people why they didn't come for the protest, they said this is
not what we want. We are not asking the Court to 'stop eviction'
because we don't have faith in the Judiciary. We want them to
remember the Constitution because they have lost their sense
of balance.

Much like the narrative offered by the Alliance, for Dunu Roy
the banner of 'Stop Evictions' emerged because 'a whole lot of
middle class individuals got involved and took the campaign in
a different direction'. It was these individuals, he said in an echo
of Kalyani's earlier musing about those that had a 'sense of faith
in the system', that privileged the Court as site of resistance.
Roy's then is a different sense of distance from the Court—he
argues that 'the people' did not see the Court as a site where
they should put their demands forward. Both these narratives
indicate a complex relationship with the Court as a site of
politics and resistance. While the first indicates a separation in
perception of the right to fight the Court in contradistinction
with almost an obligation to fight the sarkar, the second offers
an alternative reading that argues that the Court is an institution
that residents of the basti did not relate to and saw instead as a
site of a 'middle class' engagement.

The parcha produced for the protest straddles the two
narratives. Unlike most parchas written for distribution at a
demonstration, it contains no set of demands—it merely exhorts
the need for 'the Court (*adalat*), the Parliament (*sansad*) and the
Executive (*sarkar*)' to 'remember the Constitution.' The parcha
lists recent court cases against bastis, rickshaw pullers, and
industries that were shut down on grounds of pollution causing
a significant loss of livelihood to workers. It says:

> Those that work as beggars, wastepickers and recyclers, hawkers,
> labourers and rickshaw pullers—all of these have felt the stick
> (*danda*) of the Court. Is this what is written in the books of
> justice—that it is the industrious (*mehnatkash*) poor who are
> the only ones that are dirty?

Yet the demand that follows immediately after this assertion is not one that asks the Court to reverse its decisions or to rule in favour of the city's working poor but, curiously, one that asks it to remember the separation of powers. The parcha states: 'Article 50 of the Constitution directs that the State shall take steps to separate the Executive from the Judiciary. Does this not mean that the protection of nature[26] should be left to the Government while the courts dispense justice? It is important that the Court and the sansad have their own spheres of work and maintaining this balance is necessary.' This contrasts markedly against the language used in parchas against the government, where the demand is repeatedly for the government to intervene, resolve and act. In a parcha entitled '*Andheri Nagri Chaupat Raja* (Dark City, Fallen King)', for example, the parcha reads with a strident anger that is absent in the parcha directed at the Court:

> The rulers want that Delhi's map be erased of bastis, cycles and footpaths. They want foreign cars. They want to erase the innocent children that lay in the laps of the poor and make fast food supermarkets instead. ... Who makes these policies? In what closed rooms? Who are these white-cloth wearing leaders? What lines do they draw in the city? Do they even know how the poor live, in what circumstances? How they raise their families?

> Should we trust them? It is clear their maps and visions don't have any place for the labourers, industrious workers, women and the innocent. Can't we make our own maps? Come, let us accept their challenge! (Sajha Manch 2001)

## 'You Can't Just Walk into a Court'

I described earlier in this book the emergence of PILs. One specific part of that history is worth detailing here again. In a landmark Supreme Court case, *S. P. Gupta vs Union of India* (1982)—popularly known as the 'Judges Transfer Case'—Justice Bhagwati eased the rules of locus standi, i.e. the rules that governed who could appear before a Court, specifically for the regional high courts and the Supreme Court of India. He did

211

so to enable those in a 'socially and economically disadvantaged position' who were 'unable to approach the court for relief' to access justice through the highest courts of the land. Yet the Court recognised that the poor themselves often could not approach the courts personally for geographic, financial, linguistic and many other reasons.

The courts thus took on several mechanisms to bring the poor to court. Requirements for the filing process were eased to the point that that it was commonly said that, 'the court treated even a simple letter as a litigation,' taking upon itself the costs of litigation as well as the work of gathering facts and evidence. The Court also allowed, unlike in traditional legislation, parties not directly affected to speak for and represent the interests of others, presumably the poor. PILs thus opened up the door to 'ordinary citizens' to approach the highest courts of the land in matters of public interest either to 'espouse the cause of the poor and oppressed (representative standing), or to [seek] enforcement of performance of public duties (citizen standing)' (Rajamani 2007: 1, fn 4) but it also imagined civil society associations, NGOs and individuals to speak for the rights of others.

Yet despite these innovations and a long history of the presence of social movements within the courts using PIL, an argument that emerges repeatedly from activist narratives of resistance is a sense of literal and symbolic distance from accessing the court. You cannot, argued Sreerekha, of Jagori, 'walk into a court and ask it what it is doing.'[27] People's response in the basti, she argued, 'was to go to the DDA and the MCD offices. These were the spaces they recognised, the people they felt they could talk to.' Often, she added, there was also confusion about whether the eviction notice had come from the Court, the DDA or the MCD. 'The DDA officials would often pretend that it was their thing and that they were in control,' she said, 'and you didn't realise that they had no discretion until it was too late. People did know that the Court is involved somehow but there is no direct way to interact with the Court, no way of making contact. This distance makes it hard to know what can be done.'

Sreerekha argued that this distance was, in part, maintained by controlling access. She argued:

The MCD and DDA are sarkari institutions with which people have always had contact. There are offices they can approach. When you say the Court who do you mean? Lawyers. And only those lawyers who do PILs ... so there are some lawyers who they trust ... but even when something goes to Court, they cannot do anything with whatever has come out. The Court is the most distanced thing from them ... it was through lawyers only that they know.

Jawahar Raja, a lawyer who filed a number of cases in the Delhi high court attempting to prevent evictions, agrees. 'You go to Court only when the Court calls you,' he says. 'There is this certain respectful ... reverence is the word for it ... for the Court process. I think for the middle classes it isn't that bad—if you are middle class, you would have gone or conceived of going to the Court at some point or the other. You know what it is. It isn't like that for most people.'[28] Sreemoyee Nandini, another lawyer who has represented bastis, agreed: 'the ration office, the municipality, the public fair price shop, the government office ... those are the legal spaces of the poor. It is like the Court is a mythic beast, it's not a real thing.'[29]

The distance from the Court is heightened by the role played by lawyers as both interlocutors but also as reminders of the barriers to access. Lawyers embody and arguably perform a sense of legal expertise, of being the ultimate arbiters of deciding the legal process in what otherwise were spaces based on discussion, consensus and public decision-making however imperfectly they functioned at times across multiple fault lines. Kalyani recalls that the presence of lawyers became all the more marked as evictions proceeded in Pushta. 'There was a dependence on them,' she said. 'I remember conversations with Colin and Prashant, saying ... write it this way, don't write it that way ... in the petition, I mean ... and they would say, "listen, let us handle the Court thing. After all, there is an urgent priority here to get a stay against the evictions" ... I think that's the trap we all fell into.' When I asked Prashan Bhushan whether basti groups and activists are part of the discussion on framing the arguments of a petition, he asserted that though consultations occurred, at times, in the end, 'you have to fashion the petition in accordance of your own understanding of the law and rights.'[30]

Ramendra remarked that once the eviction orders had come from the Court, they knew '*ki ab mamla legal ho gaya hai* (now the matter has become legal).' When I asked him what he meant by 'becoming legal', he said that the process would become something 'out of our hands'—it will 'be about lawyers and orders, all of which we will hear about at a distance.' Ramendra and the DSS had worked with Bhushan on the eviction of Vikaspuri that began this chapter. They had lost. He recounted, at the time, working day and night with Bhushan's junior staff, giving them the logistical information they needed from the case. Those were, however, the only conversations that he had—he did not see the petition before it was filed.

Raja argues that, even if lawyers wanted to, 'there is literally no time for that kind of discussion.' Petitions, he argues, are filed often right as eviction notices have been issued or even when demolitions have begun. The sense of 'suddenness' and urgency that Kalyani recounted was so powerfully present during evictions at Pushta makes the legal process one that is a knee-jerk reaction. Yet it is perceived to be impossible to approach the Court at any other time that is not at the eleventh hour just as evictions are occurring. As Ishwar Singh argues: 'going to Court unless you had to would mean putting your hand in a beehive. It would be like asking: So, when are you coming to destroy our homes?'

## Rights in a 'Legal Sense'

Beyond the decision whether and how to negotiate with or confront the Court is the question of the claims that are to be made to it in either case. In the previous section, I highlighted the perception that lawyers possessed 'the expertise' of writing legal arguments and pointed out the distance that activists felt from participating in the framing of these arguments. In this section, I assess how this distance shapes arguments made within the courtroom on the rights of basti residents by contrasting these arguments with those made outside the courtroom by social movements. I do so in order to argue that rights understood and argued within the form of a legal petition differ from the understanding of rights within social movements both in their content as well as in the their understanding and conceptions of the claimant of rights themselves.

## Defining a Rights-Based Argument

Why should the residents of bastis not be evicted from what is, after all, not their land? Any resistance to eviction must grapple with this question as must any articulation of rights to or in the city. 'In a court of law,' argues Prashant Bhushan, 'you have to make an argument which is logical and legally sensible.' A 'legally sensible' argument in answer to the question above, he says, is this:

> Every citizen has a fundamental right to housing ... these are poor people who have no other access to housing except this ... if they had any other access to housing then this argument would not apply.

The core 'legally sensible' basis of the right to stay in place for the residents of basti, according to Bhushan, is indigence. 'It is legally unsound,' he argues, 'to use an argument as an absolute that, look, these people have been in that basti, they are workers, they have built that basti so they have a right to it. They don't. Legally, they don't.' Whether we like it nor not, he says, 'there is no absolute right to sit on government land. That right is only there if you are so poor and indigent that you cannot afford any other housing. That is the only right you have.'

Bhushan's argument is markedly different from those made by Sajha Manch and the NAPM. Responding to evictions in Mumbai, the NAPM has argued: 'In Mumbai, 60 per cent live in the slums. Shouldn't they have a right over 60 per cent of the land in Mumbai?' They argue further that the poor have a right to 'not just the physical space, but political, economic and social space. The voting rights guaranteed by the Constitution do not

215

mean that they have a say only in the political decisions—that applies to economic and social decisions as well' including the right to decide how to use and allocate urban resources including land and infrastructure (Patkar and Athialy 2005). This is a key demand within the Right to the City.

Bhushan is empathetic to this argument but, he argues, it is not 'legally sensible'. This debate rests in a particular context— there is no explicit fundamental right to housing in the Indian Constitution unlike, say, the Right to Education. When Bhushan says that, 'every Indian citizen has a fundamental right to housing,' he is relying on precedents set by the Supreme Court that has previously read the Right to Life to include the right to basic needs including shelter. Yet 'not all judges accept this,' he admits, 'not all judges believe that there is an obligation to meet basic needs as part of fundamental rights.' Bhushan's position then is an interpretation of a rights-claim that he believes can be made effectively within a Court rather than a clear textual right. This is not dissimilar to NAPM's interpretation of the rights-claim it should make—the difference lies in the contexts within which each claim must be legible and effective.

Jawahar Raja and Sreemoyee Nandini, lawyers who filed an intervention on behalf of a settlement called Sanjay Basti, present a second aspect of a 'legally sensible' argument. Raja, in fact, categorically rejects the idea of 'rights' having any purchase in the courts even in a 'legal sense'. 'I could have taken the entire argument about fundamental rights out of our petition and I don't think it would have made any difference.' Nandini agreed: 'there are so many grand pronouncements that the Court has made about fundamental rights. What do they mean? Nothing.'[31]

Raja and Nandini, in jointly drafting the petition, instead chose to make their arguments 'binding in legal sense as much as possible'. By this, they meant that they tried to limit the 'discretion of the Court as much as possible to textual law'. This was, Raja argued, 'not a place to debate what the poor deserved'. Their strategy was to 'remind the courts that, no matter what you think of the basti, or of the people who live within it, you can't just throw them out without due process.' The petition relied heavily on the process of eviction described within policies of the Executive, including commitments to resettle, notice periods and the requirement to survey the existing population before evictions. They argued: 'We knew that we were going towards a hostile Court. We wanted to just to say to them that this is the law ... you may think slums are an eyesore but you can't go just ahead and order demolitions without any relief. You may think that it's violating someone's Right to Life and a good environment but it isn't in your power to do it without resettlement as laid out in government policies.'[32]

## The Limits of 'Legal Sense'

If rights-based arguments had to be legally sensible to be used within the Court, then what kinds of arguments remained beyond the bounds of the Court? It is here that an analysis of the parchas produced by Sajha Manch proves illuminating. An argument emerges from these parchas that is markedly absent in legal petitions arguing for the rights of the poor within the Court: the need to challenge the 'cut-off date'.

In determining whether households in a JJ cluster to be evicted are eligible for resettlement, the cut-off date represents the year before which households must have settled in the JJ cluster. In other words, it measures the length of residence as a basis (as well as a pre-requisite) for eligibility for resettlement. There is an apparent contradiction in the idea of the cut-off date. If the act of occupation of public land is an illegal act, then it is so for those who committed this act before or after the cut-off date. Yet the consequences of committing the same action are different depending on when it is done. Further, the right to shelter that Bhushan argues for is based on formal citizenship in the nation-state rather than length of residence in the JJ cluster. There seems to be, on the face of it, little justification other than a desire to reduce numbers of eligible households, for the cut-off date to be logical and even, in Bhushan's terms, 'legally sensible'.

In parchas written by the Hazards Centre, one of the main members of Sajha Manch, the cut-off date is unambiguously

challenged using precisely this argument. In a parcha entitled
'*Punarvaas ki Rajneeti* (Resettlement Policies)', the writers ask:
'cut off date *jaisi cheezen sarkar tay hi kaise kar sakti hai jab
rehna ko aavaas har nagrik ka maulik adhikaar hai?* (How can
the Executive even set something like a cut-off date when the
right to shelter is every citizen's fundamental right?)' (Sajha
Manch 2010). It further asks: '*Logon ke hak kya hain aur unhe
kaise dilaya jaye? Aaj zaroorat hai sarkar ko yeh yaad dilaane ki
right to shelter yaani aashray ka adhikaar moulik adhikaar hai*
(What are people's rights and how do we attain them? Today,
it is necessary to remind the Executive that the right to shelter is
a fundamental right.)'

No petition representing residents of JJ clusters in the
Court has ever challenged the cut-off date and the exclusions
it represented for resettlement despite the fact that this issue
was central to social movements in the basti and to residents
themselves. In fact, some have separated the claims of the eligible
and ineligible residents. One such petition argues that, 'about
four to five thousand of these jhuggies [on the site in question]
have been in existence at the site for over twenty years and have
ration cards, voter cards and other documents to establish this
fact.' It then goes onto say in the very next line: 'other jhuggies
came up later, many with the help of local *dadas*, jhuggi lords[33]
and politicians, often with the connivance of the police and other
public authorities. Some of these are also post-December 31,
1998, origin and hence ineligible for any relocation benefits.'[34]
This is a remarkable exclusion in a petition meant to protect
the residents of the basti from eviction. This legal strategy
represents a different kind of calculus, one that evaluates not
just arguments that are 'legally sensible' but also claimants that
are legally defensible within Court.

The cut-off date shows the government's ambiguous
relationship with the JJ cluster. McFarlane argues that, 'it is
in the cut-off date that we see formal acknowledgement by
the state of its approach to "slums" as simultaneously violent
and regulatory, sovereign and disciplinary.'[35] Yet Court-ordered
evictions present a caveat to McFarlane's claim: it is not the
approach of the 'state' but that of the sarkar, i.e. the Executive

within it. When asked about challenging the cut-off date within the Court, Raja replied that it had been discussed but that the lawyers all felt that, 'no court would have set aside the cut-off. Even getting them to acknowledge that the government had a cut-off date was hard enough. Now telling them you must set aside the cut-off date ... it was just going too far.'

## Claiming Rights: Who Are the Poor? Who Are Citizens?

Yet the most significant differences between the conception and use of rights within and outside the courtroom lies in the imagination and descriptions of the claimants of rights, i.e. basti residents themselves. Rights-based approaches have long struggled with the question of who can effectively claim rights or, put another way, who can be recognised as a legitimate holder of rights? Many of the cases filed on behalf of basti residents share a similar description of the petitioners. It typically reads as the one excerpted below from the petition filed in the Delhi high court seeking to prevent the Vikaspuri evictions whose story began this chapter:

> Petitioner No 1 is 58 years old and has been living in the New Sanjay Camp Cluster since 1981. He works as a casual labourer in nearby industrial units and earns about Rs 3000 a month. He is having four members in his family including his wife and three sons. He does not own any land or house and therefore, demolition of his jhuggi will definitely render him and his family homeless as he cannot even afford any rented house or room in a city like Delhi. He is having the VP Singh card issued in 1990 and Voter Identity Card issued in 1998.[36]

Another petition reads similarly:

> The petitioners are poor slum dwellers. Some of them, who are male members, are earning their livelihood as daily wage workers, rickshaw pullers, barbers, etc. They are mainly landless dalit labourers who have come to Delhi for earning their livelihoods as there was no work opportunity in their villages. Thus, they are

219

very poor, earning Rs 2000–3000 a month and running a family comprising, on an average, of five members of on such meagre income. Rest of the petitioners are women who along with their children are totally dependent on the meager income of their husbands. All the petitioners are having documents like ration cards, voters identity cards, as residential proofs.[37]

Basti residents appear, uniformly, as 'poor, hapless slum dwellers' or 'unfortunate citizens'. They are 'landless dalit labourers' who come to the city only because there is no work in the village. Their families—especially women and children—are 'totally dependent' on the male members. From this location, the only rights claim they can make is precisely one that is outlined by Bhushan as 'legally sensible': a claim based on poverty that justifies their occupation of public land.

This is an anxiety shared by many lawyers. Filing for Sanjay Basti, Jawahar Raja recounts looking at the narratives of the petitioners and feeling the same anxiety. There is, he argues, this pressure to cast the poor as 'victim figures' because 'somewhere you are asking for a waiver of norms [when you ask for an eviction not to occur]. So somewhere in addition to asking for legal basis of that waiver you also need to have the sympathy of the Court.' Raja recounts reading the profiles of petitioners in his own petition carefully. 'I remember,' he says, 'specific lines I was very nervous about was somebody saying not just that they had paid someone for their hut and were also buying other durables ... a refrigerator or something ... stuff like that. ... I was extremely nervous about that ... and sure enough the judges picked up on that ... they said you know these guys are buying and selling property ... they are trading in this ... its not even their land so how can they be doing this?'

Nandini recounts discussing an argument that would talk about, 'how resourceful these people are, how little they use to survive ... to push it to a legal argument to say that this is the best use of the land. I think it was too far-fetched ... I think they would laugh ... I think there is still a strong sense of the slum being a eyesore ... I think the judge would look at you and laugh. Surely it is not that far-fetched to say that housing is in the public interest, but somehow ... .'

Nandini was prescient: none of the PILs filed on behalf of basti residents makes an argument that, in fact, these clusters are the best use of public land given that they house a large number of the city's poor. In the parcha written for the demonstration outside the Supreme Court in 2007, Sajha Manch (2007) asked:

> *Kya humara yeh farz nahi banta ki hum poonche ki 'sarvajanak' karya aur neeti kya hai? Kya samvidhaan ke mutabik hotel, mall, metro, flyover, sadak, park 'sarvajanik' hain? Ya kya sarvajanik ko samvidhaan ke saath baandne ki zaroorat hai?* (Is it not our duty to question what 'public' works and policies are? Is it that, according to the Constitution, hotels, malls, metros, flyovers, roads, and parks are 'public'? Or is it that we have to remind the Constitution what 'public' is meant to be?)

Yet this claim that bastis represent a higher priority in the determination of the 'public interest' as they provide housing was not one ever made within the Court, even within a PIL. The 'victim figure', though legally sensible, can make only a particular claim to relief and public interest: one that is based on sympathy and an exception of norms rather than any recognition of entitlements or industriousness.

In the parchas produced by Sajha Manch, however, the 'hapless slum dweller' is not to be found. Instead, the terms used are unequivocal: basti residents are described as *shehri mehnatkashi*, or just *mehnatkashi*, meaning 'industrious' or 'enterprising' individuals. Bastis are described as *mazdoor ki basti* or 'worker's settlements'.[38] The narrative of migration is described as one of development rather than simply distress, with the settlement of the basti as a key part of the narrative. As Ishwar Singh argues:

> *jab aadmi migrate karta hai toh iska koi astitiva nahi hota hai ... astitva tab banta hai jab who apne aap ko stapith karta hai ... jhuggi wala hoon ya beghar hoon ... basti banake shehar banata hai ... ameer aur gareeb ke ghar banata hai ... iss baat ko agar Court samjhe toh iss tarah ki judgment nahi degi ...*
>
> When someone migrates [to the city] then he doesn't have an identity (*astitva*) ... he makes an identity when he establishes

221

himself ... either he becomes a basti resident and becomes something or he is homeless ... in making the basti, he makes the city ... he builds the home of the rich and the poor ... if the Court understood this, they would not give judgments like this.

Migration is also implicated as a state strategy rather than simply a movement of distressed rural workers. Workers, argue Ishwar Singh, are brought to the city and often settled by contractors and government officials in bastis. The narratives of why these clusters are built differ from legal arguments. Rather than portray them as just a last resort of those in need due to poverty and indigence, the government is squarely implicated in their construction. In a parcha called '*Kala Kanoon, Kaana Kanoon*' ('Black Law, Blind Law'), Sajha Manch activists argue that 'while the court judgments have also blamed the DDA and the MCD for encroachment of their own, they have not recognised that it is these authorities that have denied housing to the poor' (Sajha Manch 2005). The parcha goes onto argue that, 'the Delhi government itself admits in its affidavit in the Court that the growth of bastis is a result of the government's failure to provide low income housing to the poor.'

The basti, therefore, in this narrative, is a result of a state failure to provide housing—a line that Sajha Manch has consistently taken and also articulated in a *People's Housing Policy* drafted by Hazards Centre on 'behalf of Sajha Manch' (2003: 1). The policy reiterates the parchas that follow it: 'the working population,' it argues, 'has not been provided with shelter by the planners and housing agencies and, hence, has had to settle on whatever land is available—much of it earmarked for residential purposes anyway' (ibid.: 10). Here, a different claim to rights emerges, one that is based not on indigence but on a history of state failure against its own claims for the provision of housing.[39]

## The Judicialisation of Resistance

Through this chapter, I have sought to assess changes in the sites, claims and strategies of urban social movements that seek to prevent eviction, or at least ameliorate the process of resettlement, when faced with Court-ordered evictions in Delhi. I argued for a diverse set of impacts.

One, in the moment of eviction, existing fault lines within urban social movements on choosing between (or simultaneously using) multiple strategies of resistance are further complicated when the object of resistance is the Court rather than the Executive. Already complex divisions on axes of gender, class and vulnerability continue to play out in the decision of how to resist a Court-ordered eviction even as activists additionally struggle with the belief that a court order cannot be contested at all, on the one hand, or arguing that it is not a site where basti residents can and should voice their demands, on the other.

Two, strategies of resistance are further compromised as the right and obligation to contest the sarkar is contrasted with the sense among activists that they don't have a right to fight the Court. This sense is strongly rooted in a sense of distance from the Court—both in the literal barriers to access ('you can't walk into a court') as well as the symbolic distance in the imagination of the social and political position of the Court in the lives of basti residents. As the lawyer Nandini argued: 'The Court is like a mythic beast, it's not a real thing.' This sense of distance is constituted in part by the role played by lawyers as both interlocutors but also symbols of the barriers to entry for the poor within the legal process. Ramendra's musing that '*ab mamla legal ban gaya* (now the matter has become legal)' implied an acknowledgment of this distance between political processes within social movements and legal processes.

Three, this distance then manifests itself in the very composition of rights-claims that are made by and on behalf of basti residents. Rights in their 'legal sense' are bound by the limits of arguments that lawyers believe the Court will recognise as legitimate. Arguments made by residents in movement spaces—particularly those challenging the cut-off dates and questioning the public purpose for which the land under the basti required—therefore cannot be 'legally sensible' though they form a core of rights-claims outside the courtroom.

Four, and finally, it is not just rights-claims that must be 'legally sensible' but basti residents themselves must be framed as legally recognisable and defensible petitioners. This has two significant consequences: the portrayal of these residents as helpless and indigent to gain what Raja described as the 'sympathy of the Court' and the exclusion of those residents that do not meet the cut-off date from any presence within the Court.

Taken together, therefore, the impact of the presence of the Court within the calculus of resistance challenges the choice of strategies; introduces new actors and decision-making processes into movement spaces; and alters the content of rights-claims and forecloses certain kinds of claimants just as it shapes the political identity and history of the basti and its residents themselves. It is this impact that I term the *judicialisation of resistance*. What are the implications of such a judicialisation?

## Re-Negotiating the Space of Political Engagement

Judicialisation challenges both the Right to the City and rights in the city. The former represents a claim that challenges the bounds of legal sensibility as seen in the inability of lawyers to challenge the cut-off date or to argue that the basti represents the highest expression of public interest. The latter highlights the distinction in negotiating *within* the state with the Executive versus the Judiciary as well as the limits that the each puts on the other. Different spaces of political engagement, in other words, foreclose certain modes of engagement as well as the possibility and forms of either negotiation or confrontation. For social movements in Delhi, these distinctions presented themselves in narratives of both a fear of and distance from the Court, curtailing the choices available to the activists within urban social movements.

The 'politics of patience' or the 'politics of negotiation', for example, are both altered in content and in implication when they face the Judiciary rather than the Executive. Claims that can be made to the sarkar, as this chapter has shown, are often not made to the Court. What does this imply for urban movements? It suggests, for one, the importance of a framework of entitlements that takes the form of textual and statutory rights.

Let me cite an anecdote to illustrate this point. I argued earlier in this chapter that there is no constitutional right to housing in India as there is, for example, a Right to Education. In a much publicised decision, the National Slum Dwellers Federation, part of the Alliance, had chosen not to join the failed National Campaign for Housing Rights that sought to create such a constitutionally mandated right to housing in the 1990s. They had refused to join the campaign because, as Mitlin and Patel argue, 'for the bulk of the [slum] dwellers, the national campaign appeared to have no immediate positive impact on their everyday lives ... . The president [of the NSDF], Jockin, could see that there were many constitutional rights that were not recognized. What, then, was the point of adding another?' (2005: 19).

It is when we see the 'state' not just as sarkar but instead as an intertwined regime of rule of both the sarkar and the Judiciary that the 'point of adding another' right becomes clearer. The absence of a statutory, legally binding right to housing was one part of what allowed the courts to reject the rights claims of the basti residents and to fail to hold the state accountable for the provision of housing. It is this absence that leaves 'indigence' as the only basis for rights claims for such residents. In engagement with the sarkar, textual rights may seem trivial due to persistent non-implementation and precisely because the sarkar often violates its own laws. Yet within the state, how is the flexibility manifested? The emergence of the Court as an actor of urban governance challenges the flexibility of the sarkar in complex ways. Movements that have long sought to tilt the informality of the 'state' in their direction armed with the power of their vote and their ability to mobilise publicly thus are faced with the need for new forms of struggle—ones that can affirm and argue for entitlements in forms recognised by the courts. If a 'politics of perpetual resistance' cannot yield sustainable gains, as Parnell and Pieterse argue, it is also unclear how the engagement they advocate can be constructed and constructive when it is not with the sarkar but with the Judiciary.

Adapting to the emergence of the Court is an immense task for social movements. Attempts at working across fault lines of gender, class, language and differential vulnerability will now further have to engage with a new fault line: legal expertise and the supposed binds of a 'legally sensible' argument. Judicialisation presents a challenge for movements to translate their rights-claims, their political identities and histories, and even their understanding of the processes of city formation and the production of urban space, into legal petitions. A critical example of this is the narrative of the production and settling of the basti itself and whether it is presented as a narrative of state failure or one of illegal acts of occupation of public land. Conversely, if movements choose not to negotiate but to confront, it then represents the need for movements to find a way to reject the power of the Court and its pronouncements—to learn, in other words, how to fight the Court on its own terms.

## Building and Losing Rights-Consciousness

The differences between rights-claims within and outside the courtroom are stark markers of the limitations of the PIL as a space of justice for the residents of JJ clusters. The PIL is a space that sought to amend judicial processes in order to further access to justice for the marginalised. Yet, as these judgments show, easing of the rules of standing and representation cannot ensure that they all are actually heard in the courtroom even if they are present as petitioners. The constraints of a judicial imagination and of the twin binds of legally sensible arguments and legally defensible petitioners again question the limits to the courtroom as a space of justice in the cities of the South particularly when it comes to the question of the production of space through the illegal occupation of land.

Yet it is not just in 'losing' within the Court that the Right to the City is lost—it is also within the impact of these judgments on the ability of basti residents to see themselves as well as be seen by others as having what Holston describes as 'the right to have rights'. This is the counter-factual, in a sense, to Narrain and Thiruvengadam's argument that even in legal losses, gains can be made by movements through building rights-consciousness. Yet, in the case of demolitions, the terms of access seem to militate against this possibility. Within the Court, basti residents were unable to appear as citizens with the 'right to have rights' but instead felt that they had to appear as 'victims' whose claim to a right to shelter and housing is based on indigence rather than contribution at least partially because this was presented to them as the only possible legal strategy. One of the reasons that lawyers like Prashant Bhushan and Jawahar Raja give for this is that these residents have no claim, or right, to occupy land that they do not own and have not paid for. Bhushan argued that to say that the residents of JJ clusters had any right to remain in bastis was 'legally unsound' unless made on the grounds of indigence. Judicially, his argument goes, the poor can appear only as particular kinds of citizens: not the mehnatkash who build the city as they are in parchas but as 'poor, hapless slumdwellers'.

This political imagination travels. As Ravi Sundaram (2009) has argued, through the circuits of media and information, the transcripts and narratives of the courtroom have become a widely accessed 'archive of the city'. The imagination of basti residents within the courtroom thus travels into the city just as the politics of the city enters the courtroom. Like the idea of the 'encroacher', the 'poor, hapless slum dweller' shapes the political locations and imaginaries that these residents are then able to inhabit outside the courtroom. Arguably then, the public debate on the rights and entitlements of the marginalised—which is, in turn, critical to establish statutory and legally defensible entitlements—is one that is impacted by judicial pronouncements that determine these rights in ways that are narrow and curtailed by the need to be 'legally sensible'.

I do not mean to suggest here that judicial losses have the power to close all political fields. As Narrain and Thiruvengadam state, and I will argue in the conclusion, social movements can and must be careful to balance legal strategy with mobilisation, action and presence outside the courtroom which could help them realise and further gains but also insulate them from the political impact of losses.

## Whither Insurgence?

Earlier in this chapter, I quoted Holston as both describing the insurgent citizenship of São Paulo's peripheries but conceding that 'not all peripheries are insurgent'. As a final note in this chapter, I ponder why. It is important here to note one distinction between Holston's insurgent citizens in São Paulo and JJ cluster residents in Delhi: a claim to property. Holston argues:

> Let me emphasize a point often misunderstood by outsiders (Brazilian and foreign): the majority of 'slum dwellers' in most Brazilian cities, of those who live in the poor peripheries, are good-faith purchasers of house lots in subdivisions (*loteamentos*) who have been defrauded in one form or another. They are not squatters and do not live in favelas. A favela is a land seizure without any payment and is only one of several types of illegal land occupation in Brazil's urban landscape. Thus, favela residents have no claims to land ownership, although they own their houses—an ownership that the state generally recognizes in various ways. (Holston 2009: 265, fn 4)

Within bastis, JJ clusters like Vikaspuri are favelas. The sarkar did, however, historically recognise their claim to land 'in various ways,' as Holston says, and this recognition has been the space of political engagement between social movements and the sarkar within Indian cities. It is this negotiation that the judicialisation of resistance challenges.

My intention here is not to discount Holston's narrative of insurgence but to explore why some spaces of political engagement and, indeed, some parts of the same peripheries do not become insurgent. In particular, I suggest that within the context of claiming space and land within the cities of the South, some form of a claim to ownership has played a critical role in determining the possibility of insurgence in the first place. This is exacerbated, as I argued in Chapter Two, when the space of political engagement is the law. Within the Court, the absence of any claim to ownership becomes the determining factor in how basti residents are seen. Judicially, the space of the city is thus read through legal regimes of property and ownership. Without a claim to some form of ownership or at least to formal payment, basti residents cannot be legally imagined as anything other than indigent citizens seeking welfare. They may claim social protection but cannot claim land. In the absence of a codified right to housing, judicialisation thus creates a pre-requisite to rights-claims: a claim not to the city but to property.

The contemporary moment and judicialisation then has thrown a set of new challenges to urban social movements: to challenge the bounds of 'legal sense', to question the accusations of 'illegality' levelled against them, to see the law and planning as sites of contestation and negotiation, to resist the Court on its own terms through perhaps the creation of new laws like a right to housing, as well as to challenge fundamental conceptions of property, ownership, the value of land and estimations of the public. New strategies will have to be conceived, new locations found, and new discourses and languages of articulation created. What is essential for both rights to and in the city is to recognise the particularities of these challenges in order to be able to effectively respond to them.

Walking by the River Yamuna where the bastis of Pushta once stood, Ishwar Singh said to me, '*ab nahi jayenge Court. Kyun jayen aisa court ke paas jo aisi judgment de jo gareeb ke astitva ko sweekar hi na kare?* (Now we won't go to Court—why should we go to a place which gives judgments that don't accept the very identity of the poor, their sense of self?)' He stood silent. A few moments later, smiling, he sang a popular slogan used by movements in public rallies: '*yeh to abhi angdai hai, aage aur ladai hai* (This is just a pitstop, there is still a long fight ahead).' The empty ground on which we stood bore testimony that the choice not to engage the Court was not ours to make—ours was only the realisation that the nature of the fight had changed once again.

# Notes

1. On my use of the term 'basti', see note 2 in Introduction, this volume.
2. Personal interview, dated 3 September 2010.
3. The Delhi Water Board, the public water utility in the city of Delhi.

4. For more on 'regularisation' of bastis as well as my use of the terms 'legal' and 'legitimate', see Chapter One, this volume.
5. The NAPM is 'an alliance of progressive people's organisations and movements, who while retaining their autonomous identities, are working together to bring the struggle for primacy of rights of communities over natural resources, conservation and governance, decentralised democratic development and towards a just, sustainable and egalitarian society in the true spirit of globalism.' See http://napm-india.org/aboutus (accessed October 2015).
6. In 2005, India passed a comprehensive RTI Act that allows any citizen to demand information from a public agency through writing a simple letter and expect a reply within 90 days. The Act has become a powerful tool in the hands of many activists precisely because of its operational simplicity and effective institutionalisation—every government department and ministry now has an Information Officer whose role is only to reply to RTI requests.
7. In 2005–06, many international NGOs (led by Habitat International and later supported by the United Nations Educational, Scientific and Cultural Organization [UNESCO]) and movements meeting in the World Social Forums drafted a World Charter on the Right to the City. See http://www.globalgovernancewatch.org/resources/world-charter-on-the-right-to-the-city (accessed 9 February 2012). In Brazil, the right to the city is a significant component as well as the underlying spirit of a federal law called the City Statute. See Caldeira and Holston (2005) and E. Fernandes (2007).
8. Officially known as 'Restore Order', the Murambatsvina campaign refers to the large-scale eviction since 2005 of slums areas in the cities of Zimbabwe. For a United Nations assessment of the forced evictions, see http://www.un.org/News/dh/infocus/zimbabwe/zimbabwe_rpt.pdf (accessed October 2015).
9. On implications for basti residents, see Datta (2012) and A. Ghertner (2011b).
10. As part of a broader Commonwealth tradition, the Judiciary in India recognises and formally designates certain lawyers as 'senior'. In the Delhi high court and the Supreme Court of India, becoming a senior lawyer requires an application to high court and Supreme Court judges who then meet and decide whether or not to confer the designation of Senior Advocate. In Delhi, the nominee has to be 40 years old, though a process of exception does exist for younger nominees. The judges vote on the nominee

having knowledge in a specialised branch of law. Having a senior lawyer represent a case is seen to strengthen the argument and chances of success measurably.

11. Personal interview, dated 12 February 2011.
12. See www.jagori.org (accessed 1 December 2011).
13. ITO is the colloquial name given to a commercial and institutional area in the northern part of the city that hosts many government offices, including the DDA and many offices of the municipal authority. Protests against the DDA are often said to happen 'at ITO'.
14. See note 10 in Introduction, this volume.
15. Ruma Pal was then a judge in the Delhi high court who authored the orders of eviction against Yamuna Pushta.
16. At the time of the first evictions at Yamuna Pushta, the BJP held power at the state level in Delhi, though the central government was with the Congress.
17. The words 'trading community' and 'traders' were used in English.
18. Small tea stalls, usually on street corners and pavements, often made with nothing more than a few bricks fashioned into a stove with a gas burner.
19. A mobile pushcart on which goods ranging from small consumer items to vegetables can be sold.
20. Ishwar Singh described Nirmaan as a 'union' though it is technically not registered as such.
21. Personal interview, dated 3 April 2011.
22. See Introduction and Chapter Three, this volume.
23. He used the word 'Court' in English.
24. Interview with Dunu Roy, dated 4 April 2011.
25. It is worth noting that while Kalyani counted both funded NGOs and non-funded collectives as part of 'institutionalised groups', Dunu held 'funded NGOs' as a separate category of institutions. Funding in this case usually implies international or domestic donor support or even, in some cases, governmental support.
26. Cases of industrial closures that led to significant livelihood losses, of eviction and of the forced (and costly) conversion of auto-rickshaws to compressed natural gas had, according to Sajha Manch and other commentators (see Baviskar 2003; Ramanathan 2004; among others) as 'environmental protection'. Hence the reference to the 'protection of nature' in the *parcha*.
27. Personal interview, dated 7 September 2011.
28. Personal interview, dated 8 October 2011.

29. Personal interview, dated 9 October 2011.
30. Personal interview, dated 2 April 2010.
31. Personal interview, dated 11 February 2010.
32. Personal interviews with Jawahar Raja, dated 11 February 2015, and Nivedita Menon, dated 10 Feburary 2010.
33. *Dada*s and jhuggi lords ('slumlords') are both terms used colloquially to define 'strong men' with strong associations with criminal activity or intent.
34. *National Alliance of People's Movements vs National Capital Territory of Delhi*, CWP 4229 of 1996.
35. McFarlane (2006), cited in Roy (2009a: 173).
36. *Dev Chand*.
37. *Ram Rattan and Ors vs Commissioner of Police and Ors*, Special Leave Petition (Civil) 3732 of 2005.
38. See, for example, Sajha Manch (2005, 2007, 2010).
39. For details on the history of housing, and low-income housing in particular, in Delhi, see Chapter Two, this volume.

# Concluding Provocations

## Inquiries from the South

I n the introduction to this book, I argued that the basti and its eviction are critical sites to understand dynamics of urbanism not just in Delhi but also across cities of the global South. I argued that the city, and the *basti* within it, provoked particular lines of inquiry. I followed four: spatial illegality and urban informality; governance, planning and planned development; configurations of urban citizenship; and landscapes of resistance and activism. I argued for planned illegalities and the need to understand spatial illegality relationally in auto-constructed cities, marking this as distinct from the discretions of informality as a form of rule. I showed how spatial illegality marks not just built form but residents themselves, thus mediating and differentiating negotiations of citizenship. I described how ideas of planning and planned development emerge as key rationalities and technologies of urban governance within rapidly changing cities. I sought to distinguish a study of urban politics where the core negotiations with the state are with the Judiciary rather than the Executive. I illustrated one consequence of this shift— the distinction for activists between resistance against the sarkar rather than the Court.

It is not my intention in this conclusion to summarise my arguments. Instead, I wish to return to two inquiries I laid out in the introduction as cross-cutting thematics: (a) inequality and the persistence of poverty as core sites of inquiry for southern urban theory; and (b) conceptions of a 'judicial urbanism'. Within the ethos of southern urban inquiry, I see these particularly as a set of questions *from* Delhi rather than *of* it; questions that can and should travel. In the sections that follow, I lay out these lines of inquiry while simultaneously making a case for why I believe they represent some of the more important challenges that cities of the South set up for urban theory.

I make one additional move. After laying out the analytical framework of each inquiry, I suggest a critical urban practice that emerges from them. I do so because—and perhaps I am guilty of it myself in this book—southern urban theory has not yet taken the difficulties of translating theory into reflexive and informed practice as seriously as it has its theoretical and analytical charge. If received theoretical concepts of place-less urban 'Theory' are ill-suited to cities of the South, the same is true for urban practice. Transforming one without the other would be setting ourselves up to fail.

As all conclusions ought to be, what follows is a beginning of thoughts, outlines of new inquiries, and hopefully, provocations for the production of new knowledge.

## Inequality and the Persistence of Poverty

I have argued through this book that bastis are the territorialisation of survival practices of income-poor residents across the cities of the South. They are the markers of a slow, incremental, auto-constructed existence that is negotiated at each step with a range of actors, including the law and the state. They are also and always markers of the difficulty and vulnerability of this incremental existence. Narratives of the agency, ingenuity and capacity of basti residents to survive and grow on very little, therefore, must be read alongside their structural exclusion from dignified work, access to basic services, decent housing and core human development opportunities. The basti marks this exclusion and its attendant inequalities—economic, social and political—as deeply as it does poverty.

In an eviction, decades of such incremental development—from kuccha to pucca, temporary to permanent, raw to fully formed—are erased. An eviction implies that a generation of urban residents like Rafiya, whose story began this book, will inherit the vulnerability of their parents rather than the fruits of their sacrifices. In assessing the impact of eviction and resettlement in Delhi, I described this as 'permanent poverty' (Bhan and Menon-Sen 2008). Evictions thus highlight a different aspect of poverty and inequality: their reproduction, persistence, or what Charles Tilly (1998) described as their 'durability'.

In this section, I argue that not just asking but *prioritising* questions of the persistence of poverty and inequality as sites and objects of inquiry is a way to 'see from the south' (Watson 2009). It is precisely because we are dealing with 'social worlds of massive and extreme inequality', as James Ferguson argues, that it is not just necessary but imperative 'to ask how inequalities are socially institutionalised' (2013: 233). In what follows, I sketch the outline of one way to structure such an inquiry that is particularly provoked by the basti and its eviction—looking at configurations and transformations of the urban welfare state.

I choose welfare for a number of reasons. Welfare, Partha Chatterjee has argued, at its simplest, represents a 'generalized obligation to care' for the poor and marginalised (Urban Poverty and Inequality Collective 2015) in order to realise a socially-determined and dynamic set of resources and entitlements needed to live life with dignity. Welfare is often invoked in debates on how to address and alleviate both poverty and inequality, particularly in the definitions of capabilities, basic needs, rights and public goods. It is able to straddle both equality of outcomes as well as of capabilities or opportunity (A. Sen 1992, 1999). It remains—even if operationally privatised—a public debate. Its simplest promise is to prevent destitution; its grandest is to make income and wealth less determinant of dignity and opportunity.

Yet the primary reason I focus on welfare in the context of this chapter is because it makes material our location in cities of the South. Questions of poverty and inequality are, of course, deeply relevant to cities in the North. Yet the socio-economic geographies of poverty, inequality and destitution are one of the most salient and empirically evident differences between cities of the South and the North. These are not just differences of degree—though the presence of large-scale destitution in many cities of the South rather than just poverty or high income inequality is not a small matter. They are differences of kind, of configurations of welfare and histories of development that have emerged as 'the consequence of historically developed economic and political relations' (Mosse 2010).

Let me take one example. Debates on an urban welfare state in the South speak of cities that, for the most part, were never marked by what Castells called collective consumption—the notion of the publicly negotiated use of shared, city-wide infrastructure and basic services for core urban needs (Castells 1977 [1972], 1983). It is this notion of networked infrastructure that theorists argue has 'splintered' within neoliberalism (Graham and Marvin 2001). Yet what does a 'splinter' look like if the network was never built? Many cities of the South were never defined by anything like collective consumption. Core infrastructures neither existed nor ever marked what it meant to be an urban resident. Everyday life in many places has not yet seen asphalt, water, electricity and brick, or has known them only for one generation. Existing infrastructures are often either tenuous, fragmented and temporary, or privately provided at great cost within enclaves.

Enough has been written about the need to move beyond the narrative of the 'retreat' of a state that never built enough roads, public housing or sewers—that had, in other words, nothing to retreat from but the promise that it would eventually provide. As I have argued in this book, even this promise now stands challenged. What then does it mean to think of transformations in welfare as the suspension of a deferred and incomplete spatio-temporal project rather than a 'withdrawal'? This question is particularly critical as many parts of the global South shift away from erstwhile resource constraints. My intention here is not to paint southern urban theory only as a study of precarity. Certainly, several cities and states are no longer simply 'resource poor'. This adds further to the need for a southern research agenda that asks how states that can no longer defer the promises of development on the grounds of resource poverty or incapacity continue to evade redistribution in the presence of not just inequality but widespread destitution.

How then should we theorise welfare from the South? James Ferguson's recent work (2013) offers an excellent starting point. Ferguson is writing about 'declarations of dependence' in South Africa at a moment when, as he says, one faces the fact that full employment and wage labour can no longer be the end of the developmental telos nor the way of life of even a large number of urban residents. Ferguson is asking a critical question: If informal employment is not a transitionary stage to full employment, then how do societies manage residents-not-workers that are also a demographic majority? What kind of politics is possible from within an impossibility of dignified and secure work? Ferguson offers one answer—new relations of dependence. Distinguishing between 'thick and thin relations of dependence,' he argues that the aim of development cannot be 'freedom' for the real problem for many is that freedom has come to represent a reality where they are 'not worth subjecting, cast off from the societal snowball ... for those thus abjected, subjection can only appear as step up' (ibid.: 231).

Ferguson's provocation is precisely the kind of unsettling that southern theory needs and can offer. Let us generalise his particular argument to a broader theoretical agenda: How do we imagine politics and political subjectivities of welfare without dignified work? What kind of urbanism is produced from a regime of chronic diminished employment? What kind of welfare regime will it require?

It is worth remembering here that subaltern urban residents in Indian cities seem able to win claims to food and basic education but not work, land, infrastructure or shelter—entitlements to reproduction but not redistribution. Evictions mark this distinction powerfully, coming at a time when the same Judiciary is expanding social rights to information, education and food. To then turn a contemporary question of developmental practice on its head: Are recent global moves to structure welfare through income grants and cash transfers really about efficiency and targeting, or, in fact, about the recognition that a contemporary welfare regime can no longer assume work contributions? To bring back Jayal from Chapter Three, is the expansion of some social rights a move to more egalitarian welfare states or an example of Marshall's 'class abatement'?

These arguments echo with those made by the recently formed Urban Poverty and Inequality Collective of which Ferguson and I are both members.[1] Seeking to interrogate new formations of the welfare state in the South, the collective seeks to depart from 'the North Atlantic welfare state and the notions of personhood on which its entitlements rest.' Instead it ponders: how do we trace 'emergent new empirical configurations' which may enable us to 're-imagine "the social" as an object both of theory and of politics' (Urban Poverty and Inequality Collective 2015: 8–12)? The collective charts out a theoretical and research agenda to interrogate new technologies of governing poverty; imagine post-labourist forms of personhood and claims to welfare; trace new relational geographies of geopolitical alignment and power; assess democratic forms of the reproduction of spatial inequality; trace altered urban and global political economies; and critique discourses of participation and governance. These are a set of inquiries from the South—clearly relevant in the North but shaped in and by the contexts from which they originate.

*New regimes of urban welfare*: Let us apply some of these inquiries in a specific site to illustrate translations of southern inquiries into critical and located urban practice. In this section, I take the case of the emergent urban welfare state in India. Historically, the Indian welfare state has largely been rurally imagined. Programmes of social security—ranging from enabling and rights-based entitlements to basic transfers seeking to prevent destitution—have been and remain focused on rural poverty and vulnerability. Even a glance makes this evident: there are no urban equivalents to the National Rural Employment Guarantee Scheme, the National Rural Health Mission or the National Rural Electrification Mission, to take just some examples.

Recently, however, the makings of an urban welfare state have begun to emerge. While still fragmented, a framework for social security—from principles and entitlements to policies and programmes—is beginning to take shape in urban areas. The list of its possible components is substantial: from the proposed urban livelihood mission to the already won Right to Education; social security for unorganised sector workers to growing debates on entitlements to housing; expansion of basic environmental services to universal health insurance as well as the initiation of cash and direct transfer programmes. Together, this range of urban interventions could potentially see the emergence, for the first time, of an integrated urban welfare regime that defines rights and entitlements for urban residents. It will be, therefore, a crucial battleground where growth-centred paradigms of urban development will negotiate questions of equity, welfare, redistribution and rights. What form should this welfare regime take?

The arguments of this book suggest that whether such a welfare state expands outcomes rather than just rights will, in part, depend on its rooting itself within the realities of contemporary Indian urbanism: auto-construction, spatial illegalities, differentiated urban citizenship, altered political economies and judicial emergence. One characteristic of the design of a welfare regime thus becomes key: the definition of 'resident'. I argued in this book that spatial illegality acts precisely as a mode of impoverishment by denying legitimacy, belonging and the right to have rights to basti residents. It imagines them, as Mary Douglas (1966) would argue, 'matter out of place'. Any 'universal' welfare regime then will have to grapple with the fact that spatial illegality will exclude a significant set of residents—either through de jure limitations or de facto procedural exclusions. The Right to Education is an important case in point. When the newly enacted right in India argues that all children are entitled to admission in a local school within a certain geographical area, is the address within a basti considered part of the 'local' geography? Fittingly, given the arguments to follow in this conclusion, this question is currently being decided in the courts.

There are two moves to be made here. The first insists on spatialising a welfare state designed for rural areas within the urban. The second is realising that, especially within the auto-constructed city, the category of 'urban' is not legally or spatially self-evident but negotiated and historically constituted in different ways. The articulation of a 'universal' welfare regime then itself must change. Two policies in India recognise this: the Rajiv Awas Yojana (RAY) and the National Urban Sanitation Policy (NUSP).

At the time of writing, the RAY is the Government of India's ambitious policy intervention on housing the poor. Reading the policy, it seems to signal a possible paradigm shift in thinking about urban residents within the history of India's developmental policies. RAY begins with a clear articulation of the right of all citizens—it uses the word—to come to and be in the city as well as have shelter within it. It acknowledges the failure of the state in keeping its own commitments to housing the poor as well as not enabling the market to reach them. It attempts through the provision of what it calls (though does not clearly define) 'property rights'. In many ways, then, RAY is an expression of a right to shelter that stands as a direct response to the 'illegality' of the poor.

RAY stands alongside another significant policy move in urban India: the de-linking the legality of a household's tenurial status with the provision of basic environmental services. Previously, public service providers were not able to legally provide, for example, environmental services like water and sanitation to settlements in the city that were seen as 'unauthorised' or 'illegal'. Spatial illegality, in other words, placed a de jure limit on access to services. New policy paradigms explicitly challenge this limitation. The NUSP states that: 'every urban dweller should be provided with minimum levels of sanitation, *irrespective of the legal status of the land in which he/she is dwelling*, possession of identity proof or status of migration.'[2]

Yet the provision of sanitation and other services cannot guarantee security of tenure. In the context of eviction, the NUSP is of little use. Here, RAY becomes critical as does the importance of re-signifying another familiar concept: property.

RAY argues that it shall improve security of tenure through the granting of 'property rights'. What is a 'property right' in an auto-constructed community with tenuous legality? Is it ownership? A right to sell and buy? A title? Is it the right to use? The right not to be evicted? Is the right necessarily individual? Can it be communal, co-operative or common? What rights does one have to land that is 'public'? How are 'property rights' related to security of tenure—the ability (in many ways as important to the poor as ownership) of being able to stay in place?

A basti unsettles self-evident notions of property into its constituent and often contradictory elements: use vs exchange, the right to own vs to remain, to survive vs to accumulate. This is precisely why innovations in re-imagining such rights and systems of valuing land are emerging from southern cities: the Zone of Special Social Importance (ZEIS) in São Paulo or the 'Permission to Use' from the Baan Mankong programme in Bangkok. I have written elsewhere about the need of a similar innovation needed for Indian cities: the Intent to Reside (ITR) approach (Bhan, Goswami and Revi 2014).

The ITR approach works on embracing universal (or quasi-universal) entitlements through evidence of an *intention* to reside in the city that includes residents at an early stage of this residence. The ITR approach is, in a sense, the antithesis to a 'cut-off date' or of the conditions in which particular residents inhabited the city. Rather than asking residents to prove that they deserve to be included as urban residents by surviving for years in the city, it includes them from the very beginning. It attempts at being more mindful of errors of exclusion within a context of universalisation and in real situations where operationalisation and implementation of services are themselves premised on conditions and modes of residence and spatial illegality.

A final point then is to imagine what claims this resident can make of and from the city. RAY and NUSP stand alongside a series of other policy interventions that address impoverishment in Indian cities. These are: the National Urban Livelihoods Mission (NULM), expanded social security schemes for informal work under the Unorganised Sector Social Security Act, the newly–constitutionally enshrined Right to Education as well as the passage of the National Food Security Bill.

Do these schemes suggest a possible opening to re-imagine, as Ferguson wanted us to do, personhood and citizenship in the configuration of the social? If urban residents are beneficiaries of livelihood promotions through the NULM or the Unorganised Workers Social Security Act, they are not just 'encroachers' but also workers. Importantly, they can then access the institutions of the state—the Executive and the Judiciary—with protected, textual and statutory rights or at least formal claims within policies and programmes. If *all* urban residents possess rights to services like water and sanitation as well as education and livelihoods, the provision of these entitlements signals the possibility of reconfiguring the presence of the subaltern urban residents as well as reframing how the basti is seen within the city. It forces even a judicial understanding of illegal settlement to contend with a set of other imperatives and rights.

These policies enable at least a partial claim of a right to the city because they are *urban* policies—they are premised on residence within the city. Unlike previous regimes of poverty alleviation, they do not exclusively identify beneficiaries as targeted groups marked by their relationship to, for example, the poverty line, or imagine urban citizens simply as rural residents out of place. They represent, in other words, new criteria for the group differentiated citizenship I discussed in Chapter Three. They use a language of universal rights and entitlements—they do not separate the basti from the city, the income poor from the elite. They make possible, therefore, practices of citizenship that argue against regimes of differentiation between different urban citizens. They allow movement towards what Jayal (2013) would call the social and civic solidarity necessary for citizenship to achieve substantial rather than just formal equality.

Finally, they suggest a different imagination of a 'worker' in line with Ferguson's call for post-labourist claims to welfare and Gidwani's provocation to think of claims that come from shack dwellers, waste-pickers and street vendors rather than from the wage labourers of the factory (Urban Poverty and Inequality Collective 2015). In a parallel to Castell's challenge to urban Marxists to think of consumption and the neighbourhood rather than just production and the factory (Castells 1977 [1972], 1983), urban welfare states imagined around informal workers suggest different geographies of work, production and consumption. These are claims to welfare-as-entitlement rather than welfare-as-charity, yet they are rooted in the realities of informal work that is, as Hariss-White and Prosperi (2014) remind us, not going to 'transition out' with economic development and rising incomes. Just as importantly, these are claims made in and to urban space, as much about the right to be in the city as to work within it. As the successful passage of the National Street Vendors Act in 2014 indicates, this is possibly a fruitful location from which to make claims to the city that both emerges from and is rooted within the cities it seeks to transform.

## Judicial Urbanism

In independent India, the Judiciary has often exceeded any constitutional imagination of a balance of powers with the Executive and the Legislature. It has been remarked, in fact, that the Indian Supreme Court is 'one of the most powerful among democratic polities' (Mate 2015) especially since the rise of PIL in the 1970s. As this book has argued, contemporary debates on the balance of powers have centred on the active and dynamic engagement of the courts—described as 'judicial activism'—in passing orders that are increasingly 'administrative' (Sathe 2002: 238) in character. PILs have seen the courts, argue scholars, 'obliterate the line between law and policy' (Muralidhar and Desai 2000) and move the 'character of the judicial process from adversarial to polycentric, adjudicative to legislative' (Sathe 2002: 235). Manoj Mate (2013) has termed this as the 'judicialisation of governance'.

This is a pattern that arguably extends far beyond India. Particularly relevant given our interest in southern urban inquiry is the argument made by John Comaroff and Jean Comaroff (2008) that judicialisation seems to be shared across diverse post-colonial contexts. Using a range of examples from the drug trade to real estate, generic drugs to evictions, they describe a 'judicialisation of politics' in much of the post-colonial world. Politics itself, they argue, is 'migrating to the Courts. Conflicts once joined in parliament, by means of street protests, mass demonstrations, and media campaigns, through labour boycotts, and other instruments of assertion, to name a few—now tend more and more to head to the Courts' (Comaroff and Comaroff 2008: 27).

This transition is occurring particularly in the post-colonial world, they argue, because of a contemporary moment marked by deepening neoliberalism, lawlessness, corruption and the 'failure' of government. Within this 'disorder', they argue, the law is fetishised. 'Legal instruments *appear* to offer a repertoire of more or less standardized terms and practices,' they claim, 'that permit the negotiation of values, beliefs, ideals and interests across otherwise impermeable lines of cleavage' (ibid.: 32). To engage with the law is no longer a choice but an inevitability, making the terms of such engagement a critical question for politics.

Their claims echo my own in different ways. In Chapter Two, I argued similarly that one of the ways in which the Judiciary claimed an ethico-moral imperative to intervene into the city was through the narrative of 'failure' of the institutions of the Executive and the 'crisis' of planned development that thus ensued. The courts, indeed, often portrayed themselves as the only alternative to an incompetent, informalised and criminalised Executive. This vision had and has significant popular appeal. It is undoubted that the Indian Judiciary continues to possess a sense of moral as well as legal authority as it expands its power and jurisdiction. In Chapter Four, let us remember, even the activist Ishwar Singh spoke of the *maryaada* (honour) of the Judiciary as an institution despite having been evicted through its orders.

How do we locate and spatialise the 'judicialisation of governance' and the 'judicialisation of politics' within the city? Throughout this book, I have marked the emergence of the Judiciary as an institution playing an increasingly powerful role in shaping the contemporary Indian city. I have shown how the courts actively produce the city, shaping the built environment,

governance, planning, rights and citizenship. I have argued—
if implicitly—that they increasingly shape urbanism.

The deepening imbrications of law and urbanism demand
careful scrutiny. Prima facie, they suggest that as the authority
and jurisdiction of the courts widen in the city, a series of
questions, interventions and processes come to be articulated
and addressed within the logics of law. The political becomes
legal, much as the activist Ramendra mused in chapter four:
'*ki ab mamla legal ho gaya hai* (now the matter has become
legal).'

How should we read this transition? One way is to bring back
a framework used in Chapter Two. As the courts increasingly
take polycentric and administrative decisions—as they govern—
in order to intervene in the city, their actions will require what
Inda (2005) summarised as the key elements of an analysis of
government: reason, technics and subjects. In other words, the
presence of the Judiciary in the city can be read through the
rationalities, technologies and subjectivities that it both draws
from and shapes. In what follows, I bring together various
arguments in the book to offer an example of each of these three
elements. I do so to suggest that, taken together, they outline
the contours of a *judicial urbanism*. At the end of this section,
I offer an opening definition of such an urbanism and suggest
that it is an important inquiry from the South.

First: rationalities. I cited Teresa Caldeira (2014) earlier in
describing how a dominant mode of the production of space
in cities of the global South—auto-construction—was marked by
'transversal engagements with official logics of legal property'.
Urban theory has understood such production primarily through
the idiom of urban informality, which Roy re-fashioned from a
defined spatial form or sector into a 'new spatial vocabulary
of control, governance and territorial flexibility' (A. Roy 2003:
157) where the state could use its discretion to 'decide what is
informal and what is not, to determine which forms of informality
will thrive and which will disappear' (A. Roy 2005: 182).

Within a judicial register, as I argued in Chapter One, this
discretion or flexibility in governance is deeply constrained and
its terms altered. The increasing importance of 'spatial illegality'

as opposed to informality to mark the production of space signals a clear shift in the spaces of political negotiation *within* the state from the Executive to the Judiciary. To apply the Comaroffs' argument would imply considering this shift as partly inevitable: in a city built within uncertain relationships with law, the courts are inevitable sites where 'transversal engagements' and their logics will conflict and have to be resolved.

Yet on what terms shall this resolution take place? Evictions make visible one set of rationalities on the basis of which the Judiciary seeks to resolve uncertainties arising from auto-construction in the contemporary moment. As Chapter Two detailed, the courts used the symptom of 'encroachment' to diagnose the 'failure' of the institutions of the Executive and the 'crisis' of 'planned development' that thus ensued. This failure is precisely a governmental rationality that legitimises judicial governance 'in relation to a truth' (Rose 1999: 25) that it, in part, constructs. A particular reading of 'spatial illegality' thus becomes a key ordering principle through which to regulate and govern the built environment. It is a principle, importantly, from within the judicial register, representing an idiom (illegality) recognisable in law rather than one outside it (informality).

Second: technologies. As the courts govern, they need technologies of intervention. The arguments of this book suggest that, in a judicial register, a greater importance seems to accrue to the presence of formal and statutory forms of law, policy and rights as technologies of governance regardless of the success or 'failure' of their implementation. In Chapter Two, I described this through the reading of 'plan in its legal position' that transformed a public and policy document into law. This translation insulated the Plan from its own systems of change and review, shielded it from public advocacy and accountability, and also allowed a simplification—to use James Scott's term—as 'a complex set of relations and processes' were reduced to a 'single element of instrumental value' (1998: 77). The Plan in its legal position bound the city as governable space, reducing the complexity of the city to all that does or does not ally with it at any given time. It became both law and ideal, stripped of history and politics.

Concluding Provocations

Studies of governance in the global South, particularly influenced by debates on informality, have long been uncertain about the value of formal (often seen as 'top-down') and legal change in contexts marked by the informal, extra-legal and unplanned. I am not suggesting that judicialisation suddenly empowers plans and policies to realise themselves exactly on the ground, or that the courts don't selectively enforce one policy or law over another. Yet, within a judicial register, the 'traces', to use a term from the first chapter, of formal and textual law become increasingly relevant as modes of political engagement in shaping outcomes in the 'real city'. Judicial emergence means it is more imperative than ever for urban political practices to grapple with new and innovative forms of planning and policy-making precisely in places where, as Sheppard, Leitner and Maringanti argue, 'it is difficult to plan and yet where planning cannot be abandoned' (2013: 895). I have argued this in different ways throughout this book, be it in the arguments in Chapter One for planners to practice 'occupancy urbanism' (Benjamin 2008), or in Chapter Four in emphasising the need for a textual and constitutionally-embedded right to housing.

A judicial register challenges different actors seeking to shape urban politics to (in an ironic parallel to basti residents) exist on paper. This is partially precisely because of the possibility of an increasingly entrenched judicial urbanism where the 'formal and legal' are no longer fictions, contrary to what Ananya Roy once argued. It also implies the need to make law rather than just be bound by it and see the creation of new law as a critical site of urban political change. This is already underway. Not only are urban social movements struggling to expand social rights and enforce constitutional protections through law, there is, as Nandini Sundar reminded us in Chapter Four, a 'growing middle-class emphasis on the rule of law and procedure, especially when it is subverted by the bureaucracy or the rich' (2011: 423). The law then is very much as Baxi described, 'a peril and a promise,' enmeshed within a broader urban politics and political economy. It can neither be reduced to a space for emancipatory politics nor one of elite control.

247

Third: subjectivity, personhood and citizenship. The law is a key site where each of us comes to understand notions of personhood and citizenship. I showed in Chapter Three that judicial pronouncements are part of shaping regimes of urban citizenship though they do not do so in isolation from broader changes in developmentalism outside the courtroom. In that chapter, I detailed how the discursive and legal category of the 'encroacher' bound the citizenship of basti residents to an act of occupation just as their vulnerability was ignored amidst a broader criminalisation. As the ideas of 'encroacher' and 'encroachment' travelled within the courtroom and the city, a particular and legal reading of presence in the auto-constructed city narrowed the possibilities of citizenship and belonging.

Yet the implications of the political becoming legal are perhaps most evident in the impact of judicial emergence on practices of resistance. As I argued in Chapter Four, there is a significant shift in fighting what activists called the sarkar—the institutions of the Executive—and the Court. This new site for struggle imposes upon movements the need to choose new strategies, negotiate new institutions and take on the twin burdens of translating rights-claims into arguments that make 'legal sense' while finding claimants that are 'legally defensible' instead of being morally and politically worthy in other registers. Strategies of resistance are further compromised as the right and obligation to contest the Executive or sarkar is contrasted with the sense among activists that they don't have a right to fight the Court. This sense is strongly rooted in a sense of distance from the Court—both in the literal barriers to access as well as the symbolic distance in the imagination of the social and political position of the Court in the lives of urban residents.

A *judicial urbanism* thus suggests a mode of urbanisation where the production of space, social struggles over the meaning of space, and the possibilities of urban citizenship are significantly determined in a judicial register. This register privileges, recognises and produces a set of (a) governmental rationalities, (b) technics and modes of political engagement, as well as (c) forms of personhood and subjectivity that draw from the logics of law. In doing so, it alters regimes of urban governance, shapes state-citizen relations, mediates regimes of value within the urban economy, and impacts the form as well as outcomes of the apparatuses of public policy and planning.

In this book, I have shown what one set of such rationalities, modes and practices look like as they are made visible in the case law on eviction. Yet this case law is only one small part of judicial interventions into the contemporary Indian city. Let me take just five of innumerable examples of other Court decisions that would add other rationalities, technologies and subjectivities. In Delhi, the removal of 'polluting' industries from the city centre led to massive livelihood losses for workers just as high-end retail commercial complexes were allowed to be built on protected green spaces in the city. In Mumbai, erstwhile mill lands stretching over acres in the heart of a land-starved city were given over almost entirely to upscale commercial redevelopment with almost no allocations for public space or low-income housing just as the courts also refused to allow extension of water supply into bastis. In Bangalore, the courts agreed to hear petitions by private developers to remove or reduce mandatory reservations on them requiring them to build certain quotas of low-income housing just as they refused to intervene to order compensation and resettlement for post-eviction households. In Chennai, it was the courts that decided where to locate land for landfills after trucks of solid waste were refused by one peri-urban community after another.

In each of these sets of cases, I have deliberately juxtaposed the complexity of competing claims to and in the city that are pivotal to the concerns of this book: inequality and citizenship. Further research needs to unearth the rationalities, technologies and subjectivities that emerge from within this broader set of urban case law in order to both empirically enrich as well as conceptually refine our understanding of judicial urbanism.

Such work is critical and timely. My intent in this book was not to study judicial urbanism. Yet I am one of the researchers working on diverse questions on Indian urbanism that have found themselves at the doorsteps of the courts. This is a telling gathering that deserves further analysis. While rich bodies of work are emerging on individual sectoral engagements with the law—PILs on environmental issues, for example, or on informal work, or on evictions—work has been slower to bring these together and suggest the Judiciary's significant (dominant?) role in shaping urbanism over the past two decades. The work of scholars like Asher Ghertner (2011b), Vinay Gidwani (Gidwani and Reddy 2011), Diya Mehra (2013), Anuj Bhuwania (2013) and Ayona Datta (2012) are all encouraging beginnings in looking seriously at the law and urbanism, particularly looking at how, as Datta frames it, 'encounters with the law in everyday life' destabilise the binaries of urban studies—'state-citizen, urban poor-middle class, city-slum, centre-periphery' (2013: 518).

Doing so must enrich not just our conceptual frameworks, however, but our practices particularly when the object of our study is inequality and exclusion in our own cities. As the introduction quoted Caldeira as saying, we cannot leave the cities of which we are citizens 'untouched, implicit, and unspoken about.'[3] If judicial urbanism offers us new inquiries, we must also translate them into critical and effective urban practice. In concluding this section, then, let me illustrate how my own study of judicial urbanism provoked one such translation. I do so by picking up where I left off in Chapter Four looking at provocations that judicial urbanism levels at urban social movements.

*Re-tooling urban social movements*: Judicial urbanism makes one thing clear: the law, and within it the Plan, must now become objects and sites of a politics of resistance in the city. How then can urban social movements respond to this new frontier of political action? I offer three thoughts on new forms of practice shaped by a need to respond to and within judicial urbanism.

One, movements must claim the city and not just the basti. Urban social movements have rarely articulated their claims as claims to and within the city. I argued in the book that lawyers defending basti residents would describe them as 'citizens of India', or still describe them as 'migrants' even when they had been urban residents for decades, in sharp contrast to petitions from elite residents who described themselves as 'citizens of

Delhi'. Urban social movements and basti residents must re-scale their arguments to the city—they must produce the city through these claims just as the courts re-scaled the determination of public interest to the scale of the city. It is in claiming an urban rather than national citizenship with the city as the primary political community of reference and belonging, to paraphrase James Holston (2008), that the presence of the poor both within and outside the courtroom can go beyond its reduction to the 'encroacher' and 'encroachment'.

If the Court has reduced the basti to the slum, then social movements must refuse this simplification. They must reinsert the basti residents into the imagination of the city as city-markers, workers, residents, tax payers, consumers and voters all at once. The emergent policy regimes discussed earlier in this chapter could allow for such a reframing to be tied with the policy directions of the Executive, a move that could both enable a new judicial discourse on the poor as well as hold the Executive accountable for the implementation of its policy landscape.

This implies the construction of new solidarities that take an urban location seriously. Social movements in Delhi have often been deeply divided along identity lines like gender and caste or along different types of rights-claims—as dalits, as women, as workers, as Muslims. The city offers the possibility of both integration as well as intersection across these claims—intersections that reflect more accurately the lived experience of its residents. After all, workers are also Muslim, women are also dalits. Can an urban location provide a useful intersection of rights-claims to the city? Do movements gain from a shared articulation that could be the basis of at least some part of their claims in a claim to the city?

Two, movements must challenge the very foundations of their exclusion: notions of property, ownership and the value of land and, in the case of Delhi in particular, of the use of public land. The idea of 'encroachment' implies that public land cannot be valued in terms of its use by, for example, the city's poorest residents as a source of shelter. Yet if we think, taking inspiration from Brazil's federal law—the City Statute—of the 'social function of property', new possibilities of valuing land emerge that give equal precedence to its use rather than reducing questions of its ownership simply to title and estimations of its value simply to its price within the land market. Within auto-constructed cities marked by a judicial urbanism, social movements have no choices but to conceptually and legally re-signify key terms such as property, illegality and informality.

By taking on conceptions and definitions of property and land within the city, social movements can alter the urban landscape as well as challenge the judicial interpretation of property as a particular form of 'ownership' rather than a range of relationships to settlement and use. This could also enable them to re-frame illegalities relationally. Yet new articulations of these relationships must also ensure that they take a form that is judicially defensible and makes 'legal sense'. What can these forms look like? On what basis can tenurial security be provided to basti residents that is judicially defensible?

Three, movements must make law. In the city, by extension, they must make the Plan or at least find means and mechanisms to reject its judicial power. The twin challenges of the judicialisation of politics and resistance in part implies that movements must empower themselves to challenge the Court on its own terms. If the Court is bound by law, then the legislative power of the Executive and Parliament must become a focus of social movements. Movements of the elite have long exercised this power by using their proximity to the law-making institutions within the state to their advantage. The path for social movements will not be so easy yet too many contemporary urban movements in India have seen institutional reform, policy changes, planning and the law as sites irrelevant to the lives of the poor who are seen to live beyond the formal world of institutional civil society, outside planning, and outside the world of 'policy' except as its distant objects. Judicial urbanism erases this distance. It brings, once again, a new set of challenges for social movements to transform, translate and locate an older claim of equality and justice in a new site in Indian politics.

## A Final Word and A Surprising Election

This book marks a moment in which the city emerged into the political imagination of the nation in India. Contemporary evictions remind us that this moment is also one in which rights have been lost, where citizenship is inegalitarian and differentiated, the promise of development is refused, and poverty and inequality are reproduced and deepened. For any effective conceptualisation and realisation of a just city, we must understand this moment in all its particularities, continuities and discontinuities from others like those that have faced us before. The task at hand then is not just to explain evictions but also to listen to what they are telling us—about the city that is as well as the city that can be.

Yet what they are telling us may also be changing even as we speak. As this book came to its final stages of editing, Delhi changed. Through 2013, the city was the focal point of massive national popular mobilisations as part of the India Against Corruption campaigns led, among others, by Anna Hazare and Arvind Kejriwal. The campaigns were complex phenomena but, despite divergent views on their ideology and efficacy, there is little disagreement that they captured and shaped a political moment. Kejriwal, with other leaders of the movement such as Prashant Bhushan (who featured prominently in Chapter Four of this book), as well as noted political scientist Yogendra Yadav, ex-senior policewoman Kiran Bedi (who would later leave the party for the BJP and contest directly against Kejriwal), and others, decided to transition from a people's movement to a formal political party. The Aam Aadmi Party (Common Man's Party) was born.

In a book that has sought to take discourse seriously, the language and politics of the AAP is un-mistakable. Their symbol is a broom. They speak the language of urban citizenship that much of this book has sought out but failed to find within the languages of the courts. Much of their political innovations as a party—as opposed to their moral high-ground as a mass movement—have drawn from efforts at deepening participatory democracy: referenda via mobile SMS messaging, mohalla sabhas on a range of issues from local governance to party ideology, a raft of volunteers to make party cadres.

In 2013, the AAP contested State Assembly elections in Delhi. They emerged as the second-largest party with 28 of 70 seats, and formed a government with support from the Congress Party. It faltered. A mere 49-days later, Arvind Kejriwal resigned as chief minister. Fresh elections to overcome a hung Parliament were called in February 2015. This time history was written: AAP won 67 of 70 seats, the largest majority any party had ever won in the city.

One of AAP's first moves was to declare a ban on evictions. It's a symbolic gesture since in Delhi's complicated federal structure as a National Capital Territory, the Government of Delhi does not have the authority to prevent evictions, for example, on land owned by the DDA. Yet the declaration matters a great deal beyond its legal and statutory jurisdictions. In a city scarred by evictions, the declaration of an elected government that evictions violated the Right to the City for many is a tremendous shift in public discourse, perception and politics. For each of the arguments of this book, the new Government of Delhi may cause foundational changes. A declaration against evictions implies an Executive that will mount a very different challenge within the Judiciary when cases of evictions return to the courts as they undoubtedly will. AAP's diagnosis of the 'crisis' and 'failure' of urban governance is a markedly different reading than the judicial narratives I discussed in Chapter Two.

In its move to replace RWAs and the Congress government's Bhagidari systems with mohalla sabhas, they have challenged the links between spatial illegality and urban citizenship outlined in Chapter Three. In their first budget, spending on healthcare and education have been tripled and doubled to be at their highest allocations ever. Manish Sisodia, presenting the budget for the government, described it as the basis of a 'development model that was driven from the bottom instead of a top-driven one as it was prepared by the public at the Mohalla Sabhas.'[4] In one sense, AAP echoes this book's own claim: to speak to and about the city from its peripheries. Does this imply a deepening of the resistance against the processes of impoverishment described in Chapter Three?

Yet AAP's emergence is also fraught. Dissent and fractures within the party have begun to emerge leading to the expulsion of two of its most visible faces: Prashant Bhushan and Yogendra Yadav. The very public expulsion has lent significant credence to accusations of Kejriwal's undemocratic leadership and intolerance for disagreement within the party and his government. Doubts abound on whether the party has the ability to translate its vision and discourse into implementation when it is up against deeply entrenched economic and power structures. AAP will have to take on the discursive and structural legacies of inequality that have marked the city's economic emergence and transformation in the last decade, many of which have been the subject of this book. How it does will shape not just the fledgling party itself but the diverse set of urban futures that will become possible for *dilliwallas*. As Rafiya would often mimick me chanting at anti-eviction protests: '*yeh to abhi angdai hai, aage aur ladai hai* (this is but a pitstop, a long fight still lies ahead).'

# Notes

1. Other members of the still growing collective include Partha Chatterjee, Ananya Roy, Vinay Gidwani, Teresa Caldeira, Maxine Molyneux, Gianpaolo Biaocchi and Richard Pitthouse.
2. Annexure 1, p. 13 of Government of India (2006). Emphasis added.
3. See Chapter One, this volume.
4. http://www.thehindu.com/news/national/delhi-budget-201516-education-health-major-focus-in-aaps-first-budget/article7354469.ece (accessed 10 September 2015).

# References

Anjaria, J. S. 2009. 'Guardians of the Bourgeois City: Citizenship, Public Space, and Middle-Class Activism in Mumbai'. *City & Community* 8 (4): 391–406.

Appadurai, Arjun. 2001. 'Deep Democracy: Urban Governmentality and the Horizon of Politics'. *Environment & Urbanisation* 13 (2): 23–43.

———. 2002. 'Deep Democracy: Urban Governmentality and the Horizon of Politics'. *Public Culture* 14 (1): 21–47.

Balibar, E. 1988. 'Propositions of Citizenship'. *Ethics* 4: 723–30.

Banting, K. and W. Kymlicka. 2006. *Multiculturalism and the Welfare State: Recognition and Redistribution in Contemporary Democracies.* Oxford: Oxford University Press.

Baross, P. 1987. 'Land Supply for Low-income Housing: Issues and Approaches'. *Regional Development Dialogue* 8 (4): 29–50.

Baviskar, A. 2003. 'Between Violence and Desire: Space, Power and Identity in the Making of Metropolitan Delhi'. *International Social Science Journal* 55 (175): 89–98.

———. 2007. 'Delhi's Date with the Common Wealth Games 2010'. *Games Monitor* 11.

———. 2011. 'Spectacular Events, City Spaces and Citizenship: The Commonwealth Games in Delhi' in *Urban Navigations: Politics, Space and the City in South Asia*, edited by J. S. Anjaria and C. McFarlane, 138–61. London: Routledge.

Baxi, U. 1988. *Law and Poverty: Critical Essays.* Bombay: N. M. Tripathi.

———. 1997. 'Judicial Activism: Usurpation or Re-Democratization?' *Social Action* 47 (October–December): 341–57.

Baxi, U. 2000. 'The Avatars of Indian Judicial Activism: Explorations in the Geographies of [In] Justice' in *The Indian Supreme Court: Fifty Years Later*, edited by S. Verma and Kusum, 156–209. New Delhi: Oxford University Press.

———. 2002. 'Introduction' in *Judicial Activism in India*, S. P. Sathe, *x–xxi*. New Delhi: Oxford University Press.

———. 2003. 'Rule of Law: Theory and Practice' in *Asian Discourses of Rule of Law*, edited by R. Peerenboom, 324–45. London: Routledge.

Bayat, A. 2000. '"From Dangerous Classes" to "Quiet Rebels": Politics of the Urban Subaltern in the Global South'. *International Sociology* 15 (3): 533–57.

Benjamin, S. 2004. 'Urban Land Transformation for Pro-Poor Economies'. *Geoforum* 35 (2): 177–87.

———. 2008. 'Occupancy Urbanism: Radicalizing Politics and Economy beyond Policy and Programs'. *International Journal of Urban and Regional Research* 32 (3): 719–29.

———. 2014. 'Occupancy Urbanism: An Anti-Planning Manifesto' in *Routledge Handbook on Cities of the Global South*, edited by S. Parnell and S. Oldfied, 309–21. London: Routledge.

Benjamin, S. and B. Raman. 2012. 'Claiming Land: Rights, Contestations and the Urban Poor in Globalised Times' in *Urban Policies and the Right to the City in India*, edited by M.-H. Zerah, S. Lama Rewal and V. Dupont, 63–75. New Delhi: Centre des Sciences Humaines.

Bhan, Gautam. 2009. '"This is not the City I once Knew": Evictions, Urban Poor and the Right to the City in Millennial Delhi'. *Environment & Urbanisation* 21 (1): 127–42.

———. 2012. 'In the Public's Interest: Evictions, Citizenship and Inequality in Contemporary Delhi'. Unpublished PhD dissertation, University of California, Berkeley, California.

———. 2013. 'Planned Illegalities'. *Economic and Political Weekly* 48 (24): 58–70.

Bhan, G., A. Goswami and A. Revi. 2014. 'The Intent to Reside: Spatial Illegality, Inclusive Planning, and Urban Social Security' in *State of the Urban Poor Report 2013*, edited by O. Mathur, 83–94. New Delhi: Oxford University Press.

Bhan, G. and K. Menon-Sen. 2008. *Swept Off the Map: Surviving Eviction and Resettlement in Delhi*. New Delhi: Yoda Press.

Bhan, G. and A. Roy. 2013. 'Lessons from Somewhere'. *Cityscapes* 4: 80–89.

Bhan, G. and S. Shivanand. 2013. '(Un)Settling the City: Analysing Displacement in Delhi from 1990 to 2007'. *Economic and Political Weekly* 48 (13): 54–61.

Bhushan, P. 2004. 'Supreme Court and PIL: Changing Perspectives'. *Economic and Political Weekly* 39 (18): 1770–74.

Bhuwania, A. 2013. 'Competing Populisms: Public Interest Litigation and Political Society in Post-Emergency India'. Unpublished PhD dissertation, Department of Anthropology, Columbia University, New York.

Blom Hansen, T. and F. Stepputat. 2001. 'Introduction: States of Imagination' in *States of Imagination: Ethnographic Explorations of the Post-Colonial State*, edited by T. Blom Hansen and F. Stepputat, 1–39. Durham: Duke Univeristy Press.

Burra, S., S. Patel and T. Kerr. 2003. 'Community-designed, Built and Managed Toilet Blocks in Indian Cities'. *Environment & Urbanisation* 15 (2): 11–32.

Butalia, U. 2000. *The Other Side of Silence: Voices from the Partition of India*. Durham, NC: Duke University Press.

Caldeira, T. 1996. 'Fortified Enclaves: The New Urban Segregation'. *Public Culture* 8 (2): 303–28.

———. 2000. *City of Walls: Crime, Segregation, and Citizenship in São Paulo*. Berkeley: University of California Press.

———. 2014. 'Peripheral Urbanisation'. Paper presented at the LSE Cities Public Lectures, London, 23 October.

Caldeira, T. and J. Holston. 2005. 'State and Urban Space in Brazil: From Modernist Planning to Democratic Interventions' in *Global Assemblages: Technology, Politics, and Ethics as Anthropological Problems*, edited by A. Ong and S. J. Collier, 393–416. Malden, MA: Blackwell Publishing.

Castells, M. 1977 [1972]. *The Urban Question: A Marxist Approach*. Cambridge: The MIT Press.

———. 1983. *The City and the Grassroots: A Cross-Cultural Theory of Urban Social Movements*. Berkeley: University of California Press.

Chatterjee, Partha. 1997. 'Development Planning in India' in *State and Politics in India*, edited by P. Chatterjee, 271–97. New Delhi: Oxford University Press.

———. 2004a. 'Are Indian Cities Becoming Bourgeoisie at Last?' in *The Politics of the Governed*, 131–48. New York: Columbia University Press.

———. 2004b. *The Politics of the Governed: Reflections on Popular Politics in Most of the World*. New York: Columbia University Press.

# References

Chatterjee, Partha. 2012. 'After Subaltern Studies'. *Economic and Political Weekly* 47 (35): 44–49.

Coelho, K., L. Kamath and M. Vijayabaskar. 2013. *Participolis: Consent and Contention in Neoliberal Urban India*. New Delhi: Routledge.

————. 2011. 'Infrastructures of Consent: Interrogating Citizen Participation Mandates in Indian Urban Governance'. Working paper no. 362, Institute of Development Studies (IDS), Sussex.

Coehlo, K. and Nithya Raman. 2010. 'Salvaging and Scapegoating: Slum Evictions on Chennai's Eaterways'. *Economic and Political Weekly* 45 (21): 19.

Coelho, K., Venkat and R. Chandrika. 2012. 'The Spatial Reproduction of Urban Poverty: Labour and Livelihoods in a Slum Resettlement Colony'. *Economic and Political Weekly* 47 (47 and 48): 53–63.

Comaroff, Jean and John L. Comaroff. 2008. *Law and Disorder in the Postcolony*. Chicago: University of Chicago Press.

————. 2012. *Theory from the South: Or, How Euro-America is Evolving Toward Africa*. Boulder: Paradigm Publishers.

Cooke, B. and U. Kothari. 2001. *Participation: The New Tyranny?* London: Zed Books.

Das, V. 1990. *Mirrors of Violence: Communities, Riots, and Survivors in South Asia*. Delhi and New York: Oxford University Press.

Datta, Ayona. 2012. *The Illegal City: Space, Law and Gender in a Delhi Squatter Settlement*. Vermont, USA and Surrey, UK: Ashgate Publishing.

————. 2013. 'Encounters with Law and Critical Urban Studies: Reflections on Amin's Telescopic Urbanism'. *City* 17 (4): 517–22.

Davis, M. 2006. *Planet of Slums*. London and New York: Verso.

De Angelis, M. 2005. 'The Political Economy of Global Neoliberal Governance'. *Review (Fernand Braudel Center)* 28 (3): 229–57.

Dean, M. 2010. *Governmentality: Power and Rule in Modern Society*, Second edition. London and Thousand Oaks, California: Sage Publications.

Delhi Development Authority (DDA). 1962. *Delhi Master Plan 1962*. New Delhi: DDA.

————. 1990. *Delhi Master Plan 2001*. New Delhi: DDA.

————. 2007. *Master Plan for Delhi-2021*. New Delhi: DDA.

DDA and G. Tiwari. 2000. 'Rationalisation of Infrastucture Standards'. New Delhi: TRIPP. Available at http://tripp.iitd.ernet.in/rp/RP_Rframe.html#dda (accessed October 2015)

## References

Deshpande, Satish. 1993. 'Imagined Economies: Styles of Nation-Building in Twentieth Century India'. *Journal of Arts and Ideas* 25 (26): 5–35.

———. 2013. 'Outside Capital, Inside the Urban?: Notes and Queries on the Politics of the Present' in *Participolis: Consent and Contention in Neoliberal Urban India*, edited by K. Coelho, L. Kamath and M. Vijayabaskar, 34–55. New Delhi: Routledge.

Devlin, R. T. 2011. '"An Area that Governs Itself": Informality, Uncertainty and the Management of Street Vending in New York City'. *Planning Theory* 10 (1): 53–65.

Douglas, Mary. 1966. *Purity and Danger*. London: Routledge.

Drèze, J. and A. Sen. 2013. *An Uncertain Glory: India and its Contradictions*. London: Allen Lane.

Dupont, V. 2008. 'Slum Demolitions in Delhi since the 1990s: An Appraisal'. *Economic and Political Weekly* 43 (28): 79–87.

———. 2011. 'The Dream of Delhi as a Global City'. *International Journal of Urban and Regional Research* 35 (3): 533–54.

Eckert, J. 2006. 'From Subjects to Citizens: Legalism from Below and the Homogenisation of the Legal Sphere'. *The Journal of Legal Pluralism and Unofficial Law* 38 (53–54): 45–75.

Ellis, R. 2012. '"A World Class City of Your Own!": Civic Governmentality in Chennai, India'. *Antipode* 44 (4): 1143–60.

Ferguson, James. 2002. 'Spatializing States: Toward an Ethnography of Neoliberal Governmentality'. *American Ethnologist* 29 (4): 981–1002.

———. 2006. *Global Shadows: Africa in the Neoliberal World Order*. Durham NC: Duke University Press.

———. 2013. 'Declarations of Dependence: Labour, Personhood, and Welfare in Southern Africa'. *Journal of the Royal Anthropological Institute* 19 (2): 223–42.

Fernandes, E. 2007. 'Constructing the "Right to the City" in Brazil'. *Social Legal Studies* 16: 201–19.

Fernandes, Leela. 2004. 'Politics of Forgetting: Class Politics, State Power, and the Restructuring of Urban Space in India'. *Urban Studies* 41 (12): 2415–30.

Foucault, M. 1991 [1979]. 'On Governmentality' in *The Foucault Effect: Studies in Governmentality*, edited by G. Burchell and C. Gordon, 87–105. Chicago: University of Chicago Press.

———. 1991 [1980]. 'Questions of Method' in *The Foucault Effect: Studies in Governmentality*, edited by G. Burchell and C. Gordon, 73–86. Chicago: University of Chicago Press.

Gandhi, M. K. 1967. *Collected Works of Mahatma Gandhi*, vol. 26. New Delhi: Publications Division, Government of India.

Ghertner, A. 2008. 'Analysis of New Legal Discourse behind Delhi's Slum Demolitions'. *Economic and Political Weekly* 43 (20): 57–66.

———. 2011a. 'Gentrifying the State, Gentrifying Participation: Elite Governance Programs in Delhi'. *International Journal of Urban and Regional Research* 35 (3): 504–32.

———. 2011b. 'Rule by Aesthetics: World-Class City Making in Delhi' in *Worlding Cities: Asian Experiments and the Art of Being Global*, edited by A. Roy and A. Ong, 279–306. Sussex: Wiley-Blackwell.

———. 2012. 'Nuisance Talk and the Propriety of Property: Middle Class Discourses of a Slum-Free Delhi'. *Antipode* 44 (4): 1161–87.

Gidwani, Vinay and R. N. Reddy. 2011. 'The Afterlives of "Waste": Notes from India for a Minor History of Capitalist Surplus'. *Antipode* 43 (5): 1625–58.

Goldman, M. 2011. 'Speculative Urbanism and the Making of the Next World City'. *International Journal of Urban and Regional Research* 35 (3): 555–81.

Government of Delhi. 2006. *City Development Plan: Delhi*. New Delhi: Government of Delhi.

———. 2009. *Economic Survey of Delhi, 2008–2009*. New Delhi: Government of Delhi.

Government of India. 1956. *The Slum Areas (Improvement and Clearance) Act, 1956*. New Delhi: Government of India.

———. 2006. *Report of the 11th Plan Working Group on Urban Housing with a Focus on Slums*. New Delhi: Government of India.

———. 2012. *Provisional Population Totals: NCT of Delhi*. New Delhi: Directorate of Census Operations.

Graham, S. and S. Marvin. 2001. *Splintering Urbanism: Networked Infrastructures, Technological Mobilities and the Urban Condition*. London and New York: Routledge.

Guha, R. 1988. 'On Some Aspects of the Historiography of Colonial India' in *Selected Subaltern Studies*, edited by R. Guha and G. Spivak, 37–44. Oxford: Oxford University Press.

Gupta, A. 2012. *Red Tape: Bureaucracy, Structural Violence, and Poverty in India*. Durham: Duke University Press.

Gupta, A. and A. Sharma. 2006. 'Introduction' in *The Anthropology of the State: A Reader*, edited by A. Gupta and A. Sharma, 1–41. Malden, MA and Oxford: Blackwell.

Harriss, J. 2007. 'Antinomies of Empowerment: Observations on Civil Society, Politics and Urban Governance in India'. *Economic and Political Weekly* 42 (26): 2716–24.

Harriss-White, Barbara and V. Prosperi. 2014. 'The Micro Political Economy of Gains by Unorganised Workers in India'. *Economic and Political Weekly* 49 (9): 39–43.

Harvey, D. 1973. *Social Justice and the City*. Baltimore: Johns Hopkins University Press.

———. 2005. *A Brief History of Neoliberalism*. New York: Oxford University Press.

———. 2008. 'The Right to the City'. *New Left Review* 53 (September–October): 23–40.

———. 2009. 'Is this Really the End of Neoliberalism?' *Counter Punch*, 13–15 March. Available at http://www.counterpunch. org/2009/03/13/is-this-really-the-end-of-neoliberalism/ (accessed October 2015).

Hazards Centre. 2003. 'A People's Housing Policy'. Available at http://www.hazardscentre.com/hazards_publications/pdf/urban_ governance_resistance/people_housing_policy.html (accessed October 2015).

Held, D. 1999. *Global Transformations: Politics, Economics and Culture*. Cambridge, UK: Polity Press.

Held, D. and A. G. McGrew. 2007. *Globalization Theory: Approaches and Controversies*. Cambridge and Malden, Massachusetts: Polity Press.

Heller, P. and P. Evans. 2010. 'Taking Tilly South: Durable Inequalities, Democratic Contestation, and Citizenship in the Southern Metropolis'. *Theory and Society* 39 (3–4): 433–50.

High Powered Expert Committee (HPEC). 2011. 'Report on Indian Urban Infrastructure and Services'. Report by the HPEC for estimating the investment requirements for urban infrastructure services.

Housing and Land Rights Network (HLRN) and Habitat International Coalition (HIC). 2011. 'Planned Dispossession: Forced Evictions and the 2010 Commonwealth Games'. Report.

Holston, James. 1999a. *Cities and Citizenship*. Durham NC: Duke University Press.

———. 1999b. 'Spaces of Insurgent Citizenship' in *Cities and Citizenship*, edited by J. Holston and A. Appadurai, 155–77. Durham NC: Duke University Press.

———. 2008. *Insurgent Citizenship: Disjunctions of Democracy and Modernity in Brazil*. Princeton: Princeton University Press.

# References

Holston, James. 2009. 'Insurgent Citizenship in an Era of Global Urban Peripheries'. *City & Society* 21 (2): 245–67.

Holston, James and A. Appadurai. 1996. 'Cities and Citizenship'. *Public Culture* 8:187–204.

———. 1999. 'Introduction' in *Cities and Citizenship*, edited by J. Holston and A. Appadurai, 1–18. Durham NC: Duke University Press.

Inda, J. 2005. 'Introduction' in *Anthropologies of Modernity*, edited by J. Inda, 1–20. Oxford: Blackwell.

Jacobs, J. M. 2002. *Edge of Empire: Postcolonialism and the City*. London: Routledge.

Jain, A. K. 2010. *Delhi under Hammer: The Crisis of Sealing and Demolition*. New Delhi: Rupa & Co.

Jayal, Niraja Gopal. 2013. *Citizenship and its Discontents: An Indian History*. Cambridge, Massachusetts: Harvard University Press.

Jeffrey, C. and C. McFarlane. 2008. 'Performing Cosmopolitanism'. *Environment and Planning D: Society and Space* 26 (3): 420–27.

Jenkins, R. 2004. 'Labor Policy and the Second Generation of Economic Reform in India'. *India Review* (October): 333–63.

Jessop, B. 1999. 'Narrating the Future of the National Economy and the National State: Remarks on Remapping Regulation and Reinventing Governance' in *State/Culture: State-Formation after the Cultural Turn*, edited by G. Steinmetz, 378–405. Ithaca: Cornell University Press.

Kale, S. 2006. 'The Political Economy of India's Second-Generation Reforms'. *Journal of Strategic Studies* 25 (4): 207–25.

Keck, M. and C. Sikkink. 1999. 'Transnational Advocacy Networks in International and Regional Politics'. *International Social Science Journal* 51 (159): 89–101.

Khanna, A. 2012. *Refracted Subject: Sexualness in Law and Epidemiology*. New Delhi: Yoda Press.

Koolhaas, R. 2007. *Lagos: How it Works*. Zurich: Lars Müller.

Kudva, N. 2009. 'The Everyday and the Episodic: The Spatial and Political Impacts of Urban Informality'. *Environment and Planning A* 41 (7): 1614–28.

Kundu, A. 2012. *Report of the Technical Group on Urban Housing Shortage 2007–12*. New Delhi: Government of India.

Lama-Rewal, S. T. 2011. 'Urban Governance and Health Care Provision in Delhi'. *Environment & Urbanization* 23 (2): 563–81.

Lefebvre, H. 2002 [1968]. 'The Right to the City' in *The Blackwell City Reader*, edited by G. Bridge and S. Watson, 367–74. Malden: Blackwell.

# References

———. 2003 [1970]. *The Urban Revolution*. Minneapolis: University of Minnesota Press.

Ludden, David. 1992. 'India's Development Regime' in *Colonialism and Culture*, edited by Dirks Nicholas, 247–88. Ann Arbor: University of Michigan Press.

Marcuse, Peter. 2009. 'From Critical Urban Theory to the Right to the City'. *City: Analysis of Urban Trends, Culture, Theory, Policy, Action* 13 (2–3): 185–97.

Marshall, T. H. 1977 [1964]. *Class, Citizenship, and Social Development*. Chicago: University of Chicago Press.

Mate, Manoj. 2013. 'Public Interest Litigation and the Transformation of the Supreme Court of India' in *Consequential Courts: Judicial Roles in Global Perspective*, edited by D. Kapiszewski, G. Silverstein and R. Kagan, 262–89. Cambridge: Cambridge University Press.

———. 2015. 'The Rise of Judicial Governance in the Supreme Court of India'. *Boston University International Law Journal* 33: 169–224.

Mathur, N. 2012. 'On the Sabarmati Riverfront'. *Economic and Political Weekly* 47 (47–48): 64–75.

Mathur, Om. 2009. *Slum-Free Cities*. New Delhi: NIPFP.

Mayer, M. 2009. 'The "Right to the City" in the Context of Shifting Mottos of Urban Social Movements'. *City: Analysis of Urban Trends, Culture, Theory, Policy, Action* 13 (2–3): 362–74.

McCann, M. 2006. 'Law and Social Movements: Contemporary Perspectives'. *Annual Review of Law and Social Science* 2: 17–38.

McFarlane, Colin. 2004. 'Geographical Imaginations and Spaces of Political Engagement: Examples from the Indian Alliance'. *Antipode* 36 (5): 890–916.

———. 2006. 'Sanitation in Mumbai's Informal Settlements: State, "Slum" and Infrastructure'. Unpublished PhD dissertation, Department of Geography, Durham University.

———. 2012. 'Rethinking Informality: Politics, Crisis, and the City'. *Planning Theory & Practice* 13 (1): 89–108.

McKinsey Global Institute. 2010. *India's Urban Awakening: Building Inclusive Cities, Sustaining Economic Growth*. New Delhi: McKinsey & Co.

Mehra, D. 2013. 'RWAs and the Political Process in Delhi' in *Participolis: Consent and Contention in Neoliberal Urban India*, edited by K. Coelho, L. Kamath and M. Vijayabaskar, 222–39. New Delhi: Routledge.

Mehrotra, R. 2010. 'Foreword' in *Re-thinking the Informal City: Perspectives from Latin America*, edited by F. Hernandez, P. Kellet and L. Allen. New York: Berghahn.

Menon, Nivedita. 1998. 'State/Gender/Community: Citizenship in Contemporary India'. *Economic and Political Weekly* 33 (5): 3–10.

———. 2004. *Recovering Subversion: Feminist Politics Beyond the Law*. Urbana, Illinois and Ranikhet: University of Illinois Press and Permanent Black.

———. 2010. 'Introduction' in *Empire and Nation: Selected Essays*, edited by P. Chatterjee, 1–20. New York: Columbia University Press.

Menon, N. and A. Nigam. 2007. *Power and Contestation: India Since 1989*. London and New York: Zed Books.

Merrifield, A. 2014. *The New Urban Question*. London: Pluto Press.

Ministry of Environment and Forests (MoEF) and Government of Delhi. 2001. *Delhi Urban Environment and Infrastructure Improvement Report: Delhi 21*. New Delhi: GoI.

Miraftab, Faranak. 2009. 'Insurgent Planning: Situating Radical Planning in the Global South'. *Planning Theory* 8 (1): 32–50.

Mitchell, Tim. 2002. *Rule of Experts: Egypt, Techno-Politics, Modernity*. Berkeley: University of California Press.

Mitlin, D. and S. Patel. 2005. 'Re-interpreting the Rights-based Approach: A Grassroots Perspective on Rights and Development'. Global Poverty Research Group working paper 22, Economic and Social Research Council, Oxford. Available at http://www.gprg.org/pubs/workingpapers/pdfs/gprg-wps-022.pdf (accessed October 2015)

Mosse, D. 2010. 'A Relational Approach to Durable Poverty, Inequality and Power'. *The Journal of Development Studies* 46 (7): 1156–78.

Muralidhar, S. 1998. 'India: Public Interest Litigation Survey 1997–1998'. *Annual Survey of Indian Law* 33:525.

Muralidhar, S. and A. Desai. 2000. 'Public Interest Litigation: Potential and Problems' in *Supreme but not Infallible: Essays in Honour of the Supreme Court of India*, edited by B. N. Kirpal, Ashok H. Desai, Rajeev Dhavan and Raju Ramachandran, 159. New Delhi: Oxford University Press.

Nandy, Ashis. 1998. 'Introduction' in *The Secret Politics of Our Desires: Innocence, Culpability and Indian Popular Cinema*, edited by A. Nandy, 1–18. New Delhi: Oxford University Press.

Narrain, A. and A. K. Thiruvengadam. 2013. 'Social Justice Lawyering and the Meaning of Indian Constitutionalism: A Case Study of the Alternative Law Forum'. *Wisconsin International Law Journal* 31 (3): 525.

References

National Sample Survey Organisation (NSSO). 1997. 'Slums in India: January–June 1993, NSS 49th Round'. Report no. 417, Department of Statistics, Government of India.

Nigam, A. 2001. 'Industrial Closures in Delhi'. *Revolutionary Democracy* 7 (2). Available at http://www.revolutionarydemocracy. org/rdv7n2/industclos.htm (accessed October 2015).

Ong, Aihwa. 1999. *Flexible Citizenship: The Cultural Logics of Transnationality*. Durham: Duke University Press.

———. 2000. 'Graduated Sovereignty in South-East Asia'. *Theory, Culture & Society* 17 (4): 55–75.

———. 2006. *Neoliberalism as Exception: Mutations in Citizenship and Sovereignty*. Durham: Duke University Press.

Parnell, Susan and Edgar Pieterse. 2010. 'The "Right to the City": Institutional Imperatives of a Developmental State'. *International Journal of Urban and Regional Research* 34 (1): 146–62.

Parnell, S. and J. Robinson. 2012. '(Re)theorizing Cities from the Global South: Looking Beyond Neoliberalism'. *Urban Geography* 33 (4): 593–617.

Patel, Sheela, C., D'Cruz and S. Burra. 2002. 'Beyond Evictions in a Global City: People-Managed Resettlement in Mumbai'. *Environment & Urbanisation* 14 (1): 159–72.

Patel, Shirish. 1997. 'Urban Planning by Objectives'. *Economic and Political Weekly* 32 (16): 822–26.

Patkar, M. and J. Athialy. 2005. 'The Shanghaification of Mumbai'. *Counter Currents*. Available at http://www.countercurrents.org/ hr-athialy110805.htm (accessed October 2015).

Peattie, L. 1987. *Planning, Rethinking Ciudad Guayana*. Ann Arbor: University of Michigan Press.

Peck, J., N. Theodore and N. Brenner. 2009. 'Neoliberal Urbanism: Models, Moments, Mutations'. *SAIS Review* 29 (1): 49–66.

Pithouse, Richard. 2014. 'The Shack Settlement as a Site of Politics: Reflections from South Africa'. *Agrarian South: Journal of Political Economy* 3 (2): 179–201.

Prakash, Gyan. 2002. 'Urban Turn' in *The Sarai Reader: Cities of Everyday Life*, edited by Sarai, 2–7. New Delhi: Sarai.

People's Union of Civil Liberties, Karnataka (PUCL-K) and Human Rights Law Network (HRLN). 2013. 'Governance by Denial: Forced Eviction and Demolition in Ejipura/Koramangala, Bangalore'. Report.

Rajagopal, Balakrishnan. 2007. 'Pro-Human Rights but Anti-Poor? A Critical Evaluation of the Indian Supreme Court from a Social Movement Perspective'. *Human Rights Review* 18 (3): 157–87.

References

Rajamani, L. 2007. 'Public Interest Environmental Litigation in India'. *Journal of Environmental Law* 20 (2): 293–321.

Ramachandran, R. 2000. 'The Supreme Court and the Basic Structure Doctrine' in *Supreme But Not Infallible: Essays in Honour of the Supreme Court of India*, edited by B. N. Kirpal, A. Desai, G. Subramanium, R. Dhavan and R. Ramachandran, 107–33. New Delhi: Oxford University Press.

Ramanathan, Usha. 2004. 'Illegality and Exclusion: Law in the Lives of Slum Dwellers'. Working paper, International Environmental Law Research Centre, Geneva.

————. 2005. 'Demolition Drive'. *Economic and Political Weekly* 40 (27): 2908–12.

Rao, Vyjayanthi. 2006. 'Slum as Theory: The South/Asian City and Globalisation'. *International Journal of Urban and Regional Research* 30 (1): 225–32.

Robinson, Jennifer. 2006. *Ordinary Cities: Between Modernity and Development*. London and New York: Routledge.

Rose, Nikolas S. 1999. *Powers of Freedom: Reframing Political Thought*. Cambridge, UK, and New York: Cambridge University Press.

Rose, N. and P. Miller. 1992. 'Political Power Beyond the State: Problematics of Government'. *British Journal of Sociology* 43 (2): 173–205.

Roy, Ananya. 2003. *City Requiem, Calcutta: Fender and the Politics of Poverty*. Minneapolis: University of Minnesota Press.

————. 2005. 'Urban Informality: Towards an Epistemology of Planning'. *Journal of the American Planning Association* 71 (2): 147–58.

————. 2008. 'The 21st-Century Metropolis: New Geographies of Theory'. *Regional Studies* 43 (6): 1–12.

————. 2009a. 'Civic Governmentality: The Politics of Inclusion in Beirut and Mumbai'. *Antipode* 41 (1): 159–79.

————. 2009b. 'Why India Cannot Plan its Cities'. *Planning Theory* 8: 76–87.

————. 2011. 'Urbanisms, Worlding Practices and the Theory of Planning'. *Planning Theory* 10 (6): 6–15.

————. forthcoming. 'Who is afraid of Post-Colonial Theory?' *International Journal of Urban and Regional Research*.

Roy, Ananya and Aihwa Ong. 2011. *Worlding Cities: Asian Experiments and the Art of Being Global* 42. Chichester: John Wiley & Sons.

Roy, Dunu. 2004. 'From Home to Estate'. *Seminar* 533: 68–74.

References

Sajha Manch. 2001. 'Andher Nagri, Chaupat Raja'. Parcha (pamphlet). New Delhi: Sajha Manch.

———. 2005. 'Kala Kanoon, Kaana Kanoon'. Parcha. New Delhi: Sajha Manch.

———. 2007. 'Samvidhaan ko Yaad Karo'. Parcha. New Delhi: Sajha Manch.

———. 2010. 'Punarvaas Ki Rajneeti'. Parcha. New Delhi: Sajha Manch.

Santiso, C. 2001. 'World Bank and Good Governance: Good Governance and Aid Effectiveness: The World Bank and Conditionality'. *The Georgetown Public Policy Review* 7:1–137.

Sassen, S. 2003. 'The Repositioning of Citizenship: Emergent Subjects and Spaces for Politics'. *CR: The New Centennial Review* 3 (2): 41–66.

———. 2006. *Territory, Authority Rights: From Medieval to Global Assemblages*. Princeton, NJ: Princeton University Press.

Sathe, S. P. 2002. *Judicial Activism in India*. New Delhi: Oxford University Press.

Scott, A. J. and M. Storper. 2014. 'The Nature of Cities: The Scope and Limits of Urban Theory'. *International Journal of Urban and Regional Research* 39 (1): 1–15.

Scott, James C. 1998. *Seeing like a State*. New Haven: Yale University Press.

———. 2008. *Weapons of the Weak: Everyday Forms of Peasant Resistance*. New Haven: Yale University Press.

Sen, Amartya. 1992. *Inequality Reexamined*. New York: Harvard University Press.

———. 1999. *Development as Freedom*. New York: Knopf.

Sen, Jai. 1976. 'Unintended City'. *Seminar* 200:39–47. Available at http://www.india-seminar.com/2001/500/500%20jai%20sen.htm (accessed October 2015).

Sharan, A. 2010. 'Spaces of Work/Sites of Danger: Environment and Urban Landscape in Modern Delhi' in *Comparing Cities: The Middle East and South Asia*, edited by K. Ali and M. Reiker, 221–49. Oxford: Oxford University Press.

Sheppard, E., H. Leitner and A. Maringanti. 2013. 'Provincializing Global Urbanism: A Manifesto'. *Urban Geography* 34 (7): 893–900.

Simone, AbdouMaliq. 2004. *For the City Yet to Come: Changing Life in Four African Cities*. Durham NC: Duke University Press.

# References

Simone, AbdouMaliq. 2008. 'The Politics of the Possible: Making Urban Life in Phnom Penh'. *Singapore Journal of Tropical Geography* 29 (2): 186–204.

Sivaramakrishnan, K. 2011. *Re-Visioning Indian Cities: The Urban Renewal Mission*. New Delhi: Sage.

Smith, N. 1992. 'Contours of a Spatialized Politics: Homeless Vehicles and the Production of Geographical Scale'. *Social Text* 33: 54–81.

Sundar, Nandini. 2011. 'The Rule of Law and Citizenship in Central India: Post-Colonial Dilemmas'. *Citizenship Studies* 15 (3–4): 419–32.

Sundaram, Ravi. 2009. *Pirate Modernity: Delhi's Media Urbanism*. London and New York: Routledge.

Swamy, M. C. K., B. Bhaskara Rao and V. M. Hegde. 2008. *Urban Planning and Development at Crossroads*, First edition. Bangalore: Books for Change.

Swyngedouw, E. 2005. 'Governance Innovation and the Citizen: The Janus Face of Governance-Beyond-the-State'. *Urban Studies* 42 (11): 1991–2006.

Tarlo, E. 2001. *Unsettling Memories: Narratives of the Emergency in Delhi*. Berkeley: University of California Press.

Tickell, A. and J. A. Peck. 1992. 'Accumulation, Regulation and the Geographies of Post-Fordism: Missing Links in Regulationist Research'. *Progress in Human Geography* 16 (2): 190–218.

Tilly, Charles. 1998. *Durable Inequalities*. Berkeley: University of California Press.

UN-Habitat. 2014. 'Forced Evictions'. Fact sheet. Nairobi: UN-Habitat. Available at http://unhabitat.org/forced-evictions-fact-sheet-no-25rev-1/ (accessed October 2015).

Urban Poverty and Inequality Collective. 2015. 'Making the Urban Welfare State: New Questions from the South'. Unpublished proceedings of a meeting of the collective held at the University of Berkeley, California, 5–6 June.

Varley, A. 2013. 'Postcolonialising Informality?' *Environment and Planning D: Society and Space* 31 (1): 4–22.

Verma, G. D. 2003. *Slumming India: A Chronicle of Slums and their Saviours*. New Delhi: Penguin.

Watson, Vanessa. 2002. 'The Usefulness of Normative Planning Theories in the Context of Sub-Saharan Africa'. *Planning Theory* 1 (1): 27–52.

———. 2006. 'Deep Difference: Diversity, Planning and Ethics'. *Planning Theory* 5 (1): 31–50.

————. 2009. 'Seeing from the South: Refocusing Urban Planning on the Globe's Central Urban Issues'. *Urban Studies* 46 (11): 2259–75.

————. 2012. 'Planning and the "Stubborn Realities" of Global South-East Cities: Some Emerging Ideas'. *Planning Theory* 12 (1): 81–100.

World Bank. 1992. *Governance and Development*. Washington DC: World Bank.

Yiftachel, Oren. 2006. 'Re-Engaging Planning Theory?: Towards "South-Eastern" Perspectives'. *Planning Theory* 5 (3): 211–22.

Young, I. M. 1990. *Justice and the Politics of Difference*. Princeton, NJ: Princeton University Press.

Zerah, M.-H., S. Lama-Rewal, V. Dupont and B. Chaudhuri. 2012. 'Right to the City and Urban Citizenship in the Indian Context' in *Urban Policies and the Right to the City in India*, edited by M.-H. Zerah, V. Dupont and S. Lama Rewal, 7–17. New Delhi: Centre des Sciences Humaines.

Zhang, L. 2001. *Strangers in the City*. Stanford: Stanford University Press.

## Selected Case Law: Petitions and Judgments

*ADM Jabalpur vs Shivkant Shukla* (1976) AIR SC 1207

*Ahmedabad Municipal Corporation vs Nawab Khan Gulab Khan and Others* (1997) 11 SCC 123

*Almitra Patel vs Union of India* (2002) 2 SCC 679

*Almitra Patel vs Union of India*, CWP 888 of 1996

*Ambedkar Slum Utthan Sangathan vs Municipal Corporation of Delhi*, CWP 6981 of 2002

*Bandhua Mukti Morcha vs Union of India* (1984) 3 SCC 161

*Chameli Singh vs State of Uttar Pradesh* (1996) 2 SCC 549

*Court in its Own Motion vs Union of India*, CWP 689 of 2004

*Delhi Builders and Promoters Association vs Municipal Corporation of Delhi*, CWP 4980 of 2001

*Dev Chand and Ors vs Union of India* CM 6982 of 2007 in *Kalyan Sanstha vs Union of India*, CWP 4582 of 2003

*Dr Upendra Baxi vs State of UP* (1983) 2 SCC 308

*Hemraj vs Commissioner of Police and Ors*, CWP 3419 of 1999

*Hussainara Khatoon vs State of Bihar* (1980) 1 SCC 81

*Jagdish and Anr vs Delhi Development Authority*, CWP 5009 of 2002

# References

*Joginder Kumar Singla vs Municipal Corporation of Delhi*, CWP 1397 of 2001

*K Chandru vs State of Tamil Nadu* (1986) AIR 204

*K K Manchanda vs Union of India*, CWP 531 of 1990

*Kalyan Sanstha Social Welfare Organisation vs Union of India and Ors*, CWP 4582 of 2003

*Maloy Krishna Dhar vs Government of National Capital Territory of Delhi*, CWP 6160 of 2003

*Maneka Gandhi vs Union of India* (1978) 1 SCC 248

*M C Mehta vs Union of India*, CWP 4677 of 1985

*M C Mehta vs Union of India*, CWP 13029 of 1985

*M C Mehta vs Union of India* (1987) 1 SCC 395

*Nav Kiran Singh vs State of Punjab* (1995) 4 SCC 591

*National Alliance of People's Movements vs National Capital Territory of Delhi*, CWP 4229 of 1996

*Okhla Factory Owner's Association vs Government of National Capital Territory of Delhi*, CWP 4441 of 1994

*Olga Tellis vs Bombay Municipal Corporation and Anr* (1986) AIR 180

*People's Union for Democratic Rights (PUDR) vs Union of India* (1982) AIR SC 1473

*Pitampura Sudhar Samiti vs Government of the National Capital Territory of Delhi*, CWP 4215 of 1995

*Ram Rattan and Ors vs Commissioner of Police and Ors*, Special Leave Petition (Civil) 3732 of 2005

*Ratlam vs Shri Vardhichand and Ors* (1980) AIR 1622

*S P Gupta vs Union of India* (1982) AIR SC 149

*Satbeer Singh Rathi vs Municipal Corporation of Delhi* (2004) 114 DLT 760

*Shantistar Builders vs Narayan Khimalal Totame* (1990) AIR SC 630

*State of Rajasthan and Ors vs Union of India* 1978 SCR (1) 1

*Sudama Singh and Others vs Government of Delhi and Anr*, CWP 8904 of 2009

*Sunil Batra vs Delhi Administration* (1980) 3 SCC 480

*Veena Sethi vs State of Bihar* (1982) 2 SCC 583

*Vineet Narrain vs Union of India* (1996) AIR SC 3386

*Vishaka vs State of Rajasthan* (1997) AIR SC 3011

*Wazirpur Bartan Nirmata Sangh vs Union of India*, CWP 2112 of 2002

*Welfare Association of Majlis Park vs Municipal Corporation of Delhi*, CWP 7758 of 2007

# Acknowledgements

The giving of thanks for a project that for most of its existence has been indistinguishable from my life itself is fated to be both deeply pleasurable and hopelessly inadequate. First, formally, to the University of California, Berkeley, for the Berkeley Fellowship; the Social Science Research Council for the International Dissertation Research Fellowship; and the Urban Knowledge Network Asia for the Visiting Research Fellowship at the University College, London. Each made this book possible. My thanks as well to the Society for Applied Studies-Centre for Health Research and Development and to Jagori, New Delhi.

To the residents of all the bastis that have taught me all I know about cities, but particularly to Rafiya, Rajesh, Deepak, and Sanjay who sat me down one day in Bawana and told me to just get on with it. To comrades in movements who didn't laugh through my trying to 'interview' them.

To a queer urban universe in Delhi and beyond without whose conversations, love, politics and ethical and moral compass, none of this would even have begun. Naming you individually would undo the collective life we have sought to bring and build together. To colleagues in Berkeley but in particular to JiaChing Chen, Mona Damluji, Ricardo Cardoso and Alex Schafran for love, inspiration, an intellectual home, comradeship and courage. To colleagues at the Indian Institute for Human Settlements, my thanks for heart and mindspace, our sense of community and to the future that is ours to make.

## Acknowledgements

To my students for reminding me always what it is really all about.

To Nezar AlSayyad and James Holston for constant challenges and probing questions at every turn. To Teresa Caldeira and Ananya Roy: friends, teachers, mentors and intellectual giants. You are, to me, the best of what public education stands for in every way and I am deeply proud to call myself your student.

To my siblings, Shereen, Abhishek and Sonam: I stand on your shoulders in all that I do. To my parents who are my oldest, wisest and greatest teachers: I cannot thank you enough for teaching me to care, to fight, to seek what is just and right, to reach beyond the possible and to want to change the world. Without that, what else would there be?

274

# Index

South Africa 15, 199, 237
space 11, 16–7, 18, 22, 24, 26–9,
    33, 36–7, 48, 75, 86, 89, 92,
    99, 102, 104, 111, 120–22,
    131–2, 141, 151, 158–60,
    167, 172, 179–80, 182, 184,
    192, 194–8, 208, 212–3, 215,
    223–4, 226, 228, 243, 245–9
    governable 22, 24, 99, 131–2,
    246
    production of 11, 16–8, 28–9,
        48, 86, 172, 182, 226,
        245–6, 248
        mode of 17, 86, 245
        political economy of 29,
        172
    urban 17, 27, 86, 151, 184
        informal 17, 86
    politics 27, 151, 184
State Bank of India (SBI) 174,
    176
Supreme Court of India 2, 6, 30,
    38, 46, 95, 97, 99, 102–5, 107,
    109–13, 116–7, 126, 131–2,
    136, 168, 189, 191, 201,
    203–5, 208–9, 211, 216, 221,
    243

temporality 24, 55, 130
tenure 10–11, 20, 52, 62, 69,
    72–4, 90–91, 162, 199, 202,
    240–41
    secure 20, 90
        de facto 10, 20, 52, 62,
        72–3, 162
        de jure 20, 52
    security of 10–11, 20, 52, 62,
        69, 72–4, 162, 240–41
transformation 8, 13, 55, 100,
    117, 134, 138, 141–2, 150,
    178, 193, 195–8, 255
    economic 100, 142
    infrastructural 141

political 100, 142
    social 196–8
transport 22, 99, 128
Trilokpuri 7

unauthorised colonies 48, 60–68,
    71–2, 76–8, 81, 87–8, 91, 135
    clusters of 65, 81
    definition of 62
    spatial pattern of 65, 81
Universal Declaration of Human
    Rights 113
Unorganised Workers Social
    Security Act 241–2
unplanned colonies 60, 76
urban
    authorities 2, 181, 189, 196,
        208
    case law 22, 98, 100, 249
    citizen/citizenship 14, 16,
        25–9, 31, 149, 151–2, 161,
        174, 181–3, 185–6, 194,
        233, 239, 248, 253–4
    development 3, 8, 28, 34, 46–7,
        52, 55, 59, 80, 137, 141–2,
        182–3, 185, 194, 239
    governance 21, 46, 89, 98,
        100, 134–8, 140, 165, 182,
        225, 233, 254
    growth and expansion 59, 81
    informality 16, 17, 20, 86, 89,
        233, 245
    interventions 24, 117, 128,
        130, 185, 239
    plans/planning 14, 16, 45
    poverty 15, 85, 96, 111, 235,
        238, 242
    social movements 32–3, 38,
        191–3, 207, 222–4, 229,
        247, 250
    spaces 11, 17, 27, 86, 151,
        167, 179, 184, 226, 243
        informal 17, 86

Index

# Geographies of Justice and Social Transformation

www.ingramcontent.com/pod-product-compliance
Lightning Source LLC
Chambersburg PA
CBHW010142270326
41929CB00020B/3335